Owning the Masters

Owning the Masters

A History of Sound Recording Copyright

Richard Osborne

BLOOMSBURY ACADEMIC
NEW YORK • LONDON • OXFORD • NEW DELHI • SYDNEY

BLOOMSBURY ACADEMIC
Bloomsbury Publishing Inc
1385 Broadway, New York, NY 10018, USA
50 Bedford Square, London, WC1B 3DP, UK
29 Earlsfort Terrace, Dublin 2, Ireland

BLOOMSBURY, BLOOMSBURY ACADEMIC and the Diana logo
are trademarks of Bloomsbury Publishing Plc

First published in the United States of America 2023

Library of Congress Cataloguing-in-Publication Data
Names: Osborne, Richard, 1967- author.
Title: Owning the masters : a history of sound recording copyright / Richard Osborne.
Description: [1st.] | New York : Bloomsbury Academic, 2022. | Includes
bibliographical references and index. |
Summary: "The story of how record companies gained
ownership of sound recording rights and examines the consequences of this
ownership for musical creation and reception"–Provided by publisher.
Identifiers: LCCN 2022018383 (print) | LCCN 2022018384 (ebook) |
ISBN 9781501345913 (hardback) | ISBN 9781501345906 (paperback) |
ISBN 9781501345920 (epub) | ISBN 9781501345937 (pdf) | ISBN 9781501345944
Subjects: LCSH: Sound recording industry–History. | Copyright–Sound
recordings–History. | Copyright–Music–History.
Classification: LCC ML3790 .O824 2022 (print) | LCC ML3790 (ebook) |
DDC 346.04/82–dc23/eng/20220415
LC record available at https://lccn.loc.gov/2022018383
LC ebook record available at https://lccn.loc.gov/2022018384

ISBN: HB: 978-1-5013-4591-3
        PB: 978-1-5013-4590-6
        ePDF: 978-1-5013-4593-7
        eBook: 978-1-5013-4592-0

Typeset by Integra Software Services Pvt Ltd.
Printed and bound in Great Britain

To find out more about our authors and books visit www.bloomsbury.com
and sign up for our newsletters.

For Iris

Contents

Acknowledgements

For their help and conversations along the way, thanks are due to Ananay Aguilar, David Arditi, Kenny Barr, Adam Behr, Matt Brennan, Maria Chatzichristodoulou, Paul Cobley, Dennis Collopy, Kyle Devine, Mathew Flynn, Peter Fribbins, Simon Frith, Ann Harrison, David Hesmondhalgh, Peter Jenner, Michael Jones, Dave Laing, Lesley Main, Lee Marshall, Justin Morey, Marcus O'Dair, Tony Rigg, Matt Stahl, Jon Stewart, Hyojung Sun, Ruth Towse, John Williamson, the IASPM community, the steering board and interviewees for *Music Creators' Earnings in the Digital Era*, my old workmates at PRS and MCPS, the team at Bloomsbury (Rachel Moore, Leah Babb-Rosenfeld and Amy Martin), Viswasirasini Govindarajan at Integra Software Services, and the Osborne family.

Sections of chapters 2 and 4 are derived in part from 'Is Equitable Remuneration Equitable? Performers' Rights in the UK' first published in *Popular Music and Society* 15 July 2017 © Taylor & Francis, available online: https://www.tandfonline.com/doi/full/10.1080/03007766.2017.1348660.

Sections of chapters 4, 6 and 7 are derived in part from 'Copyright, Royalties and Industrial Decline', first published in A. Harrison and T. Rigg (eds), *The Present and Future of Music Law*, 27–45, New York and London: Bloomsbury.

Sections of chapters 5, 6 and 7 are derived in part from 'Success Ratios, New Music and Sound Recording Copyright, first published in *Popular Music* 16/3 (2017), 393–409, © Cambridge University Press, available online: https://www.cambridge.org/core/journals/popular-music/article/abs/success-ratios-new-music-and-sound-recording-copyright/AA4D6630722DB340E7F0B3CE6F6A1C58

Introduction

The recording industry is a rights industry. This is the view held by the Congress of the United States, which lists it as one of the 'core copyright industries' (CBO 2004: 3). Similarly, the British government believes that copyright 'is central to the operations of the record industry' (MMC 1994: §1.4). It is also the opinion of academics. Patrik Wikström has stressed that it is a *'copyright* industry' (2009: 17. Emphasis in original). Simon Frith has argued 'what is at stake is the ownership of titles' (Frith 2000: 388). The recording industry admits as much. Its global trade body, the International Federation of the Phonographic Industry (IFPI), has stated that the principal aim of record companies is 'investing in copyright' (2014: 4).

This investment is derived from their contracts with recording artists. The main point of negotiation is not the artists' labour but instead the sound recording copyright that subsists in the recordings they create. It is control of this intellectual property, as well as control of artists to generate more of this intellectual property, that determines the wealth of record companies. Correspondingly, it is purchase of sound recording copyright, rather than fixed assets, that is the main determinant of the price when a company is put on sale. The value can be considerable. In September 2021, the industry's most significant copyright holder, the Universal Music Group, was valued at US$54.3 billion (Stassen 2021a).

Given its importance, sound recording copyright is a notable omission in histories of the recording industry. Authors have concentrated on the invention of technologies, the establishment of record companies and the development of artists, rather than the acquirement of rights (Barfe 2004; Millard 1995). This oversight could, however, be due to the complexity of the subject matter. In the words of Professor Ronan Deazley, who has spent a lifetime working on the topic, 'copyright is hard' (Westminster Media Forum 2017). Another complicating factor is the interaction between industry and the law. Although copyright legislation has had a significant impact on the recording industry, and the industry has impacted legislation, these developments have not always occurred concurrently. On top of this, there are the politics of sound recording copyright, which have frequently been fraught. Before outlining the structure of this book, the main task of this introduction is to provide more detail about these issues. To further guide the reader through the complexities of copyright, *Owning the Masters* includes a glossary of terms and a timeline of key dates in the legislation for music. Nevertheless, while the law and its practice can be abstruse, the overall themes of this book are straightforward. It is about ownership, control and remuneration.

Legislative background

1. Works and rights

The World Intellectual Property Organization (WIPO) defines copyright as 'a legal term used to describe the rights that creators have over their literary and artistic works' (WIPO n.d.). This points towards two factors to be borne in mind when considering this subject. First, copyright subsists in different types of 'work'. WIPO's own list ranges from 'books, music, paintings, sculpture, and films, to computer programs, databases, advertisements, maps, and technical drawings' (WIPO n.d.). Second, the authors of these works are granted an array of rights, which enable them to control different uses. Employing terms derived from Britain's Copyright, Designs and Patents Act (CDPA), these rights can be listed as follows:

- *The right to copy the work*: Also known as the reproduction right, this right addresses the reproduction of the work 'in any material form', including 'storing the work in any medium by electronic means' and 'the making of copies which are transient or are incidental to some other use of the work' (CDPA 1988: §17).
- *The right to issue copies of the work to the public*: Also known as the distribution right, this right partners the reproduction right. It is utilized in instances where the distributor of the work is separate to the reproducer of the work.
- *The right to rent or lend the work to the public*: This right addresses instances where the work will be accessed 'on terms that it will or may be returned' (CDPA 1988: §18(2)).

- *The right to perform, show or play the work in public*: Also known as the public performance right, this right addresses use of the work in venues, cinemas, shops, restaurants, workplaces and other public places.
- *The right to communicate the work to the public*: This right can be broken down into a broadcast right, which addresses various forms of transmission, including radio and television broadcasting. There is also a subset to this right, known as the making available right, which was developed to cover the transmission of interactive content online. Collectively, the communication to the public right and the public performance right are known as the performing rights.
- *The right to make an adaptation of the work*: This right addresses various means of adapting, arranging and translating the work.[1]

In most cases, these rights are granted exclusively, which means the original copyright owner has control over their use. Generally, they have four possible courses of action: they can waive their rights, allowing third parties to utilize their works freely; they can allow third parties to use their rights without payment, but in doing so can impose conditions on how the works are employed and request accreditation;[2] they can oversee the use of their rights, monetizing activity and prosecuting infringement; they can transfer control of the rights to another party, usually in return for a fixed sum and/or royalty payments. Although these options can be exercised in the same manner across the entirety of a creator's 'basket of rights' (Frith 1993: ix), they can be exercised differently for separate rights, and in different ways within rights. For example, the reproduction right covers both the ability to duplicate physical copies (which the creator might want to transfer to one party) and the ability to synchronize sounds with images (which the creator might want to transfer to a different party). The transfer of rights can be by licence (in which case the original owner retains underlying ownership but the licensee has use of the relevant rights) or

---

[1] The list of rights takes different forms in different territories. Variations include: the distribution right (some territories do not have this right; some utilize it for the distribution of physical copies only; in others it covers both physical and electronic distribution); the public performance right (in some territories this right encompasses the communication to the public right); the communication to the public right (see footnote on p. 49 for various uses of this term); the making available right (this can be a distinct right or it can form a subset of the communication to the public right and/or the distribution right); the rental right (some territories do not have this right); the adaptation right (some territories, such as the United States, have a 'derivative right' instead).

[2] This use of copyright is promoted by creative commons licensing (Creative Commons n.d.).

it can be via assignment (in which case ownership is handed over completely). The original owner can also set limits around the duration of the transfer. It can be for the life of copyright or of shorter duration.

2. Rights and music

Sound recordings represent a particularly daunting prospect for analysis, as each recording contains three sets of rights. There are the rights in the musical compositions, which in some territories are treated in a unified manner but in others are broken down into separate rights in the literary work (the lyrics) and the musical work (the melodic, harmonic, rhythmic and timbral aspects of composition). In addition, there is the main subject matter of this book: the rights in recordings themselves (known as sound recording copyright or the master rights). Third, there is the related subject of performers' rights, which are also addressed in this book. These three sets of rights are treated differently.

Musical works are placed at the forefront of legislation, ranked alongside works of literature, drama and art. They operate in accordance with WIPO's definition of copyright. The rights are granted to creative authors: composers gain first ownership in respect of the originality of their work. Their rights can be infringed by anyone who makes a copy of the work itself (as in the unauthorized reproduction of sheet music). They can also be infringed if someone is deemed to have copied the essential form of the composition (such as borrowing a musical phrase that is held to have sufficient similarity to the original work). The rights last for the lifetime of the author plus a set number of years. They are usually granted exclusively.[3]

Sound recording copyright has some correspondences with the copyright in musical works, as legislation tends to grant a similar array rights. In other respects there is divergence. In many instances, it is regarded as a secondary form of copyright, placed at one remove the copyright in literary, artistic and musical works. Even where this is not the case, the legislation has particular characteristics. It escapes WIPO's definition of copyright, as authorship is rarely

---

[3] An exception is the compulsory licensing measures that some territories apply to the reproduction of compositions in mechanical form (referring to their use in sound recordings, piano rolls, music boxes and other technological devices). In this instance, after an initial reproduction has been issued, the copyright holder is compelled to license the work to other users at a price that is legislatively determined.

awarded in respect of creativity. Correspondingly, a sound recording does not have to be original to receive protection.

Rather than granting ownership to recording artists or studio personnel, it is record companies that are 'normally' cast as the authors of sound recordings (EC 2011; MMC 1994: §2.18; Sterling 1992: §6.24). In the earliest legislation, the copyright was awarded to the 'owners' of master recordings or alternatively it was acquired by record companies through automatic assignment. By the mid-twentieth century, the rights were more commonly granted to record companies in respect of their role as manufacturers. Then, by the century's end, WIPO was declaring that the 'purpose' of sound copyright legislation was to grant ownership to 'producers' (1992: 39). When used in a legislative sense, this term has referred to the financing and organization of recording sessions, rather than the technical aspects of studio work. Therefore, the award has continued to be oriented towards record companies. The United States has provided a partial exception. Here, the originality of sound recording has been taken into account: creative recognition is given to recording artists for the 'capture' of their performances, and to studio personnel for 'capturing and electronically processing the sounds' (SJC 1971: 5). Ownership has nevertheless been determined by an 'employment relationship' in which record companies have the upper hand (SJC 1971: 5). Utilizing the work made for hire rules of American legislation, the companies have claimed authorship of recordings on grounds that they commission the work.

In all territories this corporate ownership has shaped sound recording copyright more broadly. The duration of the rights is usually tied to the date of production or issue of recordings, rather than lifetimes of creators. This copyright can only be infringed if a recording is copied exactly. Consequently, many countries (other than the United States) do not grant recordings an adaptation right. Moreover, in the case of the public performance right and the broadcast right, the interests of performers, licensees and compositional copyright holders have been taken into account. Some countries offer these rights to record companies in limited form; others grant the producer an agreed share of 'equitable remuneration' rather than an exclusive right.

There is another consequence of the corporate ownership of sound recording copyright. It has fed into the creation of performers' rights. These rights are granted in respect of the 'fixation' of performances in recorded form (Rome Convention 1961: art. 7; WPPT 1996: arts 7–10). Their duration is tied to the date of the performance or the publication of the recording, rather than lifetimes of performers. They are compensatory in nature. One reason why performers have gained these rights is because they have not been expected to have control of the copyright in recordings. Their own reproduction, distribution and making available rights have nevertheless been regarded as 'ineffective in real terms' (Cooke 2015: 27). This is because performers will be expected to assign them when contracting with record companies (Cooke 2015: 27). Performers commonly have stronger broadcast and public performance rights.[4] It is not possible for performers to assign them to a record company; they are instead guaranteed a share of the equitable remuneration. The United States again provides exceptions. It has less need for the separate category of performers' rights, as its legislation makes it possible for recording artists to claim ownership of master rights on creative grounds. As indicated above, these rights are usually assumed by record companies via work made for hire criteria, but in situations where they are retained, the rights can last for the lifetime of the performer plus a set number of years. In addition, American legislation grants performers a share of remuneration for the broadcast of their work on digital subscription services. Although the duration of this performing right is tied to the publication of recordings, it is granted in respect of creativity.

A further complication in respect of the rights in musical works, sound recordings and performances is that territories have categorized them in different ways. There is a split between the legislation of countries with common law systems (such as the United States, Britain, Canada, Australia and New Zealand) and the legislation that exists in countries with civil law systems (pervasive in Continental Europe and most of South America). The common law system of copyright was intended to serve two purposes: balancing the interests of authors (by granting them rights in their artistic creations) with those of the public (by limiting the duration of copyright and therefore ensuring that works enter the public domain and become more readily available). It has nevertheless demonstrated an ability to address business interests. Relatedly, sound recording copyright has been incorporated within the main body of the law. Civil law systems, in contrast, have a greater focus on creative artistry: the author is

---

[4]   The rental right given to performers is hybrid. This right can be assigned but it is also possible for territories to subject it to equitable remuneration despite this transfer (WPPT 1996: art. 9). To date, this has generally had little practical implication as few countries have a rental trade in recordings. Subscription services for on-demand streaming can be viewed as a formal of rental, however, and therefore it is possible that this right could be brought into effect.

prioritized above all others. This orientation is reflected in the names given to legislation; rather than using 'copyright', civil law countries are more likely to use variants of the term *droit d'auteur* (authors' rights). Corporate entities cannot be classified as authors within this legislation. In consequence, while civil law countries house the rights in compositions within the main body of their authors' rights legislation, they classify sound recordings separately under the heading of 'neighbouring rights'. Performers' rights are meanwhile treated in a secondary manner in both common law and civil law systems. In Britain, for example, they are given a discreet section of legislation, which 'studiously' avoids use of the word 'copyright' (Arnold 2015: §1.86). In civil law countries they are grouped with sound recordings as neighbouring rights. These differences are reflected in international copyright agreements. Musical works are addressed in the Berne Convention and WIPO's Copyright Treaty (WCT). Sound recordings and performers' rights receive separate consideration via the Rome Convention and WIPO's Performances and Phonograms Treaty (WPPT).

The development of the recording industry as a rights industry

A theme of this book is that the recording industry *became* a copyright industry. During the first decades of its existence, there was no copyright in sound recordings. Thereafter, recordings gradually attracted different rights, with legislation being enacted in different places at different times. Notably, despite being the world's main exporter of recorded music, the United States did not have any federal copyright legislation for recordings until the industry was nearly 100 years old; recordings were instead protected to a limited extent via state law.

Complicating matters further, the prioritization of copyright did not coincide with the creation of legislation. For the larger part of its history, the recording industry was focused on the manufacture and retail of physical recordings, procedures that have been possible in the absence of rights. Its main recourse to copyright during its early manufacturing period was to employ it restrictively, using it as a means of preventing and prosecuting unauthorized duplication. Even here intellectual property was not a necessity, as it has been possible to use criminal law, rather than copyright, to clamp down on this activity. Criminal law could only go so far, however, and as recordings became more easily and effectively reproducible, the recording industry turned increasingly to copyright legislation. It used the reproduction right to clamp down on the unauthorized duplication of records, cassette tapes and compact discs. This same right enabled it to set limits around the digital sampling of recordings. To provide further protection, the rental right was used by recording industries in most countries to stop any rental trade emerging. Nevertheless, while the industry's principal revenues were from manufacture and its main use of copyright was restrictive in nature, it did not conceptualize recordings in relation to the intellectual property they contain. They were viewed instead as goods for sale.

It is through licensing activity that copyright assumed centrality and record companies began to abstract recordings into different revenue streams. Although it has been possible to license music without rights being in place, this practice has been most effectively facilitated and monetized through copyright law.[5] Record companies initiated a more expansive use of rights in the 1930s and 1940s. The public performance right facilitated the licensing of recorded music in clubs, bars, shops, workplaces and restaurants. Television and radio licensing were underpinned by the right to reproduce as well as the right to broadcast. It was also in this period that record companies first licensed the synchronization of film images with sound, a process that was aided by their reproduction right. In the late twentieth century, the industry's licensing practices increased significantly in scope and remuneration. Synchronization licensing was expanded upon to incorporate the use of recordings in videos, advertisements and computer games.[6] More recently, the recording industry facilitated online licensing. The monetization of downloading and streaming has relied on the fact that recordings have reproduction, distribution and making available rights. Licensing revenues now exceed those for sales. This first happened in 2013, when the recording industry's annual global revenue for the retail of physical products was US$6.8 billion, and the combined revenue for the licensing of downloads,

---

[5] Two examples of licensing taking place prior to the implementation of rights are provided by the BBC in Britain. From its inception, the broadcaster entered into agreements with the Performing Right Society (PRS) for the use of compositions, albeit that the BBC 'refused to acknowledge' that radio represented a form of public performance and this was reflected in its licensing rates (Ehrlich 1989: 47). The BBC also forged licensing agreements with record companies ahead of the establishment of performing rights for sound recordings (HJC 1978: 216, note). A further example of this practice comes from the United States: synchronization licensing first took place in the inter-war period, but was not addressed by federal copyright until the 1970s.

[6] In the United States, synchronization licensing is facilitated by the derivative right as well as the reproduction right (USCO 2016a: 55–6). It is also American practice to license digital sampling via these two rights.

on-demand streaming, synchronization and public performance was US\$7.4 billion (IFPI 2022: 11). By 2021, licensing was accounting for over 80 per cent of global recording industry revenue (IFPI 2022: 11).

This move towards licensing has had contradictory effects. Copyright has gained greater importance for record companies, but in the process their hold over it has become less assured. There are two reasons for this. First, the concentration on copyright has alerted other parties to its value. Recording artists in particular have questioned why they have not gained recognition as copyright owners. Second, the recording industry's strength as a copyright industry has been derived from its strength as a manufacturing industry. The corollary of this is that, as record companies' manufacturing practices have declined, there has been greater potential for music makers to gain ownership of rights. Record companies have reacted to this situation, arguing that if they are denied the long-term security of their copyright holdings they will not have sufficient funds to invest in the music of tomorrow. In addition, they have suggested that without their centralized control of copyright there will be administrative chaos. Licensing processes will get tied up in claims and counter-claims about ownership; recordings will therefore have less chance of providing their aesthetic and economic rewards.

This rhetoric is indicative of insecurity. High-profile performers, including Prince, Taylor Swift and Kanye West, have expressed outrage that record companies have had abiding control of their master rights (Ingham 2019a; Newman 2016; Stutz 2020). These artists have made their claims, in part, on the grounds of creativity, but their main legislative impulse is that they have assumed the organizational and financial responsibility for making recordings. Other artists have made successful bids for copyright ownership. As far back as the mid-twentieth century, performers such as Ray Charles, Frank Sinatra and Dave Clark were gaining hold of their rights. This was, nevertheless, a minority position. Prior to the advent of digital technologies, artist ownership was circumscribed. In order to facilitate the manufacture and distribution of physical recordings, the majority of musicians had to sign exclusive contracts with record labels. It was control of these processes that placed copyright in the companies' hands. Downloading and streaming work differently. It is possible for artists to distribute their sound recordings online without going through traditional record company channels. If they license through DIY distributors or services companies, the artists will have ownership of copyright. This is because they are, in effect, acting as 'producers'. Moreover, because artists have recourse to these alternative routes to market, they are now better positioned when negotiating with traditional labels. One concession more regularly achieved is the shorter transfer of rights.

The politics of sound recording copyright

Recording artists have gained various types of capital from owning the rights in sound recordings. Most obviously, they have acquired economic capital. The rights have been of value in and of themselves, as indicated by the large sums obtained by performers for the outright sale of their copyright titles. Ownership has also enabled artists to negotiate superior royalty rates, either at the point of initial contract with distributors and services companies or when renegotiating terms with record companies. Performers have gained artistic capital as well. Ownership has given them a greater say in relation to the recording and presentation of their work. In addition, it has enabled them to restrict uses of their music, should they wish. Rights ownership has provided artists with symbolic capital too. For many performers, copyright has assumed centrality in their power struggles with the recording industry. Taylor Swift, for example, has spoken of the justice of having her rights ('you deserve to own the art you make') and a need to counter male dominance (she does not want her recorded work to be 'beholden to men who had no part in creating it') (Ingham 2019a). The term 'owning the masters' has been tactically employed. Although derived from an outdated equation that ownership of rights is coincidental with ownership of physical master recordings, it has gained wide usage and added resonance. African American artists, including Prince, Jay-Z and Kanye West, have equated the surrender of copyright to record companies with becoming their slaves. In Prince's formulation, 'If you don't own your masters, your masters own you' (Sutcliffe 2016: 63).

Recording artists have not been alone in objecting to the proprietorship of the recording industry. For many members of the public, it is these master rights that have provided their first experience with and lasting impression of copyright restrictions. The encounter has often been negative. During the 1980s, the recording industry attempted to criminalize its consumers, warning them that 'home taping is killing music: and it's illegal'. In the 1990s and 2000s, it used technological enforcement to restrict the public's activities: limiting the copying abilities of digital recorders and seeking to control distribution via computer coding. The early twenty-first century witnessed further criminalization, with the industry prosecuting individual consumers for the exchange of digital files. The public has also experienced an increase in the duration of sound recording copyright and a reduction in its exemptions. The activities of amateur musicians and 'prosumers' have additionally been circumscribed (Toffler 1980). Record companies have patrolled the sampling and remixing of recordings. They are battling against the 'safe harbours' that spare user-generated services from prosecution when consumers post recordings online.

Criminalization has led to activism. Despite the distinct treatment of sound recordings within intellectual property legislation, there has been a tendency to view the corporate ownership of master rights and the manner in which it has been exercised as being representative of copyright as a whole. Correspondingly, sound recordings have been utilized by those who have wished to push back against intellectual property laws. Advocates of alternative copyright systems have made them central to their debates. The rights have also provided a target to be attacked through the active promotion of 'piracy'. More generally, the politics of copyright have been polarized. Law professor Paul Goldstein has documented a split between copyright optimists, who 'view copyright's cup of entitlement as always half full, only waiting to be filled still further', and copyright pessimists, who 'accept that copyright owners should get some measure of control over copies as an incentive to produce creative works, but they would like copyright to extend only so far as is necessary to give this incentive, and treat anything more as an encroachment on the general freedom of everyone to write and say what they please' (1994: 15).

The most prominent optimists have been the rights-holders themselves. Their opinions have found sympathetic responses among policy-makers, however, particularly those who have regarded the creative industries as a vital part of their economies. Within academia, in contrast, there has been a tendency towards pessimism. There have been a number of overlapping and occasionally contradictory critiques. In respect of the public interest, one complaint is that a system that was designed to facilitate access to knowledge has become a means to 'prevent' this (Frith and Marshall 2004: 4). The public domain has been encroached upon; the private use of copyright material has been monitored and monetized. A further concern is that, even when the public has gained access to copyright material, it has not been permitted to utilize or adapt it. The fair use and fair dealing provisions of the law, which traditionally provided freedom to parody and quote, have been replaced with 'fared use', meaning that every employment of a copyright work has to be authorized and paid for (Bell 1998: 557–620). Another tranche of criticism relates to the aesthetics of copyright. The law has been condemned for promoting false and self-serving ideals. Rather than acknowledging that creative practice is collaborative and borrows from the past, copyright perpetuates the 'concept of individual genius' (Bettig 1996: 239). This has been regarded as 'a mystification that helps perpetuate possessive individualism' (Bettig 1996: 239). It also upholds a Eurocentric bias. Copyright has favoured the scripted works of lone creators. As such, it has readily embraced the melodic and harmonic aspects of musical notation but has not been 'well suited to the protection of Afro-American musicians' improvisational art or rhythmic skills' (Frith 1988: 63). A further critique focuses on the economics of copyright. It has been argued that, rather than rewarding its 'supposed beneficiaries' (the authors of creative works), copyright has been of most benefit to the 'big corporations' that have requested the transfer of their rights and bound them with one-sided contracts (Toynbee 2004: 124).

Sound recording copyright both complicates and reinforces these ideas. Ownership has enabled record companies to restrict access by making recordings 'scarce' and 'dear', thus corresponding with a traditional complaint about the monopolizing tendencies of copyright (Macaulay 1841). We can witness this in their business-to-consumer practices for physical sales, whereby they have clamped down on unauthorized manufacture and set high prices for their goods. It is also evident in their approach peer-to-peer file-sharing. This has not, however, been their only policy. When it comes to the licensing of venues, broadcasters and online services, the main intention of corporate owners has been to make their copyright holdings as widely available as possible.[7] In addition, much of this licensing has been paid for business-to-business rather than directly by consumers. Thus, there are times when it has felt as though recordings have been available for free.

Sound recording copyright has demonstrated similarly diverse tendencies when it comes to adaptation and fair use. On the one hand, the legislation

---

[7] In contrast, when performers gain control of master rights, there is evidence of them going further than corporations in relation to increasing their scope (with a desire that the term be tied to their lifetimes rather than dates of production) and being more restrictive when granting access to the work (evidencing a greater tendency to withdraw recordings from circulation). There is a long history of the latter attitude in relation to performing rights and it has also been evidence with reproduction rights. Examples are provided by the KLF, who confirmed their retirement from the music business in 1992 by deleting their back catalogue (Higgs 2012: 201). Kraftwerk have similarly utilized ownership of their catalogue to prevent early recordings being re-released.

has been more open than other forms of copyright. It has remained resolutely 'physicalist' in nature, meaning that it is only possible to infringe the rights if copying master recordings exactly (Barron 2004: 193). Consequently, the individual techniques of recording artists and studio technicians have not been protected in law. On the other hand, sound recording copyright has been strictly controlled. There has been a 'ratcheting up' of the law so there is no *de minimis* leeway (Sell 2010). The rights of the owners are trespassed upon even when copying small fractions of recordings.

Evidence has been further conflicted in respect of copyright's mystifications. Sound recording copyright has had scant regard for artistic genius. One area where this has been manifest is in the award of ownership. As noted above, rather than going to lone creators, it has most commonly been granted to corporate entities. Artists have been able to own this copyright, but their standard means of doing this has been to cast themselves as recording companies. Performers' rights have also called the individualistic ethos of copyright into question. They have been forged in a co-operative spirit, with the result that each performer on a track will gain accreditation. Also, in their original conception it was possible to distribute the remuneration to a collective body of musicians, rather than those who made the recordings. It is nevertheless worth reiterating that sound recording copyright and performers' rights have been considered secondary within legislation, a status that has been accorded because they have not been regarded as the works of individual creators.

These tendencies have also been evident when it comes to Eurocentric bias. Performers' rights and sound recording copyright have operated in a more neutral manner than the rights for original creative works. Performers' rights have generally been egalitarian: all vocal and instrumental contributions have been given near-equal recognition. Sound recording copyright has had a similar orientation due to its physicalist nature. Rhythm and improvisation have been accorded the same status as harmony and melody when it comes to creating copies of recordings. In addition, the designation of authorship has provided a means by which biases can be overturned. African American artists have been able to vanquish the legislative neglect of their improvisational and rhythmic skills by claiming master rights on business grounds.

The issue of economic beneficiaries has been the most vexed of all. On some occasions, record company personnel have been upfront about their self-interest. Walter Yetnikoff, who was CEO of CBS from 1975 to 1990, admitted it was company policy to 'Pay the artists as little as you can. Tie up the artist for as long as you can. Recoup as often as you can' (Yetnikoff and Ritz 2004: 286). Ben Katovsky of BMG revealed that the outlook of record companies towards artists has been 'what's mine is mine and what's yours is mine' (Forde 2021). Sound recording copyright has aided them in this respect, as it has been oriented so that business entities, rather than recording artists or studio personnel, can be the first owners. Yet the authorial criteria have also provided a means of measuring copyright's benefits for music makers, an increasing number of whom have been able to claim ownership in spite of these designations. Significantly, they have gained clear advantages from doing so. Copyright-owning artists have regularly been in a stronger position – economically, artistically and symbolically – than those who have not had hold of their rights.

This has not meant that the point raised by copyright pessimists is moot. It remains important to ask who profits the most: the big corporations or the music makers? Indeed, this is the lure for writing about this subject. More than any other form of intellectual property, the history of sound recording copyright is one in which creators have battled against industry to gain control. Gauging the scale of this transformation is not straightforward, however. In addition to tallying the increase in copyright-owning artists, there is a need to assess the manner in which they have acquired and utilized their rights. One difficulty in this respect is the corporate-like manner in which they have made their claims. In theory, it could be possible for recording artists to overhaul or reorient the criteria of legislation so that ownership of this copyright is accorded in respect of creative work. Yet rather than doing this, music makers have overwhelmingly sought ownership by assuming the mantle of organizers and employers. Relatedly, masters-owning artists have displayed some of the self-interest of record companies. A creative copyright would be pluralistic, with authorship being shared between the numerous artistic contributors to recordings. A corporately oriented copyright forecloses this, with the rights instead being the preserve of the most business-like creators.

A second complication is that, even though they have utilized corporate criteria to gain ownership, most music makers remain different to record companies in their uses of these rights. Record companies now gain ownership both as authors and assignees. Their purpose is to protect and exploit their portfolios of copyright titles to maximize returns. To do so, they want to retain hold of the rights for as long as possible. The desire of music makers, on the other hand, is to secure initial ownership as authors. They may share the same monetizing goals as record companies, but even with the turn to online licensing, they might not be able to achieve them on their own. Consequently, their needs may be best realized by transferal of ownership, which in many instances is still being transacted with record labels. The obtainment of authorial recognition can therefore matter less in relation to retaining control of sound recording copyright than in the negotiating power it provides.

About this book

This book shares a belief with copyright pessimists that legislation can be excessive. In particular, there have been betrayals of the common law system and its intent to serve the public. At the same time, it does not view copyright in a wholly negative light. To assess the parameters of legislation, it suggests that we look at copyright's affordances as well as its constraints. To address the ratcheting up of the law, we need to examine whether it inevitably serves corporate interests at the expense of other parties. To explore its philosophical influence, we need to assess the extent to which business and artistic practices are beholden to its beliefs. There is a need to take an evolutionary approach, not only in examining how the law has multiplied over time but also to gauge its treatment of different types of work in their different domains.

In assessing the particularities of sound recording copyright and performers' rights, the main focus is on the development of laws in Britain and the United States. In addition, this book addresses the comparative legislation in civil law countries. The opening chapter looks at the creation of the first reproduction rights for recordings at the outset of the twentieth century. Although record companies claimed these rights and thus established norms of ownership that would safeguard their businesses, there is little sense of this representing a bid for power. The second chapter turns to the inter-war period, examining developments in copyright that resulted from the introduction of radio broadcasting and electronically amplified recordings. There was rivalry over the resultant intellectual property in performances, leading to the development of neighbouring rights and performers' rights. The third chapter looks at the mid-twentieth-century introduction of tape recording technologies and the effects they had on sound recording copyright law, prompting changes in authorship criteria and a wider adoption of legislation. The fourth chapter progresses towards the end of the century, exploring an expansion in licensing activity, including the monetization of digital sampling, increased opportunities for synchronization licensing, and the development and concordance of performing rights. It also addresses the record companies' more stringent control of the reproduction right, as they sought to maximize their revenues from compact discs. The fifth chapter addresses the companies' ownership insecurities. As copyright assumed greater importance, the authorship of master rights was increasingly called into question. The companies hoped to shore up their interests through rhetoric and by changes to laws. The sixth chapter examines the introduction of online services. With the turn to downloading and streaming, the majority of record company revenues have been drawn from licensing rather than physical sales. The record companies pre-empted this situation by contributing to the development of the making available right and orienting the online market so it would operate in a similar manner to the one for physical goods. The final chapter addresses the contemporary situation. As indicated, there has been a turn towards artist ownership of master rights, not least because the recording industry has not been able to completely resist the qualitative differences of the online environment. Nevertheless, while some artists are vaunting the benefits of owning their masters, others are experiencing limitations. This has prompted questions about reform.

1

Mechanizing

Most histories of the early recording industry pay scant attention to copyright (Gelatt 1977; Read and Welch 1976).[1] When it comes to intellectual property, they address patent rights instead. And while they trace the transformation from an industry focused upon the development of recording technologies towards one that concentrated on musical recordings, they paint a picture of a business obsessed with the production of goods rather than the production of intellectual property. Simon Frith has suggested it was only towards the end of the twentieth century that the industry moved away from this model. For him, what had been regarded 'as manufacture, an industry primarily selling commodities to consumers, came to be treated… as a service, "exploiting" musical properties as baskets of rights' (1993: ix).

Michael Jones has argued, in contrast, that the recording industry 'has always been a rights industry' (2014: 52). There is some evidence for this. If we look at the British and American copyright acts of the twentieth century, we find that sound recording was repeatedly a central concern. The legislative debates set the interests of record companies against the interests of publishers and broadcasters. They brought forth interventions from leading politicians, including Theodore Roosevelt and Winston Churchill. They also involved artistic luminaries, such as George Bernard Shaw and John Philip Sousa. Sound recording was debated at meetings of the Berne Convention, the first major international copyright agreement, including the original Convention of 1886 and the revisions of 1896, 1908, 1928 and 1948. It also prompted an offshoot of Berne, the Rome Convention of 1961, which centres upon this subject.

Sound recording rights have nevertheless taken a curious trajectory. Although Britain legislated for their copyright as early as 1911, there was not a great deal of interest in this development. Elsewhere, the idea of this form of protection was rejected. In the United States, for example, sound recording copyright was

---

[1] Notable exceptions are Suisman (2012) and Sanjek and Sanjek (1991).

first debated in the opening decade of the twentieth century, but there would be no federal legislation until the 1970s. Moreover, while various other countries contemplated or created recording rights in the early 1900s, the main ambition of record companies in this period was not to secure protection. Rather, it was a *lack of rights* industry that was desired. They were not in search of copyright for their own recordings but hoped to instead avoid copyright fees for their use of songs and compositions.

This chapter examines this early period. Its first section addresses the philosophical and economic considerations that led to the creation of what came to be known as the 'mechanical right'. This right belongs to composers and their publishers, and is activated whenever a musical composition is reproduced for a recording device, whether that be a shellac record, a tin-foil cylinder, a piano player roll, a music box or any of the later formats for sound recordings. The second section of the chapter looks at means by which manufacturers fought against and set limits around this right, most notably with the development of compulsory licensing. The introduction of sound recording copyright is the subject of the chapter's third section. Given its later importance to the economics of the music industries, as well as its significant effects on intellectual property law, the origins of this copyright are curiously muted. The fourth section of the chapter addresses the earliest debates about the authorship of recordings. In this period, sound recordings both gained and were denied rights on creative grounds, with debates centring on whether corporate entities and performers can be viewed as creators.

The quest for a mechanical right

1. Copyright doctrine

Copyright law begins with the word. The British Statute of Anne of 1710 has been described as the first copyright act (Kretschmer and Kawohl 2004: 26; Sherman and Bently 1999: 207–8). It is concerned solely with 'published books and other writings' (Statute of Anne 1710). What differentiates this Statute from earlier legislation for the book trade is its inclusion of the 'encouragement of learning' as a core rationale (Statute of Anne 1710). The Statute sought to make writing profitable and reading affordable. In doing so, it created a new rights owner. Whereas printers and booksellers had previously assumed control of the rights in books, this legislation casts authors as owners. They have the 'sole liberty' to determine the publication of their work (Statute of Anne 1710). Their rights are nevertheless restricted in duration. A fourteen-year term is set by the date of publication, after which any assigned rights will be returned. The authors then have the opportunity to protect their work for fourteen more years, but at the end of this period it will enter what has become known as the 'public domain'. It was believed that the expiry of the copyright period would open up a free market for publication, leading to cheaper books and a wider literary market. American copyright law has been influenced by the ideals of this Statute, as can be witnessed in the Constitution of 1787, which states, 'Congress shall have Power… To promote the Progress of Science and useful Arts, by securing for limited Times to Authors and Inventors the exclusive Right to their respective Writings and Discoveries' (1787: art. 1, §8).

Although the Statute of Anne is foundational, it does have key differences from contemporary legislation. It does not use the term 'copyright', instead stating that authors have rights in the 'copies of printed books' (Statute of Anne 1710). Copy is a publishers' term, referring to the manuscript for a printed work (Rose 1993: 12, 58). Its usage is significant, as it points towards the trade interests that lay behind this author-oriented Act. While writers were given new status via the Statute, its main sponsors and beneficiaries were the booksellers who purchased the 'copy' of their scripts. The use of the word 'copy' is also indicative of the 'physicalist' nature of the legislation. Anne Barron has employed this term to describe rights that are centred on physical products. In contrast, she uses the term 'formalist' for rights that deal with artistic expression in a more abstract sense (2004: 193). The Statute of Anne is physicalist through and through. The duration of rights is tied to the date the book is published, rather than the lifetime of the author. It is only possible to infringe an author's work if the text is copied exactly. If caught, offenders have to submit illicit copies to the rightful owner, who will 'make waste-paper of them' (Statute of Anne 1710). They also have to pay the owner one pence for each sheet they have printed.

Barron regards this protection as 'thin' (2006: 105). It is confined to duplication and does not address plagiarism. This oversight was not, however, due to the Statute's physicalist nature alone. Within contemporary artistic practice, the reworking of material was valued rather than denigrated. Writing in 1719, Jonathan Richardson stated that no artist should 'be asham'd to be sometimes a Plagiary, 'tis what the greatest Painters, and Poets have allowed themselves' (Goehr 1992: 184–5). Peter Jaszi notes that early case law accordingly 'treated non-identical imitations as meritorious new productions by new "authors", not as infringements' (1991: 472).

Music entered into and helped transform this framework. Compositions first gained copyright protection on the grounds they too are literary works. This designation was achieved in Britain in 1777 via the case of *Bach v Longman*, which held that music 'may be written; and the mode of conveying the ideas is by signs and marks' (1777: 624). Music could therefore be regarded as one of the 'other writings' addressed by the Statute of Anne. In 1842, royal assent was given to a new Copyright Act, which would underpin British rights legislation until 1911. It encompassed music on the grounds it can be published in books. American copyright law developed similarly. Case law decisions in the late eighteenth century established that scores are texts. Subsequently, the United States Copyright Act of 1831 accepted musical compositions as a category of writing (Brauneis 2014: 10–12).

Yet music could only be regarded as a form of writing because literary copyright was no longer equated solely with its physical manifestation. A move towards a formalist conception of copyright 'involved identifying the literary object as an entity whose existence exceeded these surface details' (Barron 2006: 113). Mark Rose views this transformation as being implicit in the Statute of Anne: 'If the author was to be a proprietor and an agent in the literary marketplace, if the author was to appear in court in his own person to protect his interests, then inevitably the conception of the property owned would be affected' (1993: 65). What followed was an 'abstraction of the notion of literary property from its physical basis in ink and paper' (Rose 1993: 64). Correspondingly, new terminology began to be employed. In the wake of the Statute of Anne, the term 'copyright' was taken up in place of 'copy'. Its use, according to Rose, 'suggests an attenuation of this feeling for the manuscript as the material basis of the property; an abstract right was being formulated, a legal claim based on a general idea of the author's creative labour' (1993: 58).

Barron places the fuller formation of this thinking in the literary property debates of the 1760s and 1770s. Scottish booksellers were seeking to liberate the market by confirming the concept of the public domain; London booksellers, in opposition, were hoping to cement their dominance of the British trade by establishing a perpetual copyright in books. It was their argument that there had been common law copyright in literary compositions prior to the Statute of Anne and which continued in spite of it. They sought to differentiate literary invention from mechanical invention, as patent rights for the latter were limited in duration. In making their case, they suggested that copyright existed within literary compositions themselves, rather than in the manifestations of those compositions as published books. This brought forth new conceptions of creativity, challenging the prevailing neo-classical conceptions of artistic practice, which had little room for originality or inspiration. An artist's main purpose, according to the neoclassical viewpoint, was to imitate nature to the best of their ability (as the least mimetic of the arts, music was consequently downplayed). In seeking perpetual literary property rights, the advocates of common law protection reversed this thinking. Artistic expression was now prioritized.

The claim for common law copyright was both accepted and denied. The outcome of the 1774 case of *Donaldson v Beckett* has been disputed, but is generally taken as holding that common law copyright for authors' texts had existed in principle, but was superseded by the Statute of Anne (Rose 1993: 109–10). However, while this decision terminated notions of perpetual copyright, the debates relating to it encouraged a formalist conception of authors' rights to take hold. As a result, copyright thickened. Infringement cases had previously been undertaken in relation to the full and exact replication of the written word, but were now prosecuted on the basis of appropriating particularities of style and adapting sections of texts. In addition, as the idea of what constituted writing became more amorphous, it became possible to view copyright as encompassing more than just books. The copyright of music arrived on the back of the formalist reconfiguration of literary works. Protection also expanded beyond the unauthorized reproduction of texts to encompass other types of activity. A public performance right for dramatic works was recognized in Britain via the Dramatic Literary Property Act of 1833. Musical compositions received the same right in the Copyright Act of 1842 (1842: §20). It should be noted, however, that although copyright became increasingly formalist in nature, it retained its focus on literature and other forms of writing.

It has been argued that these legislative changes were reflective of a turn within art philosophy from neoclassicism to Romanticism. The Romantic movement accorded artists an elevated role, regarding them as bearers of unique insight and genius. Music acquired an elevated role too. It was recognized as being the most purely expressive discipline; consequently, it was believed that all arts aspired to its condition (Pater 1877: 140). Romantic artists maintained they were in advance of society and therefore only likely to be understood after they had died. They were also separate from society; the last bastions of sensitivity in an industrial revolution that had mechanized the world.

Within music, this turn was manifested in the 'work concept'. Lydia Goehr posits a paradigm shift at the cusp of the eighteenth and nineteenth centuries, at which point composers began to assume greater importance than performers. However, while they were viewed as the creators of original works, the essence of these works was somewhat obscure. Goehr writes, 'That a work's determining idea was an expression of an individually inspired genius effectively meant that its content was necessarily elusive' (1992: 222). The main remit of performers was to 'present works to us by adhering as closely as possible to the relevant scores', yet works were not 'not identical... to any one of their performances' and nor were they 'identical to their scores' (Goehr 1992: 3). This elusiveness was nevertheless imposing. A truly original work was considered inviolate.

It is Goehr's argument that when 'the ideal of originality began to regulate the activities of composers, a corresponding change was required in the concept of plagiarism' (1992: 220). Barron has countered that copyright had developed its formalist idea of 'works' prior to and independent of any 'work' concept in music. Moreover, while legislation and art theory were both centralizing the artist, they had different prompts for doing so. The Romantic elevation of artistic practice was spurred by authors themselves. In contrast, it was booksellers who promoted authorship during the literary property debates. They did so for their own ends. Few writers or composers of the eighteenth century received royalties for the sales of their 'writings'. Instead, they generally assigned all rights in their works to booksellers and publishers for one-off fees (Goehr 1992: 220). It was the assignees who stood to benefit most from any expansion of copyright.

Barron nevertheless concedes that the tenets of Romanticism and copyright law became increasingly entwined (2006: 120). This was evident in the increased legal and artistic valuation of originality and the conjoined scorn for 'mechanical' creation. Edward Young's *Conjectures on Original Composition*, first published in 1759, outlines the Romantic belief that the most important writers are those who are most expressively unique. He contrasts original composition, which 'rises spontaneously from the vital roots of Genius', with imitative composition, which represents 'a sort of *manufacture* wrought up by those *mechanics, art* and *labour*, out of preexistent materials not their own' (Rose 1993: 119. Emphasis in original).

These sentiments are echoed in the case of *D'Almaine v Boosey* (1835), which established a formalist basis for the copyright in musical works. The dispute centred on arrangements: should these reworkings be regarded as displaying independent creativity or should they be considered as an infringement of the original composition? In the 1740 case of *Gyles v Wilcox* it had been suggested that under the Statute of Anne no adaptation could be deemed 'a piracy' (*D'Almaine v Boosey* 1835: 296). *D'Almaine v Boosey* was decided differently.

Lord Chief Baron found in favour of the plaintiffs, proclaiming, 'The original air requires the aid of genius for its construction, but a mere mechanic in music can make the adaptation or accompaniment. Substantially the piracy is where the appropriated music, though adapted to a different purpose from that of the original, may still be recognised by the ear' (1835: 302).

Romantic artists led a crusade for a further expansion of copyright. In the UK, the 1814 Copyright Act had increased the term to the longest of either twenty-eight years or the life of the author. William Wordsworth, Robert Southey and Thomas Carlyle were among the authors who argued that Romantic genius would only properly be appreciated post-mortem. As a result of their campaigns, the British Copyright Act of 1842 extended the duration of copyright to the life of the author plus seven years and a minimum of forty-two years from publication. It was in Continental Europe, however, that the Romantic turn was most decisive. French legislation developed its author-centric focus when writers such as Alphonse de Lamartine and Honoré de Balzac campaigned for their rights. By 1875, the Court of Cassation was declaring that 'in a conflict of interest between the public domain on the one hand and the authors or their heirs on the other hand, we always lean in favour of the latter' (Peeler 1999: 452).

Victor Hugo built upon these foundations. As chair of the International Literary Association, he played a significant part in developing the Berne Convention for the Protection of Literary and Artistic Works. First agreed in Switzerland in 1886, this multilateral copyright convention established the principle of 'national treatment', meaning that its members would give the same protection to foreign copyright owners as they did to their national owners. The Convention continues to form the basis of much international copyright law. Betraying its origins, it is indebted to the French system of *droit d'auteur* ('right of the author'). This system can be contrasted with the copyright legislation of common law countries, such as the United States and Britain, which has sought to balance the financial interests of authors with the public's access to knowledge. The *droit d'auteur* concept, initiated by the civil law countries of continental Europe, places a stronger emphasis on the interests of creators. Reflecting this outlook, the Convention declares its intention 'to protect, in as effective and uniform a manner as possible, the rights of authors in their literary and artistic works' (Porter 1991: 2). Given these legislative roots, it is not surprising that civil law countries were prominent among its original signatories. Britain was one of the first common law countries to ratify it, doing so in 1887. The United States witnessed early Convention gatherings but did not accede until 1989. The influence has not wholly been one way, however. The Convention has influenced legislative practice in common law countries, but common law countries have also shaped the protocols of Berne.

The Berne Convention was conceived in a formalist manner, safeguarding original works rather than formats of reproduction. This had possible implications for the inventors and businesspeople who were developing new ways of distributing musical compositions. The late nineteenth century was a time of considerable technological innovation. It was the period in which sound recording was invented, the music box was elaborated and the player-piano took its mature form. Nevertheless, even though the 1886 agreement promised to protect 'every production whatsoever in the literary, scientific, or artistic domain which can be published by any mode of impression or reproduction', it exempted these devices (1886: art. 4). The agreement states that 'the manufacture and sale of instruments for the mechanical reproduction of musical airs in which copyright subsists shall not be considered as constituting an infringement of musical copyright' (1886: Final Protocol 3). As a result, the manufacturers did not need to gain authorization or pay royalties for their use of musical works.

The prompt for this exemption was diplomatic rather than philosophical. It was offered as a gesture to the host country Switzerland, which dominated the trade in music boxes. The Berne Convention has been periodically revised, however, and at a subsequent 1908 conference in Berlin it was proposed that songwriters should have 'the exclusive right' of authorizing 'the adaptation of [their] works to instruments which can reproduce them mechanically', as well as be able to control 'the public performance of the said works by means of these instruments' (Berlin Act 1908: art. 13). The makers of these instruments would henceforth be circumscribed by copyright. In addition, their devices would be branded as 'mechanical' and therefore tainted with associations of inferior artistry.

This proposal corresponded with the overall philosophy of the Convention, reflecting the belief that works of authorship should be protected in any shape or form. Yet the introduction of the mechanical right would also trouble these ideals. It led to measures that limited the scope of authors' rights and brought forth intellectual property legislation that recognized corporations as the first owners of copyright. As Benedict Atkinson has written, the Berne delegates 'discovered that if authors wanted the right to control "indirect appropriations" of musical works by mechanical reproduction, they would have to deal with a ruthless industry not inclined to give much weight to considerations of moral rights or natural justice' (2007: 48).

2. Economics

The twenty-two years between the original Berne Convention and the Berlin Conference were crucial. In 1886 there was not a recording industry as such. Thomas Edison introduced sound recording in 1877 via his cylinder-based phonograph, but commercial uptake of his discovery was slow. Two developments from 1887 represent the first stirrings of a musically focused recording industry: Columbia Records was founded (as the American Graphophone Company) and Emile Berliner patented the gramophone disc. Berliner envisioned an industry in which 'Prominent singers, speakers, or performers, may derive an income from royalties on the sale of their phonautograms, and valuable plates may be printed and registered to protect against unauthorized publication' (1888: 21). It would nevertheless be a further twenty years before these ambitions began to be realized. The sound recording trade was originally dominated by cylinder manufacturers, whose devices worked differently to gramophones. Cylinders provided a home recording function, whereas discs were restricted to professional recordings. Cylinders were also hard to duplicate, whereas reproduction was inherent in Berliner's process. It was only in the first decade of the twentieth century, as discs became ascendant, that a recording industry worthy of attracting mechanical licensing interests was established.

By 1901, the American record business had coalesced into a trio of major companies who between them controlled the main patents in discs, cylinders and their respective reproduction devices: Edison's National Phonograph Company, which remained focused on cylinder production; the Victor Talking Machine Company, which oversaw Berliner's gramophone interests; and Columbia, who by this point were manufacturing both discs and cylinders. These companies had been legislative rivals, but eventually pooled their patents via a series of licensing agreements. Despite these manoeuvres, relationships between them remained uneasy. In Britain, the recording industry was less oligopolistic, as there were fewer patent restrictions in operation. The same three businesses were nevertheless dominant. The Gramophone Company represented Berliner's interests and had reciprocal agreements with Victor; Columbia had a branch in Britain; Edison's business was first represented by the Edison-Bell Consolidated Phonograph Company and then from 1904 onwards by a branch of the National Phonograph Company.

In the years before the First World War there was significant growth in the retail of recordings and machines. Record sales in Britain reached approximately thirteen million in 1908 (Gorrell Committee 1909: 44). In the United States, the production of discs and cylinders rose from 3.75 million at the turn of the century to 27.5 million in 1909 (Sanjek and Sanjek 1991: viii). By 1911, the British record business was employing between 2,000 and 3,000 people in manufacturing and a further 15,000 as 'wholesale and retail dealers, artistes, shopmen, travellers, and the like' ('Trade Topics' 1911: 81). This was also a period of great popularity for player pianos. The leading American companies, such as Aeolian, were selling tens of thousands of copies of their most popular rolls (Henn [1956] 1960: 11 (note)).

It is understandable, then, that composers and publishers sought protection against, and revenue for, these uses of their works. The manufacturers had several counter-arguments, however. They indicated that composers would be earning money from an activity that required no extra input on the publishers' behalf. They also argued that, by purchasing sheet music, they had acquired the rights to use the compositions. More pertinently, the manufacturers contended that the publishers had previously sought their support (Gorrell Committee 1910: 53, 227). One of the recurrent features of the music industries is the balance between promotion and compensation. Some interested parties have been willing to forgo payments for uses of their works as long as those employing them are doing them greater good than harm. This had originally been the attitude of music publishers towards record companies. They viewed recorded performances of their compositions as a means to promote the sales of sheet music, and consequently requested the record companies to record their songs.

There was, however, an increasing belief among publishers that this balance had been tipped. In addition to missing out on potential copyright revenue from uses of compositions in phonographs, gramophones, piano players and music boxes, these devices were beginning to displace the sales of sheet music. It was in this context that John Philip Sousa published an influential article about the 'menace of mechanical music', arguing that recordings threatened 'to reduce the expression of music to a mathematical system of megaphones, wheels, cogs, disks, cylinders, and all manner of revolving things' ([1906] 2012: 114–15). He noted that, because composers were being 'refused a just reward for their efforts', a situation was 'almost sure to arise where all incentive to further creative work is lacking, and compositions will no longer flow from their pens' ([1906] 2012: 122). In doing so, he nodded towards the generative impulse of Anglo-American copyright legislation, while laying down arguments about newness that would be repeated in the future.

When these complaints were originally raised, it was legal practice in most countries to rebuff attempts to establish a right for the mechanical reproduction of compositions. In Britain, a precedent was set by the 1900 case of *Boosey v Whight*, which held that the perforated rolls of mechanical organs did not infringe sheet music. This ruling was viewed as applying to phonographs and gramophones as well. Belgium and Austria also held that mechanical players did not infringe copyright. The coming years witnessed some cases going the other way. In 1905, a Parisian court determined that the 'rules of plagiarism' were applicable to musical cylinders (Attali 1985: 98). Bearing in mind the contemporary exemption of music boxes from the Berne Convention, French law made clear that this ruling applied only to the reproduction of lyrics and not the reproduction of musical notation. In Italy, it was decided that the lyrical and musical aspects of mechanical devices were both worthy of copyright protection. This sentiment was echoed by the United States Supreme Court in the 1908 case of *White-Smith v Apollo*, even though it ruled against the imposition of a mechanical right. Justice Holmes stressed that 'the result is to give to copyright less scope than its rational significance' (Brylawski and Goldman 1976: K272). The year 1908 also witnessed the Berlin revision conference for the Berne Convention and its own recommendation for a mechanical right.

The manufacturers' responses

The mechanical right appeared to offer a no-win situation for the recording industry. On the one hand, composers and publishers could use it to deny access to their musical works; on the other, they could grant access, but insist upon licensing fees. The manufacturers fought back on two fronts. One policy was to deny the legitimacy of this right; another was to set limits around it.

1. Denials

Although legal cases were turning towards a formalist conception of copyright, this philosophy was not yet reflected in legislation. During the early twentieth century, the copyright laws in Britain and America remained orientated towards the protection of writings rather than works. The phonograph industry exploited this position, arguing that recordings are not texts and therefore beyond the bounds of copyright law. Its campaigns were purely a matter of convenience and entailed a repudiation of past beliefs.

Sound recording, like copyright, had begun with the word. Edison christened his sound recording device the 'phonograph', deriving the term from the Greek words for 'sound' and 'writing'. Its nearest predecessor was Edouard-Léon Scott de Martinville's phonautograph, which was patented twenty years earlier. This device operated in a similar manner to the phonograph and had a similarly derived name. However, rather than seeking to reproduce sounds, it was concerned with their 'natural stenography' (Sterne 2003: 45). Edison expressed surprise that Scott 'having gone so far' had not developed a 'talking machine', yet he too had a literary impulse (Lewis-Young 1907: 576). The phonograph was the chance outcome of other research projects, including an attempt to capture sound visually with a view to translating it into text (Conot 1979: 97). This interest persisted. Edison would flatten his cylinders into book form and take plaster casts of them, after which he would examine their 'indents' as 'an interesting study' (Asor 1878: 404).

The other developers of sound recording also thought textually. In 1888, Charles Sumner Tainter and the cousins Chichester and Alexander Graham Bell patented the graphophone, the recording machine that provided the basis for Columbia Records' business. This instrument improved upon the phonograph and was inspired by it in both function and name. Berliner's disc-playing gramophone offered a further variation on the Greek terms for sound and writing. Like Edison, he acknowledged Scott as a forebear (Berliner 1888: 3–4). He also had faith that an understanding of the groove's language could be attained. A pamphlet given away with one of his early machines states that 'Printed sound-records adapted for the purpose of studying sound-curves, and catalogues of plates will be published from time to time' (Osborne 2012: 14).

The translation of this writing remained out of reach. As early as 1878, it was being argued that it was futile 'to hope to be able to *read* the impressions and traces of phonographs, for these traces will vary, not alone with the quality of the voices, but also with the differently related times of starting of the harmonics of these voices, and with the different relative intensities of these harmonics' (Mayer 1878: 723. Emphasis in original). Intentions to decipher this language were further hampered by the commercial imperatives of sound recording. The desire with Scott's phonautograph to make 'the vibrations appear as large as possible' was replaced by a need to condense the grooves in order to maximize the playing time of both cylinders and discs (Berliner 1888: 4).

Commercial imperatives were also in evidence in the campaigns against mechanical rights. Legal cases witnessed the 'natural stenography' of sound recording being grouped with the mechanical notation of piano rolls and music boxes. The record manufacturers may once have resisted this conflation, but now utilized it for their own ends. In order to escape the textual classifications of copyright law they needed to prove that records are not writings. Consequently, the manufacturers turned from being proud purveyors of the scripture of their recordings to being defenders of their illegibility.

This policy was pursued most extensively in the United States. In 1905, President Theodore Roosevelt proposed a new copyright act. One of its early drafts included a clause to provide composers with the right to 'let for hire any device, contrivance, or appliance especially adapted in any manner whatsoever to reproduce to the ear the whole or any material part of any work published and copyrighted' (Brylawski and Goldman 1976). This mechanical right was the most vexed topic on the agenda and bore chief responsibility for the legislative debates lasting from 1906 until 1909. The record companies questioned whether it was legal within the Constitution's framework of 'writings'. Making their case at the copyright hearings, they now boasted of their failure to read records. Paul H. Cromelin of the Columbia Phonograph Company stated that 'No man living has ever been able to take a talking machine record and by examining it microscopically or otherwise state what said record contains' (Brylawski and Goldman 1976: H158). Frank L. Dyer, representing Thomas Edison and the National Phonograph Company, claimed that 'a phonograph record is not a writing because it cannot possibly be read' (Brylawski and Goldman 1976: J287). In staking out this position, the companies argued against any copyright in sound recordings. It was more important to deny a mechanical right for composers than gain a copyright of their own.

The verdict in *White-Smith v Apollo* was handed down during the hearings. At first glance, it appeared to back the record companies' claims. It held that perforated rolls could not be read and therefore were not 'copies within the meaning of the [1790] copyright act' (Brylawski and Goldman 1976: K272). The presiding justices nevertheless suggested a legislative review. Subsequently, the copyright committee heard the arguments of composers and publishers, as well as those of representatives acting on their behalf. They countered the views of record companies with two lines of thought. On the one hand, it was argued that what mattered in respect of writings was the potential of legibility. Sousa stated that 'Just as the man who wanted to scan the heavens discovered a telescope to do it. No doubt there will be found a way to read these records' (Brylawski and Goldman 1976: H23). Conversely, it was suggested that the legibility of recordings was not the real issue. The Constitution was concerned with authors' literary compositions; it did not seek to delimit the various means by which they could be manifested. Nathan Burkan, attorney for the Music Publishers Association, argued that the mechanical right was not unconstitutional as it did not 'propose to make phonographic devices a subject-matter of copyright' (Brylawski and Goldman 1976: J212). It was instead protecting the writings of composers against new forms of exploitation.

The latter argument prevailed. The final report on the Copyright Bill states, 'It is not the intention of the committee to extend the right of copyright to the mechanical reproductions themselves but only to give the composer or copyright proprietor the control… of the manufacture and use of such devices' (Ringer [1957] 1961: 5). As a result, the 1909 Act does not classify records as writings. Rather, as Lisa Gitelman has pointed out, it classifies record players, piano players and music boxes as 'readers' (1999: 145).

2. Limitations

a) The United States

Although composers received a mechanical right via the 1909 Act, their triumph was somewhat Pyrrhic. It was made subject to the first compulsory licensing provisions in American copyright law. The legislation states that once a composition has been issued on a mechanical device 'any other person may make similar use of the copyrighted work upon the payment to the copyright proprietor of a royalty of two cents' (Copyright Act 1909: §e(a)). From the publishers' perspective this was a considerable imposition. They would have no freedom in the market place. Rather than being able to sell their music to the highest bidder, they would face a limited royalty rate. In addition, once their compositions had been recorded, they would have no control over subsequent recordings of the work. Compulsory licensing meant that 'cover' versions could abound (Keightley 2003: 614–17).

The manufacturers secured compulsory licensing on two grounds. First, they argued that their vested interests should be protected (Brylawski and Goldman 1976: H158, J289). They had previously been assured there would be no mechanical right for compositions; it was against this background that their companies had been founded. These trades, with their great worth to the nation in terms of revenue generated and jobs provided, would be placed in jeopardy if there were an unfettered mechanical right. This was new territory for copyright legislation. Where previously it had been viewed as a means of protecting authors or of balancing their welfare with that of public access, it was now being suggested it should square the interests of manufacturers with those of music publishers.

The manufacturers' second argument was more decisive. They raised the spectre of monopoly, claiming that unless compulsory licensing was introduced the most powerful among them could enter into deals with music publishers for exclusive mechanical licences. Competition would be stifled, as the other companies would not be able to utilize those publishers' compositions. Here, they had evidence on their side. While most manufacturers viewed the imposition of the mechanical right as a threat, there were others who saw it as an opportunity to gain control of their trades. The Aeolian Company was the most ambitious in this respect. During the course of the copyright hearings it was revealed they had entered into exclusive licensing agreements with eighty-seven out of the eighty-nine members of the Music Publishers Association, offering them 10 per cent of the retail price of sales of pianola rolls should a mechanical right be established (Brylawski and Goldman 1976: K219, K223). It was Aeolian who sponsored the White-Smith publishing company in their case against the Apollo pianola company, calculating that any expenditure on the mechanical right would be compensated by having dominance in their business (Brylawski and Goldman 1976: H167).

There were accusations of monopoly in the recording industry too. S. T. Cameron of the American Graphophone Company argued that his company's rivals, the National Phonograph Company and Victor Records, had entered into similar negotiations with music publishers in respect of the cylinder and disc markets (Brylawski and Goldman 1976: H142). Although both companies denied this, it was discovered that Victor did have links with the Music Publishers Association. Alone among the record companies, they were proposing that sound recordings should also have a copyright of their own. They agreed to back the publishers' legislative arguments for the mechanical right in return for the publishers' support for this idea (Brylawski and Goldman 1976: H154). While the other companies stressed the illegibility of recordings, Horace Pettit of Victor was arguing that sound recording represented a 'new form of writing' that was 'within the contemplation of the Constitution' and therefore deserved to be protected by copyright (Brylawski and Goldman 1976: H29). It was a position he later reneged. Following the verdict in the *White-Smith* case, Pettit stated that, as 'the court does not consider the subjection of musical instruments to a copyright act to be constitutional', there should be neither a mechanical right nor a sound recording copyright (Brylawski and Goldman 1976: K265).

This was no Damascene conversion. Pettit's decision to adopt the same stance as his manufacturing rivals is more likely to have been occasioned by a desire to avoid the taint of monopoly, which had long caused alarm in copyright disputes. In 1841, Lord Macaulay made a foundational argument on this subject to the British parliament, as he sought to rebuff the claims of Wordsworth, Southey and Carlyle for a longer term of copyright:

> Copyright is monopoly, and produces all the effects which the general voice of mankind attributes to monopoly... The effect of monopoly generally is to make articles scarce, to make them dear, and to make them bad... It is good that authors should be remunerated; and the least exceptionable way of remunerating them is by a monopoly. Yet monopoly is an evil. For the sake of the good we must submit to the evil; but the evil ought not to last a day longer than is necessary for the purpose of securing the good.
>
> (1841)

Accusations of monopoly led President Roosevelt to intervene in the American debates (Sanjek and Sanjek 1991: 12). He signed off on the 1909 Act on condition that the mechanical right be made subject to compulsory licensing restrictions. The House Report on the Act concludes, 'It became evident that there would be serious danger that if the grant of right were made too broad, the progress of science and useful arts would not be promoted, but rather hindered, and that powerful and dangerous monopolies might be fostered which would be prejudicial to the public interests' (Currier 1909: 7). The Report also confirms there will be no sound recording copyright, stating there is no intention 'to extend the right of copyright to the mechanical reproductions themselves' (1909: 8).

b) Berne Convention countries

The conclusion to the American copyright debates overlapped with the Berlin Conference and its own debates about the mechanical right. Issues that had been aired in America were on the agenda again, not least because witnesses from the US hearings were present in Berlin. The National Phonograph Company, Victor and Columbia were each represented, despite the fact that America was not a Berne member. Delegates at the Berlin Conference heard about the hardship that would be caused to 'legitimate' manufacturing businesses if mechanical rights were enacted (Grey 1909: 14). The threat of exclusive licensing agreements was also raised. During the proceedings, accusations were made that monopolies were being established in France, Italy and Germany (Brylawski and Goldman 1976: J341-2; 'Law of Copyright' 1908: 74). It was claimed that these would-be monopolizers only offered a 'lukewarm' opposition to the imposition of a mechanical right ('Musical Copyright Situation' 1909: 726). National interests were at stake. Countries with significant record manufacturing concerns, such as Germany and Britain, campaigned for a mechanical right with compulsory licensing provisions. Other countries, such as Italy and France, who had already established mechanical licensing and did not wish to 'diminish' any rights 'enjoyed by composers', thought differently (Grey 1909: 14).

The result was a compromise. While an international system of compulsory licensing was 'emphatically rejected' (Grey 1909: 14), the Berlin Conference gave Berne members the option to make 'reservations and conditions' as they saw fit (1908: art. 13(2)). A raft of legislation then followed as signatories to Berne updated their laws to accommodate these recommendations. In Britain, a copyright committee was set up under the stewardship of Lord Gorrell. During the proceedings that followed, representatives of the Gramophone, Columbia and Edison companies repeated arguments that had been voiced in America. There was a different inflection to the debates, however. The British manufacturers realized that their aims could be best achieved if they presented a unified front, and so formed a coalition to present their case to government. In addition, they accepted the mechanical right as a given. Hence their campaign was focused on the compensation they could receive in return.

Outlining their position before Gorrell's committee, the first 'cardinal point' the British companies insisted upon was compulsory licensing, modelled on the 'precedent' set by American legislation (1910: 46). They argued that because they were 'putting such an enormous amount of additional work and money into the phonograms' and 'the saleability of the phonogram depends almost exclusively on the reputation of the artiste who *created* the record', composers 'should be satisfied with a comparatively small royalty' (1910: 50, 230. Emphasis in original). When questioned by the publisher William Boosey why the manufacturers would 'deny to the composer the protection of his property, his right to bargain for that which belongs to him?', James Van Allen Shields of Columbia raised the threat of monopolies, 'which will be to the detriment of the public as well as to the detriment of the manufacturer' (1910: 107).

The Gorrell Committee rejected these claims. It discounted the idea of compulsory licensing on the grounds that 'freedom of contract is most beneficial to the development of all kinds of industries' and because it believed the threat of monopoly was 'exaggerated' (1909: 25). The record companies' emphasis on their artists also appears to have backfired. The Committee stated that if 'the performer is of more importance to the manufacturers than the composer of the piece', the manufacturers were operating their own 'class of monopoly' by means of their exclusive recording contracts (1909: 25). The Committee also felt that, given it was 'impossible to separate the values respectively of the manufacturer's work, the performer's work and the composer's work' in each individual recording, it would be unwise to set a standard compulsory licensing rate (1909: 25).

British manufacturers were treated differently to those in Germany, which in 1910 became the first European country to legislate for a mechanical right with compulsory licensing provisions. They nevertheless persisted with their case, petitioning politicians as the Copyright Bill made its way through parliament and promoting their cause in the daily press. The proceedings became increasingly focused on workers' interests, with the record companies presenting themselves as defenders of the labouring classes. James Drummond Robertson of the Gramophone Company had earlier conjured up the 'vast number of wage-earners, dependent directly upon the prosperity of our business, without taking into account the even larger numbers of workers in the wood, metal, printing, and many other industries, who furnish the needs of our trade', and suggested that these interests must 'be weighed against the claim of a very small number of composers to be compensated for rights which were never theirs' (Gorrell Committee 1910: 228). The record companies gained the support of the Labour Party, which was becoming a significant presence in parliament having gained forty-two seats in the 1910 election. Labour's influence was strengthened further because there was a hung parliament and the ruling Liberal Party required its support.

William Boosey viewed these developments with mystification. Engaging in debates in the letters pages of *The Times*, he wrote of 'perplexing' attitudes, maintaining that 'Every vote given by the Labour Party for compulsory licence is a vote in support of capital and vested interests against the worker' (1911: 4). He argued, 'It is a vote against the right of the labourer to ask what wage he considers he is entitled to' (1911: 4). George Bernard Shaw participated in this dialogue, taking the composers' side against that of the manufacturers. He noted, 'We, being artists, are poor and politically insignificant. They, being industrialists, are rich and can bully Governments' (1911: 7). Shaw nevertheless supported the record companies' claims for recompense. Offering a comparison to the outlawing of slavery in America, he argued that the policy of compensating slave owners for abolition had been the right thing to do. He would not, however, have asked the freed slaves 'to pay the compensation' (1911: 7). Correspondingly he would not wish the imposition of a compulsory licence upon 'unfortunate composers, who have already been robbed' (1911: 7). Government should instead compensate the record companies directly.

The record companies continued to press for compulsory licensing. In his own correspondence to *The Times*, Robertson claimed that its imposition would not be to the detriment of 'poor composers' and would instead make them prosperous due to the increased licensing of their works (1911a: 10). The companies also stressed the benefit of compulsory licensing for poorer audiences, arguing that in its absence there 'would be a most oppressive monopoly, and one which would bear extreme hardship upon that class of the population who had hitherto expected to purchase replicas of works at modest and moderate prices' ('Trade Topics' 1911: 77). Their case eventually gained cross-party support. The Copyright Bill had been introduced by the Liberal Member of Parliament Sydney Buxton. In July 1911 he announced a new clause, which granted compulsory licensing on the grounds that 'giving the composer full rights would be injurious to the manufacturers and the public' ('Gramophones and Copyright' 1911: 12).

This proposal was endorsed. The 1911 Copyright Act establishes mechanical licensing with the proviso that:

> It shall not be deemed to be an infringement of copyright in any musical work for any person to make… records, perforated rolls, or other contrivances by means of which the work may be mechanically performed, if such person proves that such contrivances have previously been made by, or with the consent or acquiescence of, the owner of the copyright in the work. (1911: §19(2))

The licensing fees for this system were based on a percentage of the retail price of the 'contrivance': 2.5 per cent until 1913; 5 per cent after that (1911: §19(3)). This was in contrast to the United States, where the 1909 Act established a fixed price, originally set at two cents per recording.

Within the space of three years, a mechanical right with compulsory licensing provisions had therefore been introduced in each of the leading record manufacturing countries: the United States, Germany and Britain. This was a subject that received a great deal of attention, bringing manufacturers and publishers into conflict and introducing transformative measures to rights legislation. As such, it overshadowed another development. These debates also ushered in the earliest copyright protection for the recording itself.

The origins of British sound recording copyright

When American record companies entered the legislative copyright debates in 1906, the majority were campaigning against all forms of copyright relating to recordings. In their desire to reject the mechanical right they were prepared to forgo sound recording copyright as well. The British legislative debates took place in a different context. They followed on from the American Copyright Act and the Berlin Conference, which via the mechanical right had established the principle of intellectual property in recordings. Consequently, the manufacturers were better placed to demand rights of their own.

Sound recording copyright was first requested as part of the 1908 Berlin Conference negotiations. Representing the interests of British manufacturers, Sir Edward Grey sought 'a provision specially giving international copyright protection, in suitable cases, to gramophone discs, pianola rolls, &c.' (1909: 14). Other delegates objected on mechanical grounds, believing that 'the subject was on the border line between "industrial property" and copyright, and might conceivably be held to belong more properly to the former category' (Grey 1909: 14). The proposal nevertheless resurfaced during the Gorrell Committee's proceedings, which witnessed the British record companies' making a request for 'copyright protection for the phonogram' (1910: 229). Moreover, while the Committee originally concluded by denying compulsory licensing for the mechanical right, it compensated this by recommending that 'protection should be afforded by legislation to the manufacturers of discs, cylinders, rolls and other mechanical devices' (1909: 26). This advice was acted upon in the British Copyright Act of 1911, which created a copyright in sound recordings.

Looked at from a twenty-first-century perspective, this early campaign for a sound recording copyright appears subdued. In comparison to compulsory licensing, it was barely mentioned during the Gorrell Committee hearings. What is more, in the few times it was addressed, even the music publishers were accepting of it. This might seem strange. If compulsory licensing represented a break with copyright traditions, the introduction of sound recording copyright was more radical still. Its acceptance is nevertheless indicative of the pragmatism of British copyright debates. The publishers were happy to concede to the manufacturers' copyright in sound recordings if they gained a mechanical right of their own. Even William Boosey, who was vehemently opposed to the record companies' compulsory licensing proposals, maintained that 'The gramophone companies claim, and quite rightly, protection for their own discs' (1911: 4).

The record companies did not make this claim forcefully. Outlining their demands as they sought compensation for the mechanical right, Robertson indicated that their 'main' desire was for it to be accompanied by a compulsory licence (1911b: 4). Sound recording copyright, in contrast, was the final and apparently least of their concerns. This is evidenced by the record companies barely complaining when, in spite of the Committee's recommendations, sound recording copyright was not included in the original drafts of the Copyright Bill. They were fixated instead on the denial of compulsory licensing. In addition, when sound recording copyright was eventually recognized in the 1911 Act, the record companies did not make much of this either. The trade journal *Talking Machine News* attempted to solicit manufacturers' responses to the legislation but found there was 'a reluctance to offer any very definite opinion' ('Trade Views' 1912: 416). J. Lewis Young of the National Phonograph Company is indicative of this attitude, responding that he did not think the Act would 'make the slightest difference' to his trade ('Trade Views' 1912: 418).

Lewis Young nevertheless pointed towards one reason why the legislation could be useful, stating it was good the Act made it 'illegal to duplicate' ('Trade Views' 1912: 418). The unauthorized reproduction of records was a growing concern, albeit that even here there were reasons why copyright was not yet essential. The perpetrators tended to be rogue manufacturers, as they alone had the ability to undertake this activity (Barfe 2004: 62; Martland 2013: 40). The more widespread copying of records was still some way off, awaiting advances in tape recording technology that occurred in the mid-twentieth century. Moreover, copyright was not the only means by which protection could be secured. In America, for example, the laws of common law copyright and unfair competition were employed against unauthorized manufacture. In Britain, it had meanwhile been proposed that the mechanical right would enable record companies to prevent such production via the 'indirect' route of the composers' interests (Grey 1909: 14). Conversely, the fact that sound recording copyright was initially focused on this concern provides one reason why it received backing from publishers. As long as it was restricted to this area, it was in their mutual interest. Sound recording copyright would help concentrate the market on legitimate recordings from which mechanical licensing income could be derived (Ringer [1957] 1961: 49).

Sound recording copyright therefore entered British law with little fanfare and causing little apparent concern. It was still a radical manoeuvre, nevertheless. For the first time in legislative history, copyright was awarded directly to manufacturers. The 1911 Act states that 'Copyright shall subsist in records, perforated rolls, and other contrivances by means of which sounds may be mechanically reproduced, in like manner as if such contrivances were musical works' (1911: §19(1)). It adds that 'the owner of such original plate at the time when such plate was made shall be deemed to be the author of the work' (1911: §19(1)) and that this owner can be 'a body corporate' (1911: §19(1)). Running counter to copyright's Romantic tide, manufacturers are regarded as the authors of original creative works (1911: §1.1, §5.1).

Record companies as authors

Aside from the United States, which protects recordings as creative works, most countries now accord them sound recording copyright or neighbouring rights in respect of organizational 'production'. Rights are granted to the party that finances and organizes the recording; artistry is not the underlying factor. British record companies originally secured sound recording copyright in a different manner. Their chief rationale was to identify the creativity in recording. In doing so, they followed the Berne Convention's ethos to protect 'the rights of authors over their literary and artistic works' (1886: art. 1).

Arguing the manufacturers' case before the Gorrell Committee, Robertson noted measures that had been introduced at the Berlin Conference in respect of film. The revised Berne Convention included a right for creators of literary and artistic works to authorize 'the reproduction and public presentation of their works by cinematography' (1908: art. 14). This was similar to the mechanical right that was provided for composers of musical works. However, in addition the Convention added a separate copyright for the films themselves, stating that 'Cinematographic productions shall be protected as literary or artistic works, if, by the arrangement of the acting form or the combinations of the incidents represented, the author has given the work a personal and original character' (1908: art. 14). The conditions for establishing a 'cinematographic work' were reflective of countries with civil law systems, which required the input of creative individuals for authors' rights to be accorded. In turn, this prompted debate about which of a film's collaborators should be classified as artistic creators. Unable to resolve this conundrum, the Convention left it to member states to determine authorship. The film's director was usually put forward as a candidate, but this was not the case for the producer. The former, as a creative individual, fitted the model of an author; the latter, as a financing and corporate entity, did not.

Record companies maintained that sound recordings should be treated similarly, albeit that they maintained their own role as producers was creative. Robertson stated, 'We take a copyright work such as a translator or a cinematographer produces, or a photographer, and we put into it our own personal skill, and the skill of the artiste, and we want copyright protection for that' (Gorrell Committee 1910: 50). This reasoning provided a new inflection to legislative debates about records and writing. In America, it had been majority policy among record companies to stress the illegibility of discs and cylinders. In Britain, the arguments focused on why records are illegible. According to Robertson:

> The reason is that it is not a copy of the author's work… like a sheet of music, but it is the result of the labours of at least three separate personalities – (1) The composer who writes the work; (2) the artist who performs it for the purpose of recording the sound waves of his voice; and (3) the inventor and mechanician to whom is due the possibility of registering and subsequently producing in commercial form a means by which these sound waves, the artist's voice, may be reproduced.
>
> (1911b: 4)

These three personalities produced a composite text, which in its layered form was impossible to read. Outlining this theory, Robertson was operating in accordance with the advice of German manufacturers, who recommended campaigning on the grounds that a recording is 'the joint work of several highly skilled hands' ('Law of Copyright' 1908: 74).

The British companies wished to distinguish their creations, not only from the writings of composers but also from the scripts of piano players and music boxes. Acting as chairman for a gathering of company heads, J. E. Hough suggested that recordings are 'a reproduction of another person's translation or execution of the author's work' and unique among mechanical devices in this respect ('Trade Topics' 1911: 77). Winston Churchill, serving as president of the Board of Trade in this period, accepted this point of view, believing that 'experts could read pianola records of music without it being necessary to place the same upon the instrument which reproduced them', but 'no one could read the gramophone records' (Boosey 1931: 147–8).

The record companies argued that because composers were granted a mechanical right, the other creative contributors to a sound recording should also receive consideration. Outlining their claims for a sound recording copyright, the manufacturers had no qualms about positing themselves as creative authors. In addition, they promoted the unique expressivity of their recording artists. Van Allen Shields of Columbia stated that 'added value is given to the record not by the composer, but by the manufacturer or the artiste employed by the manufacturer' (Gorrell Committee 1910: 218). Robertson detailed the 'enormous' contributions that record companies made, including the 'arrangement of the orchestra', getting 'the sound so that is operates properly' and 'the technical production of the phonogram' (Gorrell Committee 1910: 54). Nevertheless, in identifying the personal and original character of sound recordings, it was the contributions of recording artists that he emphasized most, arguing that 'the composer has done nothing towards enhancing the value of the records; it is the artiste who does so' (Gorrell Committee 1910: 149).

Similar arguments had been raised in Germany, which in 1910 became the first country to provide a copyright for sound recordings. They were legislated for as adaptations of musical works. This policy operated in accordance with a further innovation of the Berlin Revision of the Berne Convention, which decided that 'Translations, adaptations, arrangements of music and other reproductions in an altered form of literary or artistic work… shall be protected as original works without prejudice to the rights of the author of the original work' (1908: art. 2). Consequently, the German protection of recordings was restricted to instances where performance was deemed to have had a transformative effect upon the work of composers (Ulmer and von Rauscher 1989: 434). Ownership was given to the performers in the first instance, but case law determined that their rights would be transferred to manufacturers by implied assignment (Ringer [1957] 1961: 40).

The British solution was different. The 1911 Act does not treat recordings as adaptations; they are instead given equivalence to musical compositions. Moreover, while the artistry of performers underpinned the campaign for sound recording copyright, it is not recognized in the legislation itself. The Act restricts ownership to the 'body corporate' instead.

This designation can be accounted for on a number of grounds. First, there were few arguments that the rights should go to performers (Ricketson and

Ginsburg 2005: 1207–8). The Amalgamated Musicians' Union (a forerunner to the Musicians' Union) did not campaign for their legislative recognition, a stance that can be explained due to sound recording being a minority profession and because few recording artists were union members (Williamson and Cloonan 2016: 74). Recording artists were also absent from the legislative hearings. The Gorrell Committee had numerous publisher and record company witnesses, but no musicians were present. There is also scant evidence of them entering debates in the British press. This reticence can itself be explained due to the nature of contemporary recording contracts. At this time, the majority of artists did not receive royalties and were instead paid fees for recording work, which they would receive regardless of record sales. They therefore had little concern with the unauthorized manufacture of recordings. Generally, it was the record companies whose profits were reduced by this activity and who were therefore most in need of protection. It is notable, however, that the few recording artists who did solicit politicians at this time – Enrico Caruso, Luisa Tetrazzini and Kennerley Rumford – were on royalty contracts and thus had a shared interest in the record companies' financial returns ('Copyright in Gramophone Records' 1911: 7).

Another reason why recording artists neither pressed for nor gained legislative recognition is because performance had not previously been deemed a subject fit for copyright protection. It had come to be thought of as an interpretive act rather than a creative one and hence was not addressed by the Berne Convention (Sterling 1992: 234–5). It had also been something that could not be copied. As Richard Arnold has pointed out, prior to the invention of recording technologies, 'performers did not need protection, for the only way in which their performance could be exploited was by the public paying for admission to a concert or play' (2015: §1.41). He adds that, while sound recording meant that multiple copies of performances could now be manufactured and sold, 'legislature was slow to react to this development' (2015: §1.42).

In Britain, the law also reacted in a particular way. Although the record companies emphasized the artistry of performers as they lobbied for sound recording copyright, they did not wish performing styles to be recognized within the Act. Van Allen Shields stressed, 'It is not intended that any such protection, as asked for the records themselves, shall be construed as preventing two manufacturers from recording the identical selection by identical artistes and in identical manner, so far as such identity is humanly possible' (Gorrell Committee 1910: 220). The desire instead was to prevent 'some irresponsible man, as the music pirates have been doing, to come and make a duplicate of that record and sell it under our price' (Gorrell Committee 1910: 106). The focus was on 'the particular record'; there was no desire to protect the expressivity of musicians (Gorrell Committee 1910: 220). This physicalist orientation is reflected in the grant of copyright to the owner of the 'plate' (Copyright Act 1911: §19(1)).

In addition to awarding record companies with the copyright, this orientation helped them to counter the arguments of their rivals. Publishers had complained that the companies were hypocritical in wishing to place compulsory licensing restrictions on the mechanical right while at the same time demanding unfettered legal control over their artists' recorded performances. With this conceptualization of sound recording copyright, the companies could argue that these performances were not being controlled. In theory, performers were able to record the same composition for any company they wished. Downplaying the fact that record companies could garner exclusivity through contracts rather than copyright, Van Allen Shields maintained that he did not 'advocate protection for monopolies with singers' (Gorrell Committee 1910: 107). Thus, in one stroke, the record companies were able to weaken the publishers' protests about compulsory licensing as well as negate the performative imperative of sound recording copyright. It is Rose's argument that by granting rights to authors, the Statute of Anne led to a formalist conception of copyright. Here we witness the reverse. Sound recording copyright was conceived in a physicalist manner. This made it appear more reasonable that the record companies could own it.

The deciding factor nevertheless lay elsewhere. The impetus of this copyright was compensatory. The Gorrell Committee offered it to record companies 'as a sop for rejecting arguments for the compulsory licence' (Atkinson 2007: 72). Furthermore, given the limited demand for this copyright, there is a sense in which its ownership had to be corporate. If the record companies had not been regarded as the authors, it is unlikely that they or anyone else would have pressed for it. Robertson outlined that it was 'the least compensation that the legislature can offer to our industry for surrender of its existing freedom' (Gorrell Committee 1910: 145). Therefore, while the art of recording provided the essential rationale for sound recording copyright, it was the record companies' vested interests that were at the forefront of legislators' minds.

As a means of honing this perspective, the manufacturers stressed their financial input into their performers' artistry. Van Allen Shields spoke of 'employing artistes and incurring great expense', while Robertson noted that 'The losses we suffer by the copying of our records of famous artistes, to whom we have to pay very heavy fees, are enormous' (Gorrell Committee 1910: 106, 229). Having heard this entwined talk of art and commerce, the Gorrell Committee began to communicate in a similar manner. Its report concludes that

> discs and other records are only produced at considerable expenditure by payments to artists to perform, so as to record the song, &c., and by the expenditure of a considerable amount of ingenuity and art in the making of these records; and that therefore the manufacturers are, in effect, producing works which are to a certain extent new and original, and into which the reproduction of the author's part has only entered to the extent of giving the original basis of production. Therefore, the Committee regard this as one of the things which can be the subject of copyright.
>
> (1909: 26)

This statement bolsters the record companies' claims in two respects. Expenditure and ingenuity are both valued: the Committee acknowledges the artistic originality of recording while suggesting that copyright should recognize financial investment. In addition, it makes no specific mention of who is responsible for the 'art in the making of these records'. As a result, the performers' input is occluded.

It is further obscured in Britain's 1911 Act. The legislation offers no explanation why, in this one instance, a corporate entity can be the author of a copyright work. Nevertheless, while it maintains that sound recording copyright should subsist 'in like manner' to the copyright in musical works, it still betrays the effects of granting ownership to industrial manufacturers. Compositions are placed first. This order is established temporally: songs are viewed as being written prior to their reproduction in 'contrivances'. They have a longer copyright too, lasting for the life of the author plus fifty years, whereas sound recording copyright lasts for 'fifty years from the making of the original plate' (1911: §19(1)). Composition is also prioritized aesthetically. Despite the protestations of record companies' that the scripts of gramophones and phonographs contain more complex layers of artistry than the rolls that are fed into pianolas or the pins that trigger music boxes, these devices are lumped together in the Act. It coalesces 'records, perforated rolls, and other contrivances by means of which sounds may be mechanically reproduced' (1911: §19(1)). Although sound recording is not regarded as a menace, it is described in mechanical terms.

Stephen Stewart has noted how 'Attitudes and prejudices on a subject are revealed clearly by language' (1983: 15). This is reflected in sound recording copyright legislation, where 'Even in the most favourable law, the United Kingdom law, records were called "contrivances"; in French legal language the rights of composers to a royalty on their recorded works were called "mechanical" rights which led to those royalties being referred to in Anglo-Saxon countries as "mechanicals"' (1983: 15). This terminology was derived from 'music boxes and clocks, Barbary organs, and the like' and could be regarded as being unsuited to 'the more sophisticated modes of fixation that came into existence with the development of the gramophone industry' (Ricketson and Ginsburg 2005: 641 note). It nevertheless remained pervasive. As we shall see in the following chapter, it would be taken up in a pejorative manner by performers themselves.

Conclusion

The two principal forms of copyright in recordings are entwined but have taken reverse trajectories. When first introduced, it was the mechanical right for compositions that was most contentious, with record companies resisting its imposition and publishers objecting to compulsory licensing measures. Over time, this form of licensing would become an accepted way of transacting for the use of compositions. In this respect it is notable that the idea of the compulsory licensing of musical works has lived on in Britain despite it no longer being a part of copyright legislation (Osborne 2014). In contrast, sound recording copyright was overshadowed during the early twentieth-century debates, but would gain increasing importance and controversy as the recording industry matured. Between them, compulsory licensing and sound recording copyright have done much to shape the economics and aesthetics of the music industries. They have also had a transformative effect on copyright law.

In 1928, a British governmental inquiry into compulsory licensing reported that 'The mechanical music industry has flourished remarkably since the passing of the Copyright Act, 1911… The industry as a whole shows large profits' (Report of Committee 1928: 7). The gains were not uniform, however. While most of the significant disc-producing gramophone companies had prospered, the cylinder manufacturers declined. Edison persisted with this format longer than anyone, but folded his phonograph business in 1929. Mechanical licensing may have had something to do with this. Cylinders sold for a lower price than discs and had narrower profit margins. Therefore, the introduction of compositional royalties was more of an imposition, particularly in the United States where there was a fixed mechanical licensing rate regardless of the price of the goods.

By 1928, record companies in the UK and the British Dominions were paying £200,000 in mechanical royalties annually (Report of Committee 1928: 7). As record sales grew, the market for sheet music diminished (Report of Committee 1928: 8). Publishers complained that 'The trifling royalties payable on records do not begin to compensate composers and authors for the heavy losses sustained by them on their printed copies' (Report of Committee 1928: 14). In response, the record manufacturers furnished familiar arguments, claiming that their records publicized sheet music; recording artists added a distinct artistic contribution to the work; and it was manufacturers who provided the finance for this artistry (Report of Committee 1928: 18–19). It was nevertheless the case that the status of publishers had declined. If mechanical licensing had been introduced without compulsory licensing provisions, it is possible that publishers would have used their negotiating power to become dominant in the music industries: it was envisioned they might buy out the weakened record companies (Abrams 2010: 233). In the event, the industries became oriented the other way round, as record companies would go on to purchase many of the significant music publishers.

Compulsory licensing also prompted new approaches to repertoire. Because record manufacturers were not in a position to contract for the exclusive use of compositions, they found other ways to distinguish themselves. There was an impetus to be first to market with musical works. During the Gorrell Committee hearings, it was suggested that record companies would 'wait till a thing has become popular' before making a recording of it (1910: 70). Robertson of the Gramophone Company could only cite a single composition that had been 'specially composed for the gramophone' (1910: 53). Within a few years there was a belief among British manufacturers that 'copyright law will encourage people to write specially for the talking machine'; there was also evidence that 'This has happened in America' ('Trade Views' 1912: 416). New compositions were required because there was a faster turnover of material. The patent rights of the big three companies elapsed in the early 1920s, leading to a proliferation of record labels, particularly in the United States. Compulsory licensing provisions enabled each of these companies to record their own versions of hit songs and consequently these compositions quickly became tired. It was noted that 'the sale of cheap records in particular tends to shorten the life of a piece of music, by making it "hackneyed"' (Report of Committee 1928: 8).

In addition to being first to market with new works, record companies found further means of distinguishing themselves. Rather than promoting compositions, which were accessible to all companies, they instead promoted the distinctive attributes of their recording artists. Gitelman has noted how they 'intensified their battles for exclusive contracts with celebrated performers' (1997: 283). This development was reflected in record company advertising, which increasingly promoted the creativity of artists as well as proclaiming the companies' proprietorial control. It was in the 1910s and 1920s that the term 'recording artist' rose to prominence, frequently prefigured in advertising by manufacturers' names.

The supposed ethos behind compulsory licensing was that by making repertoire available to all, it would lessen the impact of the mechanical right on smaller manufacturers. Robertson had claimed that the Gramophone Company were advocating this policy in 'a very unselfish way' as it would be the 'small fry' that would be 'snuffed out' if not protected by this means (Gorrell Committee 1910: 53). The resultant emphasis on recording artists favoured the major companies, however, as they were best positioned to offer exclusive contracts and advertise the celebrities they had signed. By 1915, the Gramophone Company was boasting how their record catalogue was 'built up on records (mostly exclusive) of the world's greatest artists' and that their 'vast … advertising never ceases' (Gramophone Company Advertisement 1915: 304–5). The most adept response that smaller companies could make was to focus on repertoire the major labels were ignoring. In America, for example, it was independent labels that issued the first blues and country music (Osborne 2012: 50–56). Yet even here the competitive danger for these companies was that the majors could usurp their repertoire, either by covering the recordings or contracting the performers (Henn [1956] 1960: 72).

As the individuality of star performers rose in importance, so too did the practice of counterfeiting recordings (Stahl 2008: 6). Songs were being compulsorily licensed to all, but recording artists were bound by their contracts. Therefore, if anyone other than the contracted record company wished to make money from the recordings of these artists, they would have to do so via unauthorized manufacture. And so, ultimately, compulsory licensing led to an increased need for sound recording copyright.

Looked at from one perspective, the creation of the mechanical right represented a triumph for authors, evidencing their ability to extend the control of their works to new media. In Britain, the introduction of sound recording copyright provided them with further gains, as it confirmed the formalist reconfiguration of their rights. Whereas the Copyright Act of 1842 had only protected composers in respect of their 'books', the Copyright Act of 1911 separated the formalist 'works' of composition from the physicalist devices that housed them (1911: §1(1), §19(1)). Lydia Goehr views this as a decisive act, suggesting it is only at this point that a 'distinction is drawn between the abstract property of the copyright and the material (concrete) objects representing it' (2007: 219).

There is another way of looking at these developments, however. They can be viewed as terminating any purely Romantic conception of copyright. The Berne Convention stepped away from its wholly author-oriented approach when accepting the principle of compulsory licensing for the mechanical right. Countries that employed these measures were balancing the interests of authors with the interests of manufacturers. Meanwhile, the British Copyright Act of 1911 can be viewed as being less momentous for recognizing the works of authors than for granting ownership of rights to corporations. In the wake of this legislation, intellectual property law would become less concerned about whether it should offer rights to record companies than with how it could go about doing so.

2

Performing

The earliest copyright legislation was concerned solely with the rights of authors to 'print' and 'reprint' their writings (Statute of Anne 1710). Public performance was the next of the rights of a copyright owner to be enacted. This right originally addressed the staging of works that had been protected by the reproduction right, but as it developed its remit expanded to include broadcasting and other mediated 'communication to the public', such as cable television and streaming.[1] These different activities have been gathered under the banner of 'performing rights'.

Although these rights have been regarded as being secondary in nature as well as in time, they have been fundamental to the evolution of sound recording copyright. By 1930, only twenty countries had adopted copyright protection for recordings: nine utilized the adaptations method first implemented in Germany; nine more adopted the British practice of recognizing sound recordings as original creative works; the final two offered protection but of 'no specific' type (Ringer [1957] 1961: 40). Until this point, any campaigns for securing copyright were focused on the reproduction right only. This limited adoption, as in many territories there was little impetus from record companies to gain this right and it was not a major concern of recording artists either.

Performance was different. By the early 1930s, the effects of radio broadcasting were beginning to be felt. Record companies argued that this medium was usurping their trade and in response sought recompense via copyright legislation. Performers were also affected. Radio had not been an inherent

---

[1] The international copyright conventions have not defined communication to the public consistently (Commission of the European Communities 1995: 54). The term was first employed in the 1928 Revision to the Berne Convention to refer to radio broadcasts (Rome Act 1928: art. 11*bis*). Usage has been broadened, to refer to cable, telephone line and fibre-optic transmissions by 'wire' alongside 'wireless' radio broadcasts (CRRR 2003: §6(2)). It has also been narrowed, in some instances referring to 'wire' transmissions only (WIPO 1992: 8). At other times this right has covered wire transmissions and public performance (WIPO 1995: 375). It has also been equated with the performing rights in their entirety, addressing wireless broadcasts, wire transmissions and public performance (Ficsor 1997: 212).

threat, as it could enhance their employment opportunities as long as 'live' music dominated the airwaves. Broadcasters increasingly turned towards records, however, and in the process thwarted the earning opportunities of performers. In addition, it became more common for venue owners to play recordings or broadcasts in lieu of live performances. Performers faced competition from other media as well. This was the period in which 'talking pictures' became popular, with the result that cinemas replaced pit orchestras with recorded sound.

These developments affected different types of performer in different ways. Recording artists could feel aggrieved because they were not gaining revenue for these uses of their work. Despite an increase in the use of exclusive contracts, it remained common for their agreements with record companies to be 'based either on a first and final payment or on a royalty on sale, all other rights being transferred to the company' (Eames 1934: 10). In respect of musicians who did not make recordings, the public performance, broadcast and cinematic use of recordings posed a greater threat: it was costing them jobs. Both types of performer took a greater interest in copyright matters, competing with record companies, and sometimes each other, for the performing rights.

Performing rights prompted discord elsewhere. Rather than being ranged against unauthorized manufacture, as was the case with reproduction rights, they were imposed upon broadcasters and venue owners. These businesses objected to the imposition of legislative measures, adopting a stance similar to that of record companies when the mechanical right was introduced. They maintained that their vested financial interests should be protected and sought unrestricted access to a full repertoire of works. In addition, they argued that their use of music was beneficial for record companies and recording artists, as the publicity it provided helped to generate record sales.

Composers and publishers also complained. They had generally been supportive of sound recording's reproduction rights, as they underpinned their own mechanical licensing revenues. Performing rights were another matter. They feared that any such rights for sound recordings would be used restrictively, thus thwarting the performance opportunities that recorded compositions could enjoy. They also worried that these rights might be imposed expensively, with the effect of diminishing the licensing money available for their own performing rights. At times, the composer-publisher interests stood resolutely against the establishment of performing rights for sound recordings. Alternatively, they insisted that any such rights should operate in a different manner to their own and be regarded as inferior.

These arguments are explored in this chapter. Its first half ranges from the mid-nineteenth century until the Second World War, looking at the performing rights for compositions before turning to attempts to create similar rights for sound recordings. In doing so, it covers developments in the United States, Britain and Continental Europe. The second half looks at legislation for sound recordings that was implemented in the mid-twentieth century: the Austrian Law of 1936, the Italian Act of 1941 and the British Act of 1956. It also addresses the Rome Convention of 1961. These Acts and the Convention evidence the new conceptions of neighbouring rights and performers' rights. In addition, they demonstrate an increasing confluence between British and Continental Law. An absence should be noted, however. In America there were no performing rights for sound recordings until 1995. Until this point (and beyond), it would prove impossible to reconcile the various parties involved.

Campaigning for performing rights

1. Performing rights for compositions

Most countries established performing rights for compositions long after they created rights of reproduction. It would also be a considerable period of time before composers and publishers enforced these performing rights.[2] In Britain, a reproduction right for compositions was created in 1777, but was not accompanied by a public performance right until 1842, which in turn was not regularly utilized until the establishment of the Performing Right Society (PRS) in 1914. This collecting society has operated on behalf of the collective interests of composers and publishers, negotiating blanket licences with the users of their works and administering the resulting revenue. In the United States, musical compositions received a reproduction right in 1831, but no public performance right until 1897. The American Society of Composers, Publishers and Authors

---

[2] France was the pioneer in, and partial exception to, this field. In 1791 it became the first country to legislate for a public performance right and did so before establishing a reproduction right, which was not created until 1793. France was also the first country to establish a collecting society for the performance of musical works. The Société des auteurs, compositeurs et éditeurs de musique (SACEM) was founded in 1851.

(ASCAP), founded in 1914, and Broadcast Music Incorporated (BMI), founded in 1939, have served an equivalent function to PRS.

There is a reason for the delays. Publishers viewed performance as a means of promoting the sales of sheet music, rather than something that required compensation or which they needed to restrict. They would pay artists to promote their hits, advertising them with title pages that proclaimed 'as sung by...' (Ehrlich 1989: 6). It was only when sheet music sales suffered a downturn in the first decade of the twentieth century that they looked for other forms of revenue (Ehrlich 1989: 13–14). One response was to press for the mechanical right in sound recordings. Another was to activate their public performance right.

During this period, music publishers were not viewed sympathetically. It was commonly held that they overpriced sheet music and exploited their composers (Ehrlich 1989: 10). As a result, they hid behind these composers as they campaigned for performance revenues. Speaking to the *Daily Telegraph* at the launch of PRS, the publisher Oliver Hawkes suggested it was songwriters who were mounting 'an irresistible wave [for this licensing activity] which no publisher could stop' (Ehrlich 1989: 18). Composers benefited from this co-option, as public performance revenues were of 'economic advantage to both parties' (D'Alton 2012: 166). Publishers had traditionally kept all royalties for sales of sheet music, paying composers one-off fees for the purchase of their works. Collecting society money, in comparison, would be split three ways. The model in most European countries was to divide it among works so that a third went to the composers, a third to the lyricists and a third to the publishers. In America, the policy of ASCAP was to give a quarter to composers, a quarter to lyricists and half to publishers.

It was with the growth of radio broadcasting that revenue from these societies became significant. Although this medium had been developed in the nineteenth century, the first national broadcasting systems and organizations were not established until the 1920s. Radio then spread rapidly. Following the creation of the British Broadcasting Company in 1922, the number of British listeners holding licences rose from 200,000 in 1923 to 2,600,000 in 1929, and then doubled in the next five years (Jones n.d.). In the United States, radio listenership increased from sixteen million in 1925 to sixty million in 1932 (ILO 1939: 8).

In response, music publishers sought an expansion of their public performance rights to incorporate broadcasting. This was achieved in America via case law in 1925, and in Britain via cases taking place in 1927 and 1934. Their position was bolstered by a further revision of the Berne Convention, agreed in

Rome in 1928, which granted composers 'the exclusive right of authorizing the communication of their works to the public by radio-diffusion' (Rome Act 1928: art. 11*bis*(1)). Aware that countries wanted different levels of restrictions on broadcasting, Berne members were granted latitude about its implementation. It was insisted, nonetheless, that composers and lyricists should receive 'equitable remuneration' (1928: art. 11*bis*(2)).

As radio grew in importance there was less demand for sheet music from professional and amateur players alike. This can be demonstrated by the fate of the six leading British music publishers, who suffered a decline in sales revenues from £537,000 in 1921 to £185,000 in 1935, due 'almost entirely to broadcasting' (Ehrlich 1989: 66, 87). Relatedly, the publishing industry no longer considered the public performance right to be secondary. By 1940, the gross annual collections of PRS had reached £619,000, with broadcasting contributing more than half of this amount (Ehrlich 1989: 160).

In addition to providing an exclusive right that addresses in-person performances of compositions, the Berne Convention has protected composers in respect of performances of sound recordings. The mechanical reproduction right, introduced in Berlin in 1908, was accompanied by a mandate to protect the 'public performance of the said works by means of these instruments' (Berlin Act 1908: art. 13(2)). British record companies campaigned against its implementation, intimating that it would be self-defeating for music publishers. They suggested that, if used in a restrictive manner, it would thwart the valuable publicity that the performance of recordings could give to sheet music sales. As part of the compensation package for the imposition of mechanical licensing, Robertson of the Gramophone Company insisted that the purchaser of a record should have freedom to play it 'in public, and not merely in his private room' (Gorrell Committee 1910: 48).

Robertson nevertheless downplayed the importance of the proposed public performance right, suggesting it was 'not a matter that would affect us personally as manufacturers' (Gorrell Committee 1910: 48). There may have been some truth in this. Although the public performance of records had been popular in the late nineteenth century, the record business became oriented towards domestic use. By the early 1900s, companies such as the Gramophone Company in Britain and Victor in America were marketing their machines as elegant adornments to the home. They produced gramophones in which the amplifying horn was enclosed, transforming the instrument into an acceptable piece of furniture. One effect of enclosing the horn was that the overall volume of the gramophone was reduced.

More generally, the application of recording machines for public performance was limited due to the quietness of both discs and cylinders. Public performance still remained a part of phonographic life, however, and was experiencing a revival at the time of the Gorrell Committee hearings. Robertson conceded it was becoming 'very popular' on the Continent (Gorrell Committee 1910: 48).

The inter-war period witnessed greater transformations. Broadcasting became the most popular technological means of consuming music and thus had a direct impact on the fortunes of the recording industry. It also impacted upon the public performance of recordings. Broadcasters employed the electric recording processes of microphones and amplifiers ahead of record companies, who, until the mid-1920s, used the acoustic recording methods of recording horns, diaphragms and the incision of needles. The successes of radio encouraged record companies to introduce electric recording, which was launched in Britain and America in 1925. Its adoption led to an increase in volume: played back-to-back with acoustic recordings, electric records were louder. They were soon accompanied by electric playback equipment, providing consumers with increased levels of volume control. As a result, records were more frequently used for public entertainment (Laing 2004: 76). Witnessing these changes, the record companies accepted that composers should have a performing right for recordings. What was more important to them, however, was to have a corresponding right of their own.

2. Performing rights for sound recordings

All industrialized countries encountered a drive for sound recording's performing rights, as well as arguments among record companies and performers over who was most deserving of ownership and recompense. The results nevertheless varied. One reason for this was the contrasting rights philosophies that had developed. Another was that countries differed in terms of the legislation they had enacted for sound recordings. The campaigners were also ranged against business forces that had differing degrees of power.

a) The United States

In America, there were many attempts to establish sound recording copyright legislation. The period between 1906 and 1951 witnessed thirty-one separate bills addressing this subject, all of which failed. The earliest concerned the reproduction right only and received little support from record companies, who believed the law of unfair competition provided adequate protection against unauthorized manufacture (Ringer [1957] 1961: 11). Responding to the Perkins Bill of 1925, which sought to protect sound recordings as adaptations of compositions, J. G. Paine of the Victor Company stated he was 'not sure' manufacturers wanted this copyright as they already had the benefits of state protection (Ringer [1957] 1961: 22).

There was a problem with placing faith in unfair competition, however, as it provided no legislative platform to build on when seeking a performing right. This weakness became apparent in the early 1930s, when the effects of radio increased. Sales of recordings were decimated, slumping from 65,000,000 in 1929 to 10,000,000 in 1932 (Countryman 1949b: 249). The Great Depression was a factor, but according to sound recording historian Roland Gelatt, broadcasting was 'the major cause' (1977: 255). Consumers were turning to free commercial radio for their access to music, rather than spending money on cylinders and discs. Moreover, American radio stations were not making extensive use of recordings. This was due partly to government restrictions, which were not lifted until 1940, and was partly through choice, as consumers preferred broadcasts of in-person performances (Countryman 1949b: 249). Facing these circumstances, the record companies threw their lot behind another tranche of legislative bills, arguing that they should be owners of sound recording rights.

They faced opposition from ASCAP, which reprised arguments that records are not writings and should therefore be considered 'unconstitutional' in copyright terms (Ringer [1957] 1961: 27). ASCAP feared the creation of a rival performing right for sound recordings, believing it would reduce the share of licensing revenue available for composers and performers, and might be employed restrictively. The manufacturers were also opposed by radio companies, who had no quarrel with a reproduction right but were resolutely opposed to legislation that would affect their industry (Ringer [1957] 1961: 26). Their cause was more decisive in America than it would be in Europe, due largely to the different broadcasting methodologies that had developed. In Europe, most countries introduced public service broadcasting. American broadcasters noted the effects of this, arguing that in these circumstances 'a performance right is merely a transfer from one government entity to another and has no significant impact on the business of broadcasting in those countries' (HJC 1994: 72). In their own country, in contrast, a commercial broadcasting system was in place. This engendered greater self-interest about the economic consequences of copyright. During the inter-war period, the National Association of Broadcasters (NAB) campaigned against any performing right for record manufacturers, maintaining there would be 'real hardship' for small radio stations if licensing fees were imposed (Ringer [1957] 1961: 27). Meanwhile, the larger broadcasters became enmeshed with the record companies. The Radio Corporation of America (RCA) purchased Victor Records in 1929; Columbia Records provided the major financial backing for the Columbia Broadcasting System (CBS) in 1927, and was bought out by the broadcaster in 1938.

The cause for a performing right was weakened further by division between record companies and recording artists, as well as between different types of performer. When the subject was first broached, the manufacturers sought complete control of this right. Recording artists contested this, forming their own organization in opposition. In 1934, the bandleader Fred Waring founded the National Association of Performing Artists (NAPA), which utilized state law and federal legislation to seek a performing right for musicians. At state level, Waring recalled the British literary copyright debates of the mid-eighteenth century, using common law copyright as a means to defend his interests. In America, common law copyright has applied to works deemed to be unpublished. There was uncertainty, however, whether the unauthorized broadcasting or duplication of records voided this status. In 1937, Waring triumphed against the WDAS Broadcasting Station in Pennsylvania in a case which held that the 'not licensed for radio' statement on his records gave him the right to restrain the broadcast of recordings (Ringer [1957] 1961: 14). Although this ruling established law in Pennsylvania and set a precedent for other states to follow, its influence came to an end in 1940, when the bandleader Paul Whiteman lost a similar case.

In respect of federal legislation, NAPA supported the Daly Bill of 1936, which offered a different perspective to earlier copyright debates. Previous bills had sought to protect 'contrivances by means of which sounds maybe mechanically reproduced' (HJC 1978: 31). The Daly Bill, in comparison, proposed to protect as 'writings' all 'interpretations, renditions, readings, and performances of any work, when mechanically reproduced' (HJC 1978: 31). Its focus was upon performers rather than manufacturers of machines. This orientation met with resistance from record companies, who believed any rights for recordings should be theirs alone. In addition, despite the fact that the Daly Bill was careful to stipulate that its rights for performers would not 'interfere or curtail the right of the authors of any composition or work used for such rendition or interpretation', it encountered opposition from ASCAP, which repeated its argument that a performance is 'incapable of being considered a "writing"' (HJC 1978: 32, 33).

Following the Whiteman decision, NAPA became active promoters of legislation, urging six separate bills between 1942 and 1951. These were oriented towards recording artists and thus encountered further resistance from record companies, who repeatedly insisted upon having ownership of the rights. NAPA's cause was not aided by the American Federation of Musicians (AFM), who had backed the Daly Bill, but dropped their legislative support for recording artists in 1940, when James Caesar Petrillo assumed leadership. By this time a division had emerged between musicians who made recordings and those who were suffering from technological unemployment. Their fortunes were polarized because record sales were no longer in decline.

In America, the revival of the recording industry was due largely to the popularity of jukeboxes. These machines were first marketed in 1927, but initially made slow headway: only 12,000 were sold in the first three years (Sanjek and Sanjek 1991: 41). It was with the repeal of Prohibition in 1933 that sales flourished. The United States had quarter of a million jukeboxes by 1939, which in turn led to an increase in record sales. An estimated 33 million discs were sold in 1938, around half of which were destined for this trade (Gelatt 1977: 273; Millard 1995: 169–70). The machines were used in venues as an inexpensive alternative to musicians. Furthermore, as the jukebox restored the fortunes and popularity of recordings, American broadcasters increasingly turned to records for the content of their shows (Countryman 1949b: 250). This activity provided publicity for record companies and recording artists, but caused difficulties for musicians who relied on performance income alone.

The public performance of records was resulting in unemployment of 'catastrophic proportions' (ILO 1939: 5). A report compiled in 1939 by the International Labour Organization (ILO) outlined how 'Dance halls, cafés and similar establishments more and more frequently used recorded or broadcast music and were thus able to dispense with the services of the orchestras which they had previously employed' (1939: 5–6). Musicians faced the additional threat of talking pictures: the arrival of sound film meant that cinemas 'ceased to employ them' (1939: 6). The ILO pointed out that 'whereas in most branches of production the depression has been characterised by obvious under-consumption, never in history has the public listened to so much music and so many entertainments as to-day' (1939: 6). The problem, from this viewpoint, was not the public's appetite for entertainment but instead that it had become mechanized.

At an international level, musicians' unions campaigned on behalf of the unemployed and in the process developed an anti-recording stance. They denigrated the 'dehumanized entertainment' that 'canned' music provided, promoting instead the virtues of witnessing musicians in the flesh (Anderson 2004: 234, 235). The unions developed the use of the term 'live' music as a signifier for in-person performances, implying by comparison that recordings were dead (Fleischer 2015: 333; Thornton 1995: 41–2). It made numerical sense for them to concentrate on musicians who were negatively affected by the advances of recordings, rather than support recording artists in their campaigns for performing rights. In America, for example, the AFM had 200,000 members, only around 5,000 of whom gained a 'substantial' income from record sales, whereas ten times this amount were encountering hard times (Countryman 1949a: 71; 1949b: 262 (note), 288). Petrillo prioritized 'the fellow that is going out of business' (HJC 1978: 1099). To this end, he proposed a collective fund, which would combat the effects of 'mechanical devices' (Countryman 1949b: 270). The money would be used in support of unemployed musicians and to promote 'musical talent and culture' through a series of free concerts (Countryman 1949b: 270).

Rather than seeking redress via a performing right, the AFM targeted the processes of reproduction. In August 1942, Petrillo called his members out on strike, barring them from making recordings. His chief request was a tax upon record sales, which would provide money for the collective fund. The Union held out for over two years, by which point each of the major record companies had capitulated to its demands, as had more than 100 independent labels. Thereafter, the tax on records provided significant returns: by 1947 it had already generated US$3,700,000 (Countryman 1949b: 274). It nevertheless placed the AFM in a paradoxical situation. Although the fund provided a salve for struggling musicians, it blunted the Union's 'critique of recordings' (Anderson 2004: 248). By aligning its revenues to record sales, the AFM had become wedded to the advances of 'mechanical' music.

In the wake of the settlement, the use of records in jukeboxes and radio broadcasts continued to proliferate. It was reported that some musicians, including Duke Ellington, Tommy Dorsey and Paul Whiteman, were making more money as disc jockeys than from concert performances (Countryman 1949b: 280). The American government meanwhile enacted legislation attempting to curb any further industrial action by the AFM. Responding to both threats, the Union called another strike, which lasted from January to October 1948.

It resulted in a compromise solution with the recording industry. The fund could continue, but it would have to be administered by an independent trustee. Against this background, the cause for a performing right foundered. Following the rejection of the last of the NAPA-sponsored bills in 1951, there was a hiatus in attempts to secure protection against performances of recordings.

b) The UK

Events in America can be contrasted with Britain, where campaigns had a different basis due to the introduction of sound recording copyright in the 1911 Act. Although it was initially enacted for the reproduction right only, this measure enabled British companies to employ judicial law to determine whether they had a performing right as well. With the support of other labels, the Gramophone Company launched a test case in 1933, which was mounted against Stephen Carwardine & Co, a coffee proprietor that had been playing recordings to its customers. Justice Maugham decided in the companies' favour, reasoning that because the 1911 Act established copyright in records 'in like manner' to the copyright in musical works, the owners had the same array of rights (*Gramophone Company v Carwardine* 1934: 460). He did stress, nevertheless, that the rights in recordings should be subordinate to those in compositions (1934: 460–61).

Maugham made his case on both economic and artistic grounds. He maintained it would be wrong for broadcasters and venues to 'obtain, without doing anything more than buying a record, the advantage of the work, skill and labour expended by the makers of gramophone records for the purposes of a public performance' (1934: 461). He also outlined how

> It is not in dispute that skill, both of a technical and of a musical kind, is needed for the making of such a record as the one in question. The arrangement of the recording instruments in the building where the record is to be made, the building itself, the timing to fit the record, the production of the artistic effects, and, perhaps above all, the persons who play the instruments, not forgetting the conductor, combine together to make an artistic record, which is very far from the mere production of a piece of music.
>
> (1934: 455)

Maugham's judgement echoes that of the Gorrell Committee in 1909. He mixes up technology and musicianship while combining the contributions of record manufacturers and recording artists. Furthermore, although he places a different emphasis to the Committee – arguing that the musicians' input should be regarded 'above all' – his determination of ownership is the same. The performing right, like the reproduction right, should be the preserve of record companies.

Within six months, the leading British manufacturers had joined forces to found Phonographic Performance Limited (PPL), the collecting society that would administer their performance revenues. As owners of the performing right, they were legally entitled to the entire licensing proceeds, yet they decided to allocate a 20 per cent share to their recording artists. This was a considerable proportion, given that only the most successful artists in this period had royalty contracts and those few who did were receiving average payments of 10 per cent of the retail prices of their records (Martland 2013: 196). Moreover, this figure would fall rather than rise as more artists moved towards royalty deals.

S. J. Humphries, PPL's chair, explained his society's policy to *The Times*, stating that 'although no legal right of the performing artist can be admitted, the claim that recognition should in some way be given to the artist in public performance is just and reasonable' (1934: 10). According to PPL's own history, 'This intelligent and far-sighted decision was particularly remarkable because of its voluntary nature, bearing in mind that there was no legislative or other external pressure on PPL at the time' (2004: 15). Nevertheless, as with the co-option of composers by music publishers, this arrangement with performers was both tactical and necessary. PPL made the payment because it feared the Carwardine case might be overturned. Maugham confessed he did 'not think the answer to the question is free from difficulty' and noted the defective manner in which the original legislation for sound recording copyright had been drafted (1934: 460). In light of this legal uncertainty, PPL invited negotiations with the Musicians' Union (MU) and other performers' organizations, leading to the 20 per cent payment for recording artists. In addition to bolstering the record companies' cause, the allocation to performers helped it to appear rational. Performers were more seriously affected than record companies by the increased public performance and broadcast use of recordings.

In campaigning on behalf of the technologically unemployed, the MU was in tune with unions internationally. Its manifestation of this policy was different to that of the AFM, however. Rather than concentrating on reproduction revenues, the MU targeted the performing right. During its 1945 delegate conference, the Union declared its intention to obtain payment for the public performance and broadcast of records, and 'Acquire some measure of control over the issuing of licences, and the conditions upon which licences are issued by PPL' (Musicians' Union Executive Committee 1947: 35). These objectives led to a new agreement with the collecting society, forged the following year. Henceforth, revenue would be split 67.5 per cent to record companies, 20 per cent to recording artists and 12.5 per cent to the MU. The Union entered these negotiations in a strong position. It had suffered a dip in membership at the time of the original PPL arrangements, but became an organization of significant numbers. In addition, British record companies were mindful that the Union might undertake industrial action, taking heed of the activities of the AFM.

The MU's early constituency was 'pit musicians who played in theatres, music halls and cinemas'; the type of performer negatively affected by the advances of recorded music (Williamson 2015: 169). It originally utilized its 12.5 per cent share of PPL income to subsidize a series of May Day dances and provide financial support for orchestras, opera societies and military bands. The Union also developed an oppositional policy. It believed records should be 'essentially for domestic use' and therefore sought to curb their employment in public (MMC 1988: §6.20(c)). This strategy can be witnessed at the 1945 conference, where a further proposal was announced. The Union wanted to 'Effect limitation of the extent to which gramophone records may be used for public entertainment' (Musicians' Union Executive Committee 1947: 35). Its arrangements with PPL included the stipulation that major music venues would only gain licences to use recordings if their events also employed performers (Whitford 1977: 398). The Union also insisted upon 'needletime' restrictions, which limited the number of hours that recorded music could be played on British radio, with the aim that broadcasters would hire live musicians for the rest of their musical output. The MU was able to make these demands because Britain established an exclusive performing right for recordings. Although the record companies owned this right, the Union could utilize the PPL agreement for its own ends.

c) Continental Europe

Continental Europe provided a further model for the performing right, entailing an abandonment of earlier procedures for protecting sound recordings. Most civil law countries that introduced sound recording legislation had done so by following the practice of Germany, which recognized recordings on the basis they are adaptations of musical compositions. Exclusive rights were given to recording artists in the first instance, but it was held that the rights should be automatically assigned to their record companies. Hungary and Switzerland adopted this procedure in the early 1920s, with Italy following suit in 1928.

When the revision conference for the Berne Convention was held in Rome in 1928, its Italian organizers sought to incorporate this model within the international agreement. They drafted an Article which proposed that 'When a musical work is adapted to mechanical instruments with the aid of interpretative artists, the latter also shall benefit from the protection which the adaptation enjoys' (ILO 1939: 28). This idea was justified on grounds that:

> It is indeed incontestable that gramophone records in particular owe a great part of their commercial value to the reputation of the performing artist, so that protection against the reproduction of the performance recorded on the disc is of considerable practical importance. We believe that legislation should be adapted to meet this necessity, even though in theory the transient art of a performer can hardly be compared with the work of a writer or a painter.
>
> (ILO 1939: 29)

The proposal gained support from German, Swiss, Irish and Norwegian delegates at the conference, but was rejected by the Hungarians and 'resolutely opposed' by the French (ILO 1939: 123). The British delegate admitted that the value of records was increased by the contribution of a performer 'if he was a famous virtuoso', but did not approve this proposal as they had a suggestion of their own (ILO 1939: 123). The delegate reprised the request made at the 1908 Berlin Conference, arguing that the Convention should protect sound recordings 'as original works' and grant ownership to manufacturers (Ricketson and Ginsburg 2005: §8.112). Ultimately, it proved impossible to incorporate either proposal in a Convention that was 'intended solely to safeguard the rights of authors' (ILO 1939: 32). The Berne Bureau did offer some encouragement to performers, however, proposing that alternative means be found to protect them. The 1928 Conference expressed a '*voeu*' (wish) that governments 'should consider the possibility of action' to safeguard their interests (ILO 1939: 30).

Having witnessed its potential to grant recording artists with 'far-reaching' powers, the manufacturers in civil law countries turned against the adaptation method for protecting recordings. They also fretted that assignment from artists was not happening 'as a matter of course' (Ulmer and von Rauscher 1989: 434).

More broadly, as broadcasting grew in importance, the companies developed an increasing interest in sound recording rights. The recording industry organized its first intentional congress in Rome in 1933, which led to the formation of the IFPI, whose founding mission was to 'preserve' existing rights, to 'promote' legislation for new exclusive rights (in particular performing rights) and to 'create' legislation in countries that did not protect sound recordings (Alloway 1983: 9).

Although the IFPI was headquartered in London and senior staff from the British company EMI dominated its original executive, the organization's legislative thinking was spearheaded by Italians, with input coming from the recording industry association Confindustria and officials in Benito Mussolini's fascist government (Fleischer 2015: 333). The lawyer Amadeo Giannini was one of the guiding lights. He believed that two forms of legislation were conceivable for sound recordings: they could be protected as industrial products or as works of art. Giannini urged record companies to pursue the latter course, as it would provide a better means of securing performing rights, which could be rejected for industrial products on the basis they are not commonly performed. He also suggested that the companies should receive credit as authors. This was because they fulfilled 'an artistic task in the series of decisions behind each recording: selecting the melodies to be recorded, selecting the musicians to enlist, selecting the room with the appropriate acoustic and the placement of microphones' (Fleischer 2015: 333).

Giannini's ideas were 'immediately countered' by the International Confederation of Authors and Composers (CISAC) (Fleischer 2015: 333). This umbrella body, consisting of various national collecting societies for drama and music, was vigilant in respect of any competition to the rights of authors. CISAC insisted that 'the exclusive right of ownership, vested in the author and derived from his creation of the work, by its very nature admits of no sharing with the rights of persons contributing to the technical preparation, reproduction and technical transmission of works of the mind' (ILO 1939: 125). Aiming for conciliation, Confindustria organized a meeting between CISAC and the IFPI in 1934, at which it was agreed that record companies would campaign for 'a new kind of *sui generis* right' which would not compete with authors' interests (Fleischer 2015: 333). The result has variously been described as the 'neighbouring right' (from the French *droits voisins*), 'related right' (from the German *verwandte Schutzrechte*) or 'connected right' (from the Italian *diritti conessi*). It has given protection to works that are allied to the subject matter of the Berne Convention but which are not viewed as containing the same 'human genius' (Porter 1991: 1). Rather than protecting 'intellectual creation', it is 'industrial' and 'technical' factors that are borne in mind (de Sanctis and de Sanctis 1989: 461).

In parallel with this development, the rights for performers were also reconceptualized. The situation in Continental Europe had similarities to that in America and Britain, with the cause increasingly coming under the sway of the technologically unemployed. Following a meeting of European musicians' unions in Brussels in 1929, a dual policy was formulated. On the one hand, the unions would promote 'live' music; on the other, they would seek a tax on 'mechanical' music, targeting venues and movie theatres that were replacing performers with recorded sound. The unions viewed this issue as a matter of 'labour legislation' rather than intellectual property, as indicated by their enlistment of the ILO for support. This organization had been set up in 1919 as a tripartite agency to balance worker, employer and governmental interests. It was first approached by the International Union of Musicians in 1926, with the request that it investigate the situation of performers in 'preparation of a course of action to be recommended to all Governments' (ILO 1939: 27). The ILO took up this cause, 'inspired by a felt need to protect performers against the threat to their livelihood', and viewing it, 'not as a matter of copyright, but rather as a social and economic problem' (HJC 1978: 414).

Meanwhile, the Belgian convenors of a Berne revision conference, scheduled to take place in Brussels in 1936, made their own interpretation of the wish that had been expressed in Rome. They proposed a new Article for the Convention, which stipulated that a performer's 'interpretation of a work ... shall be protected in a manner to be prescribed by the internal legislation of each country of the Union' (ILO 1939: 30). This prompted a backlash from CISAC, which determined at its Congress in 1937 that its members 'oppose, by every means which their rules permit, the admittance of... performers to any share in the right of authors over their works' (ILO 1939: 125). In the following year, CISAC was demanding that 'in the revision of the Berne Convention any amendment tending directly or indirectly to recognize or approve such an extensive right for performers may be rejected' (ILO 1939: 125).

In response, the musicians unions were conciliatory. They had originally campaigned for exclusive performing rights but revised this approach in light of CISAC's complaints and those of other organizations for authors. By the late 1930s they were 'particularly anxious' to make clear that any rights for musicians would not interfere with those of composers (ILO 1939: 69).[3] This prompted the creation of what have become known as performers' rights, a category of intellectual property that has had the potential to incorporate a range of subjects, including the moral rights of performers and the bootleg recording of live performances. In the ILO's original formulation, however, the focus was on public performances and broadcasts. As with the neighbouring rights of record companies, performers would not be given authorial recognition in respect of these activities. They would instead gain 'a right *sui generis*' (Porter 1991: 17).

The ILO proposed an international convention on this subject, which was due to take place in 1939. Although this meeting was curtailed by the outset of the Second World War, the organization managed to lay down the 'elementary basis' for provisions it would recommend to governments (ILO 1939: 93). In place of an exclusive right, performers would gain a 'right to remuneration' (ILO 1939: 93). The ILO stipulated it should be 'determined locally' whether this money should be paid 'individually to specified performers' or utilized for collective needs (1939: 95). The rationale for payment was consistent, nonetheless. Remuneration would not be awarded in recognition of creative authorship. It was required instead as mitigation for the competitive threat of mechanical music. Musicians were owed this money because of the 'profound change that the new techniques of phonographic recording and broadcasting have brought about in the conditions under which they perform' (ILO 1939: 1).

Legislative developments

1. The Austrian Law of 1936

In 1936, Austria became the first country to legislate for sound recordings under the banner of 'related rights'. In doing so, it provided legislative protection for recordings but denied them the status of works. The 1936 Law grants ownership

---

[3] Musicians' representatives in Britain originally pressed for performers' rights on similar grounds. Writing to *The Times* in May 1934, Frank Eames, general secretary of the Incorporated Society of Musicians, stated, 'The main principles on which this claim might be based are that the performers' rights should be independent of, and secondary or subsidiary to, the composers' rights, should comprise a fair remuneration for the use of the artists' work, and that performers should have the right of protesting against performances which might be prejudicial to their reputation' (1934: 10). Although these demands were negated by the PPL agreement, the decision of the collecting society to recognize the 'interests of the artist in the public performance of records' and to enter into 'immediate negotiation with the Incorporated Society of Musicians, and with other representatives bodies' was arrived at in response to Eames' intervention (Humphries 1934: 10).

of the reproduction right to the 'Hersteller' (manufacturer) (Copyright Law 1936: art. 76(1)). The performing rights, in contrast, do not have an owner. The Law instead provides a grant of 'angemessene Vergütung' (reasonable remuneration) (1935: art. 76(3)). This measure is reflective of various interests competing in this area. It aims to placate composers and publishers by ensuring the rights are not exclusive: neither record companies nor performers have the power to limit the public performance or broadcast use of recordings. It seeks to appease broadcasters, who do not have to negotiate for the use of individual works. They do have to make the 'reasonable' payment, however, which is determined by negotiation of licensing agreements. This remuneration acknowledges the interests of record companies, as it is paid to them in the first instance. It is also indicative of performers' interests, as a share is due to them.

2. The Italian Law of 1941

Five years later, Italy enacted its own 'connected rights' legislation. The 1941 Law gives ownership of the reproduction right to the 'produttore' (producer), defined as 'whoever makes the original disc or similar original device playing sounds or voices' (Legge 1941: §78). The performing rights are reflective of Italian political thinking. Mussolini's government disagreed with the ILO's policy of allowing workers to self-organize, as it was incompatible with Fascist notions of centralized governmental control (Fleischer 2015: 334–5). Consequently, Italy held its own performers' rights convention to counter the one planned by the ILO. One of its outcomes was the Samaden Proposal of 1939, which fed into the Italian Law. This Proposal differs from the ILO's work in several respects. First, whereas the ILO focused on the economic plight of performers, the Italians sought to balance the interests of record companies with those of recording artists: the two parties are brought together in the Proposal and are each accorded remuneration in the 1941 Law. Second, the ILO had been undecided whether remuneration should be distributed to individual musicians or to a collectivity of performers: the Italian Law gives it to recording artists. Third, the ILO was engaged by musicians' unions; in contrast the Samaden Proposal had the backing of the IFPI. Lastly, while the musicians' unions of Europe had originally been focused on public performance, the Italian legislation does not provide performers with remuneration for this use of their recordings: their 'equitable compensation' is for broadcast only (1941: §80). Producers gain an additional compensation for the use of recordings in public places (1941: §73), thus indicating 'a clear hierarchy' of recipients (Fleischer 2015: 336).

3. The British Copyright Act 1956

The 1956 Act is a curious amalgam. On the one hand, it is reflective of British thinking about performing rights. There is no equitable remuneration; record companies are instead given exclusive control of these rights, while the interests of performers are not addressed directly. On the other hand, it is influenced by the neighbouring rights philosophy of Continental Europe. The Act was developed from the 1951 report of the Gregory Committee, which refers to rights in sound recordings as 'ancillary' and states that 'consideration should be given to the question whether rights of this kind should not be described by some term distinguishing them from copyright in its primary sense' (1952: §181).

Although the Committee recognized the 'very high degree of skill (in part technical, in part musical) called into play in recording music' (1952: §145), it concluded that recordings 'approximate more closely to industrial products than to original literary or musical works' (1952: §88). The Committee recommended a shorter term for sound recording copyright than the fifty years established in the 1911 Act, which it regarded as being 'unnecessarily generous' (1952: §87). In addition, it reported a view that the manufacturers' performing right was 'embarrassing', believing that 'an arguable case' could be made for its 'abolition' (1952: §143, §176). Evidence was given by PRS, who complained that the restrictive use of this right had a negative effect on the earnings of its members (1952: §149). After much wrangling, the Committee eventually supported its retention, but insisted it be 'subsidiary to the primary right of the composer or author' (1952: §181).

The 1956 Act is less hierarchical but still treats sound recordings differently to composers' rights. Compositions are addressed in the first part of the Act, which concerns 'copyright in original works'. The 'copyright in sound recordings, cinematograph films, broadcasts etc.' is covered separately in the second part. Unlike the 1911 Act, the 1956 legislation does not use the term 'author' to describe the first owner of sound recording rights and there is no originality requirement for establishing protection. The Act states instead that the 'maker' will be 'entitled' to own the rights, adding that 'a sound recording shall be taken to be made at the time when the first record embodying the recording is produced, and the maker of a sound recording is the person who owns that record at the time when the recording is made' (1956: §12(4)(8)). In this respect, it echoes the 1911 Act, which awards ownership to the owner of the 'original plate'. The 1956 Act also retains the fifty-year term of copyright for sound recordings. It separates the public performance right into two categories: 'the performance of the work in public' and 'the broadcasting of the work' (1956: §2(3)). Here, musical works and sound recordings are treated similarly: in both cases the copyright owners are given exclusive controls. The record companies' control was opposed by PRS, who said it would be 'regarded as an aberration in other countries which have not taken the same false road' (PRS 1956: 18).

The 1956 Act contains no rights for performers, with the result that British musicians had to look beyond copyright law for protection. In respect of the reproduction of their performances, they had been accorded limited measures via the Dramatic and Musical Performers' Protection Act of 1925, which criminalized the unauthorized recording of their live performances. The main beneficiaries of this Act were not musicians, however, as indicated by its chief sponsor being the Gramophone Company. British record companies had a reproduction right, but it offered no protection against the bootlegging of their artists' performances; hence they sought and secured criminalization of this activity. The 1925 Act would be consolidated by the Dramatic and Musical Performers' Protection Act 1958, which remained the principal statute for British performers until the CDPA of 1988.

In respect of the performing rights, these positions were reversed. British musicians utilized the rights of record companies to promote their own interests. They did so via the PPL agreement, which continued to provide their main means of redress. Aligning themselves with unions in Europe, the MU had campaigned for legislative recognition of performers' rights in the run-up to the 1956 Act, suggesting that any such measures would be 'additional to and not necessarily in derogation from' the copyright owned by record companies (Gregory Committee 1952: §155). The Gregory Committee was nevertheless reluctant to grant more rights in this area, believing that the performing right for sound recordings had been enforced with 'the minimum of consideration' for licensees (1952: §150). They stated that 'the stringency of the control, of which so many complaints have been made, owes its origin to no question directly related to copyright, but springs from the relations which exist between the gramophone companies and the Musicians' Union' (1952: §151). Restrictive practices were, in fact, the main focus of the Union's performing rights activity. The Committee found that the MU was 'not so much concerned with the payment of fees (although the Union appears to benefit from this) as with the question of control' (1952: §154). As a result, it feared that any additional rights given to performers would 'be used as an additional barrier to the enjoyment of gramophone music by the public generally' (1952: §176). Instead of granting rights, the Committee suggested that 'some way must be found of limiting, by statute, the opportunities of exploitation flowing from the present interpretation of the term "public performance"' (1952: §150). To this end, it recommended that an independent tribunal should oversee the activities of PPL and PRS, which was realized in the 1956 Act (1952: §200).

During the genesis of this legislation, the MU 'lobbied furiously' for the retention of the PPL agreement, combining forces with British record companies to achieve this end (Williamson 2015: 180). Ultimately, the Act did not tamper with this alliance, not least out of fear of engendering industrial disputes (Gregory Committee 1952: §185). The MU maintained its collective and compensatory use for its share of the funds. In 1961, it launched a campaign using the slogan 'keep music live', which thereafter consumed a substantial amount of its PPL money (Williamson 2015: 188). The Union's attacks on recorded music became increasingly virulent: it described recordings as a 'grave threat', 'a serious danger' and an 'ever-present menace' (Thornton 1995: 42). This stance is borne out in a BBC report from the 1960s, which refers to the Union's 'out-dated attitude that recording is evil' (Williamson and Cloonan 2016: 156).

Although the MU was criticizing its core product, the recording industry still found the PPL agreement to be mutually beneficial. It remained essential for British record companies to bolster their claims for performing rights by demonstrating that these rights acted in the interests of performers. In addition, the MU provided support in administering the revenue (MMC 1988: §7.40). The agreement, as the Gregory Committee indicated, was also the foundation of good industrial relations. Moreover, the record companies realized that as long as it was in place 'the Union was willing to place its case for statutory performers' rights on the back burner' (Williamson 2015: 181). Following the 1956 legislation, there was no organization in Britain campaigning on this front. The report compiled by Justice Whitford ahead of the 1988 CDPA is indicative, stating that his committee had 'not been asked to consider the grant of any new [performers'] rights' (1977: §409).

4. The Rome Convention (1961)

Performers' rights were on the agenda elsewhere. When the postponed Berne revision meeting was eventually held in Brussels in 1948, the Belgium government pursued requests from international musicians' unions to establish them within the Convention. The recording industry meanwhile made an effort to get its own interests recognized within Berne. Facing the usual objections from author-publisher interests, both requests were denied. The conference instead expressed two *voeu*, which initially appeared to offer more hope to musicians than manufacturers. It was held that performers interpreted compositions with 'artistic character'; the conference therefore recommended that studies 'be actively pursued, especially in regard to the protection of performing artists' (Ringer [1957] 1961: 45). The record companies' input to recordings was regarded as being industrial in nature. As a result, it was proposed that governments should 'study the means to assure, without prejudice to the rights of the authors, the protection of manufacturers of instruments for the mechanical reproduction of musical works' (Ringer [1957] 1961: 45). Despite these differences, the Permanent Committee of the Berne Union ultimately combined the interests of the two parties, suggesting the study be based on Italy's Samaden Proposal.

Concurrently, the ILO's separate initiative for a performers' rights convention was re-instigated. In the same year as the Brussels conference, the musicians' unions of Europe formed the International Federation of Musicians (FIM), which promoted 'strategies against mechanization' and sought collective compensation for the performance of recordings (Fleischer 2015: 338). In March 1949, FIM prompted the ILO to organize a meeting to discuss performers' interests, proposing that musicians should have exclusive rights. By nature, the ILO has been a consensus building organization, bringing together workers and employers to jointly resolve their issues. As such, the IFPI were called to this meeting. This organization objected to any Convention that would address performers' rights in isolation, suggesting that the interests of record companies and performers should be combined. The outcome was that the Samaden Proposal, which had originally been conceived in opposition to the ILO, received the organization's approval as the starting point for an international agreement. There followed a series of draft Conventions, eventually leading to the Rome Convention of 1961, which addresses the protection of broadcasting organizations, performers and 'producers of phonograms'.

This Agreement defines its terms. A 'phonogram' is 'any exclusive aural fixation of sounds of a performance or of other sounds' (1961: art. 3(b)). Phonogram also provides the initial for the (P) symbol, which signifies the owner of sound recording rights (1961: art. 11). 'Producer' was selected by delegates in preference to the British suggestion of 'maker', but has nevertheless been employed in a manufacturing sense (ILO, UNESCO and BIRPI 1968: §1654). It is applied to 'the person who, or the legal entity which, first fixes the sounds of a performance or other sounds' (1961: art. 3(c)). The guide to the Convention states that 'the accent is on an industrial and not a personal activity' (Masouyé 1981: §3.9). The Convention also makes clear that 'when an employee of a legal entity fixes the sounds in the course of his employment, the employer legal entity, rather than the employee, is to be considered the producer' (ILO, UNESCO and BIRPI 1968: 40). Thus, in the 'normal case' any rights granted to a producer are the preserve of a 'recording company' (Masouyé 1981: §10.4).

In theory, the Rome Convention was a consensus-building enterprise. It was jointly organized by three organizations that had studied this topic: the ILO; the United Nations Educational, Scientific and Cultural Organization (UNESCO); and the United International Bureaux for the Protection of Intellectual Property (BIRPI) (the latter organization had responsibility for administering the Berne Convention until being succeeded by WIPO in 1970). The Convention was inclusive in its discussions. Forty-one countries participated. Representatives of performers' organizations, record companies, broadcasters and CISAC were also present. The authors of the Convention aimed for balance between the interacting rights of the three major parties involved (Arnold 2015: §1.55).

It could be argued that performers deserved the greatest accord, with their status as creative individuals giving them the greatest affinity with authors of original works. They nevertheless emerged in the weakest position, most notably in respect of reproduction rights. The Rome Convention gives broadcasters an exclusive reproduction right for their radio productions (1961: art. 13). An exclusive right is also granted to phonogram producers, who receive it for the 'reproduction of their phonograms' (1961: art. 10). The artistic work of performers is not recognized. Moreover, while producers are granted their reproduction right in the phonogram itself (1961: art. 10), performers are limited to 'the possibility of preventing' the 'fixation' of their performances and the reproductions of these 'fixations' (1961: art. 7). In addition, they can only prevent this activity if it has happened without their consent. The measures therefore do not apply to recordings that they have been contracted to make for record companies; the focus is instead upon the bootleg recording of live performances and radio broadcasts.

There was opposition to this inferior casting. The American delegate believed that performers should have an exclusive reproduction right of their own (ILO, UNESCO and BIRPI 1968: §1054). This proposal was nevertheless rejected by author-publisher organizations, who successfully insisted that their own interests be preserved and prioritized. Article 1 of the Convention states that any protection granted 'shall leave intact and shall in no way affect the protection of copyright in literary and artistic works' (1961: art. 1). There was also fear that performers would use the power of assignment to hand their rights to labour organizations. The guide to the Convention states that this 'weapon in the hand of the union would be, it is felt, disproportionately large' (Masouyé 1981: §7.6). In addition, the delegate from Britain argued that exclusive performers' rights would not accord with his country's legislation, which established its limited measures for performers through criminal law rather than copyright law (ILO, UNESCO and BIRPI 1968: §1058).

Performers have had greater potential for parity when it comes to performing rights. Rather than granting exclusive controls for broadcast and public performance, the Convention proposes that an 'equitable remuneration' should be paid to both producers and performers (1961: art. 12). Securing this payment had been of greater importance to musicians' unions than gaining ownership of a reproduction right. More broadly, this was the 'most important provision' in the Convention as well as the most 'most difficult' to achieve (ILO, UNESCO and BIRPI 1968: §1280.1). Although the performing rights proposal was restricted to equitable remuneration, the representative of CISAC still raised complaints, suggesting that small venues would not be able to afford it and 'would therefore simply cease to use phonograms in their establishments' (ILO, UNESCO and BIRPI 1968: §1270.2). In his opinion this 'would be to the detriment of authors and of the general public and of no benefit to performers and phonogram producers as, in the long run, less recordings would be purchased by possible users' (ILO, UNESCO and BIRPI 1968: §1270.2). Delegates from Monaco and Tunisia complained that equitable remuneration would thwart the broadcasting interests in their developing countries (ILO, UNESCO and BIRPI 1968: §1260.2, §1267). The Monacan delegate objected on the grounds that 'Broadcasting constituted the most powerful means of publicity for the sale of phonograms' and therefore no licensing fees should be paid (ILO, UNESCO and BIRPI 1968: §1260.1). He nevertheless noted a difference between record companies and performers in this respect. Although broadcasting benefited phonogram producers, 'every time a performer made a recording he was, as it were, attending his own burial' (ILO, UNESCO and BIRPI 1968: §1261.2).

In return, the performer and record company interests outlined why they felt equitable remuneration was necessary. The representative of the IFPI made an economic case for rewarding record companies, stating that 'many broadcasters fully recognized that they simply could not function without the help of phonograms, and it was therefore only fair that they should pay a reasonable price for such essential assistance' (ILO, UNESCO and BIRPI 1968: §1278.1). The representative of FIM insisted that performers should receive remuneration 'as a matter of common justice' (ILO, UNESCO and BIRPI 1968: §1277.4). If it were not granted, 'the consideration which had been given to the subject for thirty-five years would have been wasted' (ILO, UNESCO and BIRPI 1968: §1277.4).

The Rome Convention reflects the fact these competing interests cannot be fully reconciled. Signatories can choose whether to pay the remuneration to performers, to record companies or to both (1961: art. 12). Some countries, such as Brazil, originally reserved remuneration for performers only. Others, including Sweden and Germany, divided it equally. The Intergovernmental Committee for the Convention laid out a Model Law in 1974, which recommends a fifty/fifty split based on the notion that 'equality is equity' (ILO, UNESCO and WIPO 1982: 23–5). This division has not been mandatory, however, and can be undermined by the fact that the Convention allows countries to 'not apply' its equitable remuneration provisions (1961: art. 16). Moreover, even in situations where the remuneration is split equally, there can be inequality elsewhere. The Convention does not prevent countries from creating exclusive performing rights in sound recordings, nor does it stop them from giving these rights to one party only, as Britain had done in respect of its manufacturers.

There was another 'burning question' that was discussed at Rome but obscured in the Convention itself: how should the performers' share be utilized? (Masouyé 1981: §12.17). The Convention guide, published in 1981, states, 'It would certainly seem, from a logical point of view, that the remuneration should be payable only to those who have contributed their performances to the records used for broadcasting or public performance' (Masouyé 1981: §12.17). The feeling about this matter was different in 1961. During the hearings, the Norwegian delegate detailed that it was too costly and difficult to 'effect distribution directly to each performer and to each phonogram producer', and insisted that the Convention permit collective remuneration, as had been established in his country's 1952 copyright law (ILO, UNESCO and BIRPI 1968: §1259.4). This position is supported in the Model Law of 1974, which recommends a collective fund for developing nations, stating that if it 'were to be implemented in any other way, the bulk of the remuneration might be payable to foreign performers or producers from highly developed countries' (ILO, UNESCO and WIPO 1982: 24).

Given its flexibility, it would be wrong to label the Rome Convention as imposing a neighbouring rights philosophy. As J. F. da Costa has stated:

> The States party to the Convention are free to protect the rights of the different categories by various means: copyright legislation, the recognition of neighbouring rights, other systems linked to intellectual property, administrative or penal measures, labour legislation, the laws on unfair competition, and the like. Nor is there anything to prevent a Contracting State from utilizing a different system for the rights of each category.
>
> (1976: 81)

This flexibility can be witnessed in the British response. The UK was one of the original signatories to the Convention but its ratification initially had little effect on domestic practice. Parliamentarians believed the country's existing copyright law provided sufficient coverage and consequently there was no need 'to change our own Act of 1956' (Arnold 2015: §1.61). The British delegate at the Convention emphasized how the PPL agreement had led to harmonious relations between record companies and the MU, 'which might not otherwise be possible' (ILO, UNESCO and BIRPI 1968: §1262.2). He 'could not support a Convention which would make compulsory a law providing for payments to performers' (ILO, UNESCO and BIRPI 1968: §1295).

Elsewhere there were differences in the way equitable remuneration was implemented. Some countries, such as Denmark and Austria, evolved a system of remunerating performers individually for the performances of their recordings. The Federal Republic of Germany, in contrast, based its performing rights payments on performers' revenues from record sales and session fees (HJC 1978: 184). As a result of these variations, the Rome Convention's national treatment measures were hard to implement. The Agreement was intended to stimulate the international exchange of royalties: adherents were supposed to collect and distribute revenues generated by foreign recordings in accordance with their own domestic laws (1961: art. 2). Signatories were nevertheless entitled to withhold these royalties if domestic laws were discrepant (1961: art. 16). Consequently, many member states of the Rome Convention entered into bilateral agreements, conducted according to the 'London principles' drawn up by the IFPI and FIM in 1969. If mutual exchange of performers' royalties were not possible, the revenue for foreign performers should 'remain in the country in which it has arisen' (HJC 1978: 189).

Britain was affected by these measures, as its performing rights legislation was rarely paralleled abroad. A further impediment to the exchange of performer royalties was the MU's collective use of funds. This precluded accord with any country that distributed remuneration on an individualized basis (HJC 1978: 205). As a result, most Rome Convention adherents withheld 50 per cent of the licensing revenues for the use of British recordings in their countries. PPL responded in kind, retaining half of the money it accumulated for recordings made abroad (MMC 1988: §2.3). However, as Britain was a net exporter of recorded music, it tended to lose out from the mutual withholding of receipts. American record companies and performers fared worse. The United States did not have its own performing rights legislation and did not ratify the Convention. Thus, it missed out on remuneration at home and abroad. As had been the case with the various meetings of Berne Convention, American interests were represented at Rome (the register of copyrights, Abraham Kaminstein, was reporter for the Convention). Yet, in spite of its malleable provisions, the Convention still did not accord with American copyright philosophy.

Overall, uptake of the Convention was slow. By 1971, it was only in force in ten countries. This limited acceptance has been attributed to its 'complex history and arbitrary nature', as well as to its 'pioneer character' (Davies 2012: 214; Porter 1991: 22). As Gillian Davies has noted, it laid down 'standards of protection that did not exist in many countries, so that most States had to legislate to create some or all of the rights' (2012: 208).

Conclusion

The slow uptake of performing rights should not divert us from the profound effects they had on sound recording legislation. In America, it proved impossible to reconcile the various parties who had interests in this subject. Record companies and recording artists were in competition over the rights; recording artists and performing musicians were in conflict over the means of compensation; publishers' organizations and broadcasters stood in opposition. As a result of this intransigence, the overall campaign for sound recording copyright was thwarted. Moreover, when the United States finally created a sound recording copyright in the early 1970s, it did so in a manner that most countries had abandoned. The legislation recognized recordings as artistic works.

Elsewhere there was transformation. By 1971, eight countries, including West Germany, had adopted the neighbouring rights method of protecting recordings. In most cases, record companies gained exclusive reproduction rights, but rather than gaining similar exclusive rights for performances they were given a share of 'equitable remuneration'. Other countries adopted the British method, laid down in the 1956 Act, of awarding the 'maker' of the sound recording exclusive reproduction and performing rights. In general, both methods of legislation were of benefit to record companies. Authorship was no longer granted in respect of artistry, but instead in recognition of economic, manufacturing and organizational input. As a result, record companies had less need to highlight the creative endeavours of recording artists in order to proclaim their own interests.

Parallel with these developments, recording artists in these countries lost their chance to secure exclusive rights in sound recordings that recognized their creativity. As well as being thwarted by the new legislative philosophy of the record companies, their own campaigns were overtaken by the drive for performers' rights, whose principal achievement, where established, was equitable remuneration. This conceptualization gained praise from J. A. L. Sterling, who worked for the IFPI from 1954 to 1974. He commended the ability of performers' rights to 'cut the Gordian knot' of competing interests: they provide musicians with legislative recognition, but there is no need to apply the 'criteria of "originality" or "creativity" as a condition of protection' (Sterling 1992: §7B.06). There was a side effect to this policy, nonetheless. The focus of these rights was to compensate performers, rather than protect the artistry of performances. The impetus was anti-recording in nature. Musicians' unions did not campaign for a creative copyright for recording artists and generally stood aside while record companies made copyright claims of their own.

It would be wrong to portray the campaigns for performers' rights as being wholly retrogressive, however. The benefits of collective funding for musicians should not be gainsaid. Also, while the overall revenues from equitable remuneration were at first relatively minor, the proportional share that most countries accorded to performers was considerable. When it came to their contracts for physical sales, the royalty rates of recording artists were by the 1960s averaging between 1 per cent and 5 per cent of retail prices (HJC 1967: 545; Napier-Bell 2014: 261–2). Their rates for equitable remuneration, in contrast, were commonly 50 per cent of the broadcast and public performance licensing revenues. Moreover, the British method of compensating artists via the PPL agreement should not be regarded as placing them in an inferior position to those who were equitably remunerated. Although they gained a smaller share of performing rights revenue than artists elsewhere (32.5 per cent as opposed to half), they had greater control of the musical environment. The MU utilized the exclusive rights of record companies to gain restrictions on the use of recordings in public venues and radio broadcasts.

More broadly, developments in this area are indicative of the contrasting characteristics of different rights. The turn to performance increased the importance of copyright to record companies, as intellectual property provided the most effective means of licensing their repertoire. The companies' control of performing rights was nevertheless more questionable than their control of reproduction rights. When it came to justifying the latter, they could point towards their investments in manufacture and their vulnerability to free-riders. Their demands for performing rights, in contrast, were largely dependent on the suggestion that third parties were making money from recordings without paying for their use. Performers were more obviously affected by developments in this area, particularly those who were threatened with 'technological unemployment' (Masouyé 1981: XVII). They were also well placed to make claims for recompense, either by employing record companies' exclusive rights or by campaigning for equitable remuneration.

We shall see similar patterns again. As performing rights increase in importance, record companies and performers have greater need for copyright protection. In addition, the dynamic between them changes. This is not, however, the only means by which their copyright interests have coalesced and conflicted. Another means by which this has happened is with the reorientation from manufacture to production.

3

Producing

Sound recording rights were born out of technology and have been shaped by successive technological developments. Record companies were first granted the right of reproduction – either as authors or assignees – with the primary intention of safeguarding them against unauthorized manufacture. Following on from this, record companies and musicians sought compensation for performances of recordings, whether via radio broadcasts or through loudspeakers in venues. This chapter addresses a third technological development: tape recording.

The roots of this technology go back to 1898, when the Danish inventor Valdemar Poulsen introduced the first magnetic recorder. It took until the Second World War before its wider capabilities began to be realized. When Allied forces freed Radio Luxembourg from Nazi control in September 1944, they uncovered the magnetophone, a recording machine of 'extraordinary capabilities' (Gelatt 1977: 287). The post-war cancellation of German patents meant this technology could be exploited abroad. In America, it was originally utilized for broadcast purposes. Among the earliest adopters was Bing Crosby, who financed the development of the Ampex tape recorder, which was modelled on the magnetophone and first employed in 1947 to record his network radio shows. Tape recording was introduced to American recording studios the same year. The earliest machines could record one 'track' of recording information only, but by 1954 two-track machines had been introduced, thus facilitating overdubbing processes.

Tape recording influenced sound recording copyright in several ways. Significantly, it changed the notion of the master recording. This was important as the master has provided the basis of ownership. Prior to the introduction of tape recording, studio work was concentrated on capturing a live performance directly to a master disc. This disc would then initiate the duplication procedure, with record companies creating 'positive' and 'negative' versions of it, leading to the creation of a 'stamper' disc from which multiple versions of the recording could be pressed. Tape recording added a further stage before this process got underway. Studio personnel would create a final mix of the recorded work, referred to as the 'master tape', indicating that this was the sound source for the duplicative master. This term was soon abbreviated to 'master', and before long it was this tape master rather than the master disc that became the focus of ownership. Although both types of master have resulted in the 'fixation' of performances, they have different connotations. The master disc initiates reproduction, carrying with it associations of manufacture. The master tape represents the culmination studio work and is an artistic creation. Ultimately, sound recording is a physicalist form of copyright in which the physical object has changed.

Related to this development, tape recording contributed to a restructuring of the recording industry. In the first half of the twentieth century, the leading record companies carried out the majority of functions in-house. As well as discovering and financing talent, they developed recording and listening technologies, and were makers of cylinders and discs. Hence, they were referred to as manufacturers and this term along with its variants of 'maker' and 'producer' was utilized in copyright and neighbouring rights legislation. Tape recording fostered compartmentalization. Within major labels it became common for activities to be separated into the divisions of artists and repertoire (A&R), manufacture and sales. When it came to the independent sector, an increasing number of record companies concentrated on A&R only. Although they contracted recording artists, organized studio sessions and oversaw the creation of master tapes, they would not handle the manufacture or promotion of their recordings, hiring third parties to perform these duties instead. This compartmentalization prompted a new use of the term 'producer'. It began to be employed in relation to sound recordings in the same manner it was used in the theatre and film industries. Here, rather than being the manufacturer of a product, the producer operates as an arranger and organizer. It is their role to source talent, locations and funding so that a production can take place.[1]

---

[1] The different inflections can be witnessed in the British Copyright Act of 1956, albeit that here they are applied to the word 'maker' rather than producer. The owner of sound recording copyright is a maker of physical entities, defined as 'the person who owns that record at the time when the recording is made' (1956: §12(8)). The owner of film copyright is a maker of productions, defined as 'the person by whom the arrangements necessary for the making of the film are undertaken' (1956: §13(10)(b)).

This definition would eventually be utilized in international sound recording rights agreements but appears to have first been employed in the recording industry to refer to independent record producers. These individuals and companies hired recording studios to make master tapes, which they would lease or sell to record labels for wider distribution. This practice was facilitated by tape recording, which spurred an increase in the number of studios available for private hire. As 'producer' began to be defined in organizational rather than manufacturing terms, the horizons of sound recording rights expanded. Ownership was no longer confined to record companies. It could reside with any party that booked a studio to oversee the creation of master tapes.

There were other means by which the possibilities for rights ownership were widened. Tape recording advanced the art of recording and consequently brought new conceptions of sound recordings as creative works into play. During the acoustic era of 1877–1925, the auditory role of studio personnel was restricted to positioning musicians and repurposing instruments so they could effectively be heard. Electric recording brought greater levels of control, but prior to the introduction of tape technologies this was largely confined to balancing the inputs of microphones. Judgements of creative authorship centred on musicians' performances and whether their arrangement constituted an original contribution above and beyond the written composition. The record companies were also regarded as expending their skill in the realization of master discs. The leaders among them developed and refined their methodologies for making physical recordings, demonstrating considerable ingenuity as they did so. This work was nevertheless regarded as industrial rather than artistic, thus raising questions whether sound recordings were worthy of authorial rights. Tape recording changed this situation. As well as distancing recording practice from associations with industrial manufacture, it brought the artistic manipulation of sound into play. Tape could be spliced, layered and reversed; recordings could be augmented with effects. With these developments, studio personnel joined performers as the potential owners of works-based sound recording rights.

A further transformational use of tape occurred beyond the confines of recording studios. Unauthorized manufacture had been limited in the era of direct-to-disc recording. This was because record companies owned the majority of pressing plants. In addition, the production of discs was costly and required heavy machinery. As a result, record companies in some countries felt little need to campaign for reproduction rights. Tape affected this situation in two respects. First, with the separation of manufacture from A&R, the opportunities for unauthorized manufacture increased. Second, the disc was no longer the only recording format on sale. In addition to being employed in studios, tape was utilized for consumers, with the earliest reel-to-reel recorders being issued in 1949. The first playback machines were similar in bulk to their studio counterparts, however, and the broader public use of tape only accelerated when the format became portable. This was achieved with the compact cassette (introduced by the Dutch company Philips in 1962) and the eight-track cartridge (launched by a consortium of American companies in 1964). Although record companies released pre-recorded music on each of these formats, they also viewed them as a threat. In comparison to discs, these formats were simple and inexpensive to reproduce, leading to an expansion in counterfeiting activity. Facing this development, a greater number of countries called for sound recording copyright legislation.

This chapter traces these transformations. Its first half addresses the use of magnetic tape machines in recording studios and the means by which they altered conceptions of production and ownership. The second half looks at the introduction of federal sound recording copyright legislation in the United States.

The diversification of production

The United States provides a case study for the effects of tape recording on the recording industry and changes in uses of the term 'producer'. It was here that the challenge to vertically integrated, oligopolistic companies happened earliest. Richard Peterson has charted the growing influence of independent labels, from a low-point in 1948, when four major companies were responsible for 81 per cent of hit records in the country, to the end of the following decade, when the independent sector secured 64 per cent of the same market (1990: 106).

It would be misleading to suggest that this development was wholly determined by technology. There were generic developments in rhythm and blues and country music that the independent labels were quicker to react to than the majors. In addition, there were structural changes within the music and broadcast industries, including the promotion of a wider range of genres by publishers and radio companies, which helped facilitate the diversified output of the independent labels. Tape recording nevertheless had an impact. In parallel with the rise of independent labels, the number of independent studios increased (Broven 2009: 168, 297–8). Tape encouraged this development, as it was 'simpler, cheaper, and more flexible' than direct-to-disc recording (Kealy 1979: 12). Tape also provided means by which these studios could advertise themselves. As well as capturing regional sounds, tape recording provided a way of developing them. It allowed for diversification in recording techniques, resulting in the distinct sonic characteristics of recording studios, which in turn helped them to attract clients.

In America the question of ownership of the masters continued to be resolved outside of federal law. Until the early 1970s, state laws of unfair competition and common law copyright provided the principal means of preventing unauthorized duplication. The Pushman Doctrine, which was upheld in several states, was an indicator of who the rights owner should be. It determines that ownership of common law copyright is coincidental with physical ownership of the original work. When it came to sound recordings, this meant that the rights would be owned by record companies in the majority of cases. This was not inevitable, however. If a recording had been created in an independent studio and had not been financed by a record label, control of the rights would reside with whoever had hold of the master tapes. As a result, the horizons of ownership widened. Studio owners, songwriters, publishers and artist managers all began to lay claim to the masters. Significantly, it was by this means that recording artists also first obtained ownership of recordings.

The practice of independent studio owners varied. Some offered their studios for hire, while others created studios so they could helm their own sessions. The latter would scout for talent and prospect for hits. If it looked as though one of their recordings might be a success, they had two options for optimizing its potential. They could sell ownership of the masters to a record label. Conversely, if they wished to retain the rights, their best means of doing so was to establish record companies of their own. Sam Phillips of the Memphis Recording Service pursued both routes. The masters to the early 1950s recordings he made with Howlin' Wolf were purchased by Chess Records in Chicago, and those he recorded with B. B. King were sold to Modern Records in Los Angeles. Later recordings by Elvis Presley, Jerry Lee Lewis and Johnny Cash were issued on his own label, Sun Records.

There were a number of reasons why an independent studio might be hired. In some instances they were booked by record labels who were seeking particular recording ambiances, equipment or staff. Alternatively, the labels might use them for convenience's sake. They were also utilized by songwriters and publishers who wished to realize their compositions in recorded form. Tape recording provided an artistic motivation for doing so. As studio techniques rose to prominence, records came to be purchased as much for their sonic qualities as for the compositions and performances they contained. Seeking control over these new auditory dimensions, there was a desire among composers and publishers to oversee the recording of their work. Tape recording also provided an economic spur. Advances in recording techniques had a negative effect on sheet music sales. For many consumers, the only faithful reproduction of a composition was now its recorded version. It also became increasingly difficult for amateur performers to recreate mediated sounds. Against this background, songwriters and publishers began to issue their own recordings, hoping that sales of these records would offset the decline in sheet music revenues.

Among the first writers to do so were Jerry Leiber and Mike Stoller, authors of hit compositions such as 'Hound Dog', 'Yakety Yak' and 'Kansas City'. Throughout their partnership they retained a focus on studio work, famously remarking that they 'wrote records' rather than songs (Leiber, Stoller and Ritz 2009: 299). As well as embracing the aesthetic aspects of recording, they sought its financial rewards, having been 'screwed' out of royalties when placing compositions with independent labels (Broven 2009: 233). As a result, they set up their own label Spark Records in 1954, which they hoped would serve as an outlet for their work. They were not able to gain widespread distribution, however, and sold ownership of the masters to Atlantic Records the following year. As part of this deal, Leiber and Stoller were hired to make recordings for the label, but a novel aspect of the agreement was its freelance nature. They were entitled to record masters for other companies as well, including majors such as RCA Victor.

There had been precursors. Berle Adams entered into a similar agreement with RCA in 1949, and Syd Nathan of King Records had previously hired a number of freelance recording staff (Broven 2009: 31, 136–7, 146). Bob Crewe and Frank Slay were also working in this manner at this time (Oldham 2003: 39). In each instance, the freelancers would organize the recording sessions and provide finished master tapes to record companies. In return, they would receive royalties relating to the successes of the recordings, rather than salaried wages. What appears to have been distinct about Leiber and Stoller's arrangement is their insistence on being credited as 'producers'. This required negotiation. Atlantic Records baulked at the idea, suggesting 'director' was a more appropriate term. Atlantic believed that the record label could more appropriately be regarded as the producer, due to the fact that it 'put up the money' (Brown 2008: 58). The songwriters eventually prevailed, albeit with limits to their status. Within the film industry, it had become common for organizer-producers to be regarded as owners of rights (Vaidhyanathan 2001: 102). Leiber and Stoller oversaw the development of their recordings, but were not granted ownership of the masters, which instead resided with Atlantic and the other labels with whom they worked.

The music publishers Don Kirshner and Al Nevins went further. After founding their publishing company Aldon Music in 1958, they quickly gained successes with hit records written by their songwriting partnerships, including those of Neil Sedaka and Howard Greenfield, Carole King and Gerry Goffin, Jeff Barry and Ellie Greenwich, and Barry Mann and Cynthia Weil. The amount of money that recordings of these writers' works could generate was limited, however, as the compulsory licensing rate remained the same as when introduced in 1909. Seeking to increase their earnings, Aldon Music embarked on independent record production, negotiating deals with record labels for the use of the master recordings they created. This initiative began with the release of Neil Sedaka's 'The Diary' on RCA Victor in 1958. Standard artist royalty rates at this time were one cent per record, but Aldon gained five cents for their independent productions (Napier-Bell 2014: 261–2). In addition, they licensed the use of the masters for a set period of time, rather than assigning them outright. This meant that the record company would control them for the term of the agreement, but on expiry of the licence they would revert to the publishers. It was a decisive act. Simon Napier-Bell believes these agreements represent the first occasion that record companies were coerced into forgoing ownership of the masters (2014: 261–2).

Aldon's example led other music publishers and studio producers to set up production companies or record labels of their own. This included Phil Spector, who, in addition to issuing recordings on his own Philles label, freelanced for other record companies. American practice also had an influence abroad. In Britain, the major record companies retained a great deal of control. By the end of the 1950s, there were four principal labels in operation: EMI and Decca shared 80 per cent of the retail trade in records; Philips had 12 per cent; Pye 6 per cent; the remainder of the market was shared between 'about 25 small labels' (Frith 1987: 278, 287). In contrast to the United States, rock 'n' roll did not increase the independents' share. The major companies were instead able to 'integrate' this music, as they licensed the records of American performers and developed the most significant homegrown acts (Frith 1987: 288). Tape recording did allow for some diversity, nevertheless. A small number of independent studios began to open. There were also producers who were independent of the record labels' contractual control. Freelancers such as Joe Meek and Tony Meehan would oversee their own sessions, hoping to assign their completed masters to one of the major companies in exchange for fees and royalty percentages (Oldham 2000: 135–6).

Andrew Loog Oldham, the former manager of the Rolling Stones, appears to have been the first such British producer to gain ownership of copyright as well (Oldham 2003: 51). Acting on the advice of Phil Spector, he signed a contract with Decca Records in 1963 that entitled him to record the Rolling Stones independently and retain ownership of their recordings via his production company Impact Sound. Philip Norman notes that 'Such a deal had not been proposed in the whole history of British recorded music. It was a measure of Decca's desperation to launch the "new Beatles" that Oldham's conditions were accepted' (2001: 97). This agreement was imitated by other independent producers, including Mickey Most (for records he produced for the Animals and Herman's Hermits) and Shel Talmy (working with The Who). Under the British Copyright Act of 1956, ownership of sound recording copyright resided with the 'maker' of the master recording (1956: §12(8)). These independent producers could satisfy this criterion, as they developed the original master tapes. The Rome Convention was also flexible enough to grant them ownership, as it has embraced producers who work independently of record company employment (1961: art. 3).

There is another aspect of the American producer deals that influenced the wider recording industry. According to Napier-Bell, the agreement constructed by Kirshner and Nevins introduced a new clause to label contracts (2014: 262). Previously, the costs of recording sessions had been borne by record companies. In contrast, Aldon received advances from labels to finance their sessions, but these funds would need to be recouped before they saw any royalties. This arrangement was mirrored for other producer deals and became more pervasive, with record companies in Britain and America adopting the practice for their contracts with performers (Sanjek and Sanjek 1991: 88). Ultimately, this manoeuvre encouraged recording artists to campaign for ownership of recording rights. As Napier-Bell notes, 'In the case of Don Kirshner's records, after fifteen or twenty years, the rights in the master recordings were returned to him. For artists, those rights stayed forever with the record company. It seemed absurd – the artist was now paying the cost of making records but the record company owned them' (2014: 262).

Although this aspect of record deals would become increasingly contentious, it was not the main contractual concern of popular music recording artists in the 1950s and early 1960s. The majority were instead focused on their royalty rates, deductions and fees. In respect of artists signed to independent production companies, there was disgruntlement that they were getting the inferior shares of these agreements. The licensing record company would pay a royalty for their use of the recordings, which would be divided between the production company and the performers. Oldham's licensing deal with Decca, for example, resulted in his production company receiving an 8 per cent royalty rate on record sales, while the Rolling Stones' share was 6 per cent, one quarter of which was retained by their managers as commission (Goodman 2015: 90).

The Rolling Stones were still on a higher royalty than acts signed directly to major labels. The Beatles provide a case in point. They had a traditional contract with EMI's Parlophone label, which included no advance payments. The group therefore received royalties on the initial sales of their records, rather than having to wait for costs to be recouped. The royalty rate was nevertheless only one penny per single, approximating to three per cent of sales revenues. This was reduced further, as 15 per cent of these revenues would be withheld from the group in lieu of 'records returned and/or damaged in transit and/or used for demonstration or advertising purposes' (Lewisohn 2013: 647). Similar deductions would remain a feature of record contracts long after shellac records and vinyl discs dominated the market.

For African American performers, these conditions could be particularly onerous. They would regularly be subject to punitive contractual terms, particularly when signed to independent labels. Although the companies would pay modest fees for the recording work, there were instances in which they effectively denied the artists any subsequent payments, as low royalty rates were cancelled out by excessive deductions (Stahl 2015: 349–51). The situation of the artists was compounded by the lack of sound recording copyright legislation in the United States. The masters would commonly be owned by record company proprietors; the musicians therefore had no 'extra-contractual, statutory intellectual property claims on their recordings' and were bound solely by the terms of their agreements (Stahl 2015: 352). As well as bargaining from a position of weakness, they would regularly sign contracts in the absence of legal representation.

In this period, it could be more profitable to be a session musician than a performer with an exclusive recording deal, as union rates could better the royalties that signed artists received (Perry 2021: 18; Thompson 2018: 37).

As a mitigating factor, record labels encouraged their contracted artists to view recordings as a means of publicizing their concert performances. Art Rupe, the head of Little Richard's label Speciality Records, instructed his staff to 'Impress upon the artist that if they succeed, the publicity of having their records played constantly all over the U.S.A. will make them in demand for personal appearances. Impress on them not to look in the records for income, but to the profitable personal appearances' (Broven 2009: 477).

The most determined, successful and independently minded artists did have a possible route out of these contractual shortcomings, however. They could establish independent production companies or record labels of their own. One example is provided by the jazz musicians Max Roach and Charles Mingus, who set up Debut Records in 1952 'in an effort to maintain artistic and economic control over their output' (Brennan 2020: 170). Ray Charles was motivated similarly when he moved from Atlantic Records to ABC-Paramount in 1959. His new label had previously entered into an independent production deal with Bob Marcucci of Chancellor Records, from whom they licensed Fabian and Frankie Avalon master recordings. This deal was emulated for Charles, who was offered a 75:25 split (in his favour) of record sales revenues, albeit that these payments were used to recoup all 'basic costs' (Lydon 2004: 168). He was contracted 'not as an artist but as a producer of his own records' and is alleged to have used this status to demand ownership of the masters (Lydon 2004: 167, 168). ABC-Paramount conceded on condition they be licensed to them exclusively for a period of five years. Recalling Charles's deal, Susaye Greene of his backing singers the Raelettes commented, 'He was the first artist to own his own masters. You are free when you own your own music; if you don't, then you're somebody's slave' (*Soul America* 2020).

This was a rare instance of an African American artist gaining superior contractual terms. Charles succeeded in negotiations where Frank Sinatra had failed. Seeking to improve his agreement with Capitol Records in the late 1950s, Sinatra requested creative control of his recording sessions and ownership of his recordings. When these negotiations broke down, he first responded by attempting to purchase Verve Records, where he intended to operate independently. Failing in this endeavour, Sinatra eventually found a way to secure ownership of his recorded work. He set up Reprise Recordings in 1960 as a vehicle for his own recordings, as well as to sign other recording artists.

Charles also bettered the terms achieved by Sam Cooke. Having witnessed that rights ownership was accorded to independent film producers, Cooke's manager Allen Klein encouraged his artist to adopt this model and license his recordings via a production company rather than sign directly to a record label. In 1963, RCA Victor made an agreement on this basis, but insisted on having an exclusive licence for a period of thirty years. This contract was not wholly to the benefit of the artist. Klein argued that, for tax purposes, it would be better for the production company to be set up under his name rather than Cooke's, a manoeuvre that ultimately denied the musician and his estate ownership of the masters (Goodman 2015: 46).

In the same year as Cooke's deal took place, Dave Clark of the Dave Clark Five became the first unsigned artist in Britain to contract with a record company and secure ownership of sound recording copyright. Setting a precedent for artists in the digital era, some of whom have had a strong hand negotiating their first recording contracts because they have built up followings online, Clark was able to use the success of his band as a live attraction when setting his terms (Williams 2008: 10). As the independent producer of his own recordings, he established licensing deals with Columbia in Britain and Epic in the United States. In doing so, Clark managed to negotiate a royalty rate four times higher than that of the Beatles and secured the return of his master rights after a period of three years (*Dave Clark Five* 2015).

Another method by which successful artists improved their situations was to seek new recording deals and use them as an opportunity to bargain for superior royalty rates. In situations where these were achieved, it was the practice of some artists to re-record their back catalogue, hoping that consumers would purchase the newer, more profitable versions of their work. The effects of this practice could be negated, however, as on occasions their former labels would reissue the original recordings to compete with the new versions. Paul Anka found a way of circumventing this. In 1964, he paid more than a quarter of a million dollars for ownership of his original ABC-Paramount masters. His primary intention in doing so was to keep these older recordings out of circulation, as he did not want them to compete with the re-recordings and new records he was making ('Anka Buys' 1965: 6).

Although the idea of purchasing recordings to restrict their use might appear peculiar today, it underlines the musical economy of this era. Musicians' earnings from recordings were centred almost entirely on fees and royalties relating to their latest releases. The recording careers of the majority of popular music artists were expected to be brief, with an estimated 'lifespan' of eighteen months to two years (Marshall 2013: 586). This short-term outlook can be witnessed in the agreements that independent producers negotiated. The Cooke deal had an unusually long licensing period, but it was more common that the transfer would last between three and five years, the time in which companies thought popular music recordings were likely to retain popularity. The labels set similar time limits on some of their other contractual terms. One means by which they clamped down on re-recordings was by introducing clauses that precluded artists from recording the same titles for other companies until three to five years after the originals had been made.

These were singles-based mentalities, keyed to the fast turnover of sales charts and radio playlists. There would be a turnaround in the late 1960s, when sales of popular music long-playing albums exceeded those of singles for the first time (Osborne 2012: 111). This format had a longer sales life and therefore encouraged artists and record companies to focus on the longevity of careers, as well as the duration of rights ownership. Albums also brought higher financial returns, leading to a reversal in the relationship between recorded music and live music. Whereas record companies had previously suggested to artists that recordings were promotional tools for their live appearances, they were by the 1970s willing to underwrite loss-making concert appearances with 'tour support' (Frith et al. 2019: 61). This was undertaken in the belief that performances would generate vinyl album sales.

To secure revenues from these albums, the record companies had to combat the threat from another recording format. The late 1960s turn towards long-playing records was accompanied by an increase in the manufacture and circulation of unauthorized tape recordings. With this development, the world's principal creator of recorded music finally established a sound recording copyright of its own.

Sound recording copyright in the United States

1. The development of sound recording copyright

There are two main phases in the development of the American legislation. First, the period between 1906 and 1951, which witnessed the failure of thirty-one bills that proposed the introduction of sound recording rights. The second phase lasted between 1955 and 1976, encompassing the long process of revising American copyright law. This reform programme was initiated with thirty-five studies, including a 1957 report by Barbara A. Ringer, assistant chief of the Examining Division in the Copyright Office, which addressed the subject of sound recordings and decided legislative protection was 'desirable' (1957 [1961]: 47). It concluded with the Copyright Act of 1976. For sound recordings, these periods moved in opposite directions. The first began with bills that proposed a reproduction right, but ended up concerned with performing rights. The second began with an insistence on performing rights, but sound recording copyright was eventually secured by focusing on reproduction and distribution rights only.

In America, the opponents of sound recording copyright made a consistent claim: records are not writings and therefore cannot receive protection under the terms of the Constitution. This argument was advanced by music publishers in the early twentieth century and was reprised by ASCAP in the mid-1930s. Broadcasters used it too. As late as 1978, the NAB employed it as part of their broadside against performing rights (HJC 1978: 153). By this time, however, the tide had turned. In an influential article published in 1945, Zechariah Chafee stated, 'The copyright clause of the Constitution should be construed so as to permit Congress to protect by appropriate devices any literary or artistic work which deserves such protection' (1945: 735–6). It was established that 'there was no constitutional obstacle to protecting a sound recording as the writing of an author' (USCO 2011: 9). Rather, it was the deliberate choice of the 1909 Act to debar recordings from protection and this decision could be reversed. The study period for reform concluded with a 1965 Bill that suggested an overhaul of copyright, including legislative recognition for sound recordings. The Register of Copyrights Arthur Kaminstein stated, 'there is no doubt in my mind that recorded performances represent the "writings of an author" in the constitutional sense, and are as fully creative and worthy of copyright protection as translations, arrangements, or any other class of derivative works' (HJC 1965: 1863).

Although the 1965 Bill argued for a copyright for sound recordings, it was only intended to cover the act of reproduction. Kaminstein warned that if performing rights were included this would trigger 'a wave of protest that would be likely to tear this bill apart' (HJC 1965: 1863). Legislators feared opposition from radio broadcasters, whose lobbying power had only increased with time. It is also arguable they now had stronger claims against performing rights. During the 1930s there was evidence that radio diminished the popularity of recordings, but a reversal was quickly apparent. In 1942, Capitol Records initiated the practice of issuing free copies of recordings to radio companies, believing that broadcast provided a stimulus to record sales (Broven 2009: 22). Recording artists endorsed this view, and were in the habit of visiting radio stations as a key aspect of their promotional work (HJC 1994: 94).

Performing rights continued to be the main legislative interest of record companies and performers, nonetheless. Both parties desired remuneration for the broadcast of their recordings. Performers additionally sought greater control over this use of their work. Learning from the failure of the pre-war legislative process, there was an attempt to present a united front. In 1967, the Recording Industry Association of America (RIAA) proposed an amendment to the Copyright Bill, which addressed the subject of performing rights. Influenced by the Rome Convention, it outlined how 'royalty proceeds will be split equally between the record manufacturer on the one hand and the musicians and artists on the other' (HJC 1967: 480). The National Committee for the Recording Arts, a successor group to NAPA, endorsed this proposal. It also received backing from the AFM, who by the early 1960s had healed the rift between 'members engaged in recording, and those who were not' (HJC 1978: 28). As a result it supported the cause for performing rights. However, in spite of this show of unity, the record companies and recording artists did not achieve their aim. When federal legislation for sound recordings was secured in 1971, it did not address the broadcast or public performance of recordings.

The opponents of performing rights mounted their opposition on constitutional grounds, but had no such qualms when it came to a reproduction right. In this respect, they were satisfied that recordings could be considered as writings. This apparently contradictory outlook can be explained by consistency elsewhere. As Ringer noted, the main focus of all parties was 'economic self-interest' ([1957] 1961: 37). Composers and publishers endorsed the reproduction right because they stood to gain greater mechanical royalties if recordings were effectively protected. Broadcasters backed it because it did not affect their trade. The NAB even suggested there was a 'demonstrable need' for it to be enacted (HJC 1978: 437).

This need only became apparent in the late 1960s. Until this point, the unauthorized manufacture of recordings remained a minority activity. As long as the market was focused on the production of vinyl, it was only possible for those with access to manufacturing machinery to duplicate discs. This meant the major companies' recordings were generally secure, as they had control of their own duplication processes. Independent companies were more vulnerable because they were reliant on the trustworthiness of contracted manufacturers. In the 1950s and early 1960s there was evidence of a nascent trade in unauthorized pressings, most notably in instances where there was a need to utilize numerous pressing plants to satisfy the demand for a hit. The record companies still placed their faith in state legislation, however, believing their interests were sufficiently protected by the law of unfair competition. Musicians additionally had recourse to common law copyright. The Paul Whiteman decision of 1940 was reversed in the 1955 case of *Capital Records v Mercury Records*, which determined that recording artists had 'perpetual' rights that could 'not be lost by publication' (Ringer [1957] 1961: 16).

By the end of the decade this faith appeared misplaced. Unauthorized manufacture took on new forms with the compact cassette and eight-track cartridge. Where previously the duplication of recordings was costly and required heavy machinery, these formats enabled small-scale operators to enter the trade. State laws were inefficient against them, as perpetrators could easily cross boundary lines, thus negating decisions made in local trials. When sales of these formats increased in the late 1960s, the record companies demanded federal legislation. They were further motivated by the international nature of this activity. Unauthorized cassette recordings were being imported into the United States. Correspondingly, American recordings were counterfeited abroad, leading the RIAA to complain that 'the chaos currently existing in the international market for American recordings will reach the point that these markets will no longer be available to the legitimate American recording industry' (HJC 1971: 61, 65). An international agreement on unauthorized duplication was mooted, but the United States could only participate effectively if it had sound recording legislation of its own. A final prompt towards federalization was provided by decisions in the 1964 cases of *Sears, Roebuck v Stiffel* and *Compco v Day-Brite Lighting*, which placed doubts on the validity of using state law protection.

The record companies' urgency was stifled by the copyright revision process, which by the late 1960s had become tied up in debates about cable television. In response, they requested bespoke legislation. Senators John McClellan and Hugh Scott adopted their cause, introducing a Bill in February 1971 that proposed to 'prohibit piracy in sound recordings'. The record companies made much of their economic travails in the hearings that followed. They argued that in 1970 alone the unauthorized manufacture of recordings had resulted in an 'estimated' loss of US$100 million worth of sales (HJC 1971: 1). In addition, the RIAA calculated that tape recordings now constituted about a quarter of their business and suggested this figure should be higher but a quarter of tapes in circulation were 'unauthorized duplicates' (HJC 1971: 25). They claimed that a record company would normally invest between US$180,000 and US$200,000 in the manufacture, distribution and promotion of each album release, but a 'pirate need only spend $300' to create copies (HJC 1971: 26). The companies also highlighted the damage caused by the trade in vinyl bootlegs, a practice that was becoming widespread following the 1969 releases of the unofficial Bob Dylan collection *Great White Wonder* and the Beatles' outtakes album *Get Back*. According to their calculations, the former recording sold 250,000 copies and the latter 100,000 (Marshall 2005: 116).

Although it was maintained that 'the entire music industry supports this bill', the proposal did encounter opposition from 'legal pirates': tape companies who had not been authorized by record labels to issue copies of their recordings, but insisted they were law abiding because they paid compulsory licensing fees for their use of compositions (HJC 1971: 6, 93). They campaigned for the same protection as had been granted to the recording industry when the mechanical right was introduced. A new copyright would be acceptable, but only if it were subject to a 'reasonable' compulsory licensing fee (HJC 1971: 73). The tape companies complained that if the Bill were allowed to pass as it stood, it would enable the major record labels to 'dictate extortionate licensing terms' and entrench their monopolistic power (HJC 1971: 73). These arguments received support from Senator Philip Hart, who complained that the legislation was being enacted solely to protect 'the investment of risk capital in the recording industry' (HJC 1971: 75). He pointed out that American copyright law was not supposed to serve this purpose and was instead 'limited to the protection of authors and inventors for the purpose of encouraging the disclosure of inventions and the publication of writings' (HJC 1971: 75).

Having weighed these arguments, the Senate Judiciary Committee decided that sound recordings deserved protection and were 'clearly within the scope of the "writings of an author"' (1971: 4). In October 1971, Public Law 92–140 was enacted, introducing a copyright in sound recordings as an amendment to the 1909 Act. Its measures came into force in February 1972, and were carried over almost wholesale into the Act of 1976, which still forms the basis of US copyright law. As with its introduction in other countries, the legislative protection for sound recordings was transformative in nature. Alex S. Cummings has noted that 'a new rationale for copyright' was being developed, 'one that aimed to protect the value of capital, favored longer periods of protection, and expanded property rights to new and different kinds of expression' (2010: 681).

2. Limitations

The 1971 legislation states that its measures are 'limited' in nature (SJC 1971: 6). One of these limitations is its 'significant temporal restriction' (USCO 2011: 12). When it came into force, the legislation was not retroactive, meaning that pre-1972 recordings did not receive federal protection. In addition, although the legislation respects an 'aggregation of sounds' rather than the 'physical object' of the record itself (meaning that ownership of rights is separate to ownership of the master recordings), the copyright is physicalist in nature: the owner is 'limited to the right to duplicate the sound recording in a tangible form that directly or indirectly recaptures the actual sounds fixed in the recording' (SJC 1971: 5, 9). Other recordings, meanwhile, are free to 'imitate' or 'simulate' any sounds that have been made (SJC 1971: 9). The Law is also limited in its intent. Its purpose is to provide protection 'against unauthorized duplication and piracy' (HJC 1971: 1). It addresses the unauthorized copying of commercial releases, but does not encompass the recording of live shows or the duplication of recordings that have not been officially released, and is thus ineffective against bootlegs (Marshall 2005: 116). Moreover, while it grants the owners of sound recording copyright an exclusive right to reproduce their work, it does not provide them with performing rights (SJC 1971: 9).

'Limited' is nevertheless also a misleading term. In the first instance, the reproduction right does not stand alone: it is accompanied by a right of distribution. This provision was deemed necessary for instances where the reproduction was authorized, but a separate party was undertaking distribution without the right owner's consent. Second, the legislation had the potential to expand. The duration of the term could be extended and the number of exclusive rights could increase. The 1971 legislation acknowledges its neglect of performing rights. The Senate Judiciary Committee report indicated that this subject would 'be considered subsequently when the committee acts on the legislation for the general revision of the copyright law' (HJC 1978: 52). Third, although its focus is on controlling 'piracy' and preserving 'legitimate' sales, the Law serves 'other purposes' as well (HJC 1971: 1). Principal among these is the ability to facilitate the assignment and licensing of sound recordings, whether between different record companies or for synchronization with the moving images of films, television programmes and advertisements. Fourth, unauthorized manufacture was a significant concern. Although the legislation was initiated to solve a local problem, a global dimension was borne in mind. The 1971 Law was passed two weeks ahead of the Convention for 'the Protection of Producers of Phonograms against Unauthorized Duplication of Their Phonograms' (more commonly known as the Phonograms Convention). Consequently, the United States could sign an international agreement it had urged and which includes 'provisions that correspond closely' to its copyright Law (HJC 1971: 8).

In the introduction to the Phonograms Convention, its contracting parties proclaim unity in their concern about 'the widespread and increasing unauthorized duplication of phonograms' and the 'damage' this is causing to 'authors, performers and producers of phonograms' (Phonograms Convention 1971: 1). The Convention is oriented towards the latter party, however. While it safeguards any extant authors' rights, neighbouring rights and performers' rights in domestic laws, its measures are focused solely on phonogram producers, who alone are granted protection against 'the making of duplicates', 'the distribution of such duplicates' and 'the importation of such duplicates… for the purpose of distribution to the public' (Phonograms Convention 1971: arts 2 and 7). It contains no performing rights or equitable remuneration rules.

The 'simplicity and flexibility' of this Convention rendered it less controversial than the Rome Convention and it quickly attracted a greater number of adherents (Whitford 1977: 21). It had the full backing of the IFPI, which desired 'a ratifiable international agreement to ensure action against the rising problem of record piracy' (Alloway 1983: 11). The IFPI also assumed that this Convention was effective. Although the organization remained vigilant in its 'worldwide campaign against piracy', it believed, somewhat mistakenly, that with its adoption the protection of the major recording markets had 'largely been achieved' (Stewart 1983: 17).

3. Authorship

Although there was crossover in the development of the Phonograms Convention and the American sound recording Law, there is some variance when it comes to the designation of authorship. By 1971, three main approaches to the protection of sound recordings were in evidence: the 'old' copyright system, formulated in the British Act of 1911, under which sound recordings are treated 'in like manner' to other art forms and regarded as original works (1911: §19(1)); the authors' rights system, which rejects this idea of originality and instead protects recordings because they 'neighbour' original creative works; and the 'new' copyright system, developed in the British Act of 1956, which has similarities to the neighbouring rights system, as it abandons the criterion of originality for sound recordings (Sterling 1992: 160). The Phonograms Convention is reflective of these latter two systems. It follows the Rome Convention in granting rights to the 'producer', who is defined as 'the person who, or the legal entity which, first fixes the sounds of a performance or other sounds' (1971: art. 1(b)). The American Law operates differently. It rests on a constitutional pledge to protect the original 'writings of an author' and consequently utilizes the 'old' system of copyright (Copyright Act 1909: §4; Copyright Act 1976: §101(a)). Ownership is granted to 'authors of sound recordings' in respect of their creativity (HJC 1971: 1).

This designation reignited arguments about the artistry of sound recordings, although with different inflections to earlier debates. When the first sound recording legislation was developed at the beginning of the twentieth century, record companies had utilized recording artists in order to provide evidence of their own creativity. By the early 1970s, the two parties were ranged against each other. Moreover, the artists appeared to have the stronger claim to be owners of this works-based copyright. They could be posited as individual creators, thus satisfying the Romantic tenets of authorship. Their cause was also bolstered by American common law judgements. Finding in favour of Waring in his 1937 case, Judge Stern argued for the 'distinctive and creative nature' of performance, while suggesting that manufacturers would fail to satisfy a creativity criterion (HJC 1971: 15; Ringer and Sandison 1989: 657). This position was reinforced by the 1955 Capitol Records decision. Judge Learned Hand recognized the 'wide choice' a musician has in interpreting a score, and therefore viewed a performer's rendition as being 'quite as original a "composition" as an "arrangement" or "adaptation" of the score itself' (HJC 1967: 1176). Recording artists additionally had the support of the Copyright Office. In her 1957 study, Ringer stated that 'from the creative viewpoint, the claims of the performers appear to outweigh those of the manufacturers' ([1957] 1961: 48).

These arguments focused on the ability of recording artists to enhance compositions through their performative choices or interpretive styles. They could be persuasively made in the mid-twentieth century when jazz was the leading form of popular music in the United States. Testifying before the Subcommittee of Patents, Trademarks and Copyrights in 1967, the pianist Bobby Troup suggested, 'Jazz is much more than just printed notes. In many cases, it is the complete lack of printed notes... It is the taking of the bare "framework" of a tune – the basic chord progressions – and then using this skeleton to weave an original melody that becomes a creation in itself' (HJC 1967: 830).

A performative claim could also be made in respect of classical music. Judge Stern praised the conducting work of Toscanini and the musicianship of Paderewski, believing they 'definitely added something to the work of authors and composers' (HJC 1971: 15).

It is arguable, nevertheless, that the first auteurs of recorded music were not musicians, but instead resided among the studio personnel who explored the manipulative possibilities of tape recording. The expansion of this art form was led by independent producers, including Phil Spector in America and Joe Meek in Britain. Indeed, such was the prominence of studio work in their activities and others like them that 'producer' developed a distinct recording industry application, whereby it was applied to the helming of studio sessions and described a position akin to the director of a film. Here it took on a life of its own and was adopted by studio personnel in a variety of employment situations, including the salaried staff of record companies who oversaw in-house recordings. As a result, three overlapping uses of the term 'producer' were utilized within the recording industry: manufacturer-producers (who might also have organizational oversight of the recording sessions), organizational producers (who might also have creative oversight of the recording sessions) and studio producers (some of whom might be independent, raising the funding for their recordings and contracting artists, while others would come under a record companies' employ and, although they might have an A&R role in signing artists, would not bear financial responsibility for the recordings).

Aware that the artistry of record manufacture was being refuted, American record companies rallied behind their in-house studio producers to stake their own authorial claims. During the hearings for the 1965 Bill, Goddard Lieberson of Columbia Records argued that a 'hit record is the concept not of the artist, not of the songwriter, but of… the recording man and his engineer, in company with an arranger', adding that the role of the studio producer had been growing in importance in the 'last 5 or 10 years' (HJC 1965: 938). Alan W. Livingston, president of Capital Records, stated similarly that there was a 'creative contribution' on the part of the head of the studio staff: 'He is the musically trained person who determines what song is to be sung by what performer, determines the nature and instrumentation of the orchestra, selects the arranger, and often makes many technical and musical contributions to the performance itself' (HJC 1965: 949). By 1967, Clive Davis had become president of Columbia and he too was making claims about creativity. In doing so, Davis echoed the sentiments of Judge Hand, but pointed towards record companies' decision-making processes rather than those of musicians. He noted, 'the musical composition is in the form of a few notes and words. It must be significantly embellished upon to make a successful recording. The proper studio and acoustics must be used; the sound engineer must do his job' (HJC 1967: 520). Arguments such as these led Ringer to revise her opinions about creativity. By 1971 she was acknowledging that 'the contributions of the record producer to a great many sound recordings also represent true "authorship"' (HJC 1971: 11).

The 1971 Law reflects this position. It outlines two strands of artistry: the performance that is 'captured' and the capture of this performance, including its processing, editing and compilation into an 'aggregation of sounds' (SJC 1971: 5). It remains silent, however, on who is the rightful author of the work. The Senate Judiciary Committee's report for the 1971 amendment notes that 'the bill does not fix the authorship, or the resulting ownership, of sound recordings, but leaves these matters to the employment relationship and bargaining among the interests involved' (1971: 5).

By the time of the Law's enactment, the record companies were no longer bargaining on creative grounds. The elevation of the art of studio work had led to a decline in the in-house system of making recordings, as it encouraged studio producers to branch out on their own. Rather than being permanently contracted to record companies, many of them elected to become freelancers, offering their services for fees and a share of the royalties. Moreover, rather than using record company studios, they increasingly turned to facilities that were independently owned. These methods of working first rose to prominence in the mid-1960s and were fairly widespread by the time the legislation was enacted. As a result, it became increasingly difficult for record companies to claim any creative authorship in sound recordings, which instead was more likely to reside with recording artists (for their recorded performances) and with independent studio personnel (for 'setting up the recording session, capturing and electronically processing the sounds, and compiling and editing them to make the final sound recording') (SJC 1971: 5).

American law facilitates the idea of 'joint authorship'; thus, these two parties had the potential to collectively wrest copyright from record company ownership. This did not happen, however. Although the American Law revived the 'old' system of protecting sound recordings, the record companies were still able to claim ownership via business means. The Committee had indicated the manner in which creative authorship could be subsumed: rather than accenting artistic practices, the focus could be on the 'employment relationship'. Record companies and independent producers could brand their recordings as 'work made for hire'.

4. Ownership

The concept of work made for hire was introduced to US copyright law in the 1909 Act (1909: §62). It enables an employer to become the author of their employees' creative labour and therefore owner of the associated rights. Siva Vaidhyanathan has argued that the introduction of this 'corporate copyright' represented the 'real "death of the author"' and that 'Authorship could not be considered mystical or romantic after 1909' (2001: 102). Peter Jaszi, in contrast, regards the work made for hire doctrine as a 'distorted' version of Romantic ideals, in which the employer is 'cast as the visionary, and the employee as a mere mechanic following orders' (1991: 488). The recording industry would appear to side with Vaidhyanathan. In 1990, the president of the RIAA declared that 'authors' rights are dead': the main objective of his organization was to gain protection for manufacturers and it cared 'little about the banner under which rights are protected' (HJC 1994: 85 (note)).

American record companies have nevertheless had to be mindful of the nuances of copyright law. Although sound recordings were not protected under the 1909 Act, it has been suggested that, had they been included, early employment relationships in the industry would have classified them as work made for hire (USCO 2011: 108–9, 144). Record companies had full oversight of record production: they hired artists and selected their repertoire; the recording sessions took place on record company premises and were supervised by company staff. Correspondingly, work made for hire authorship was proposed in some of the early debates about sound recording copyright. The Daly Bill of 1936 suggested that any rights accorded to recording artists would automatically be assigned to their record companies (Ringer [1957] 1961: 28). The companies put forward a similar idea in their performing rights amendment to the 1967 Bill (HJC 1967: 506). Legal cases also tended to view recording artists as employees, establishing a rule that, unless specified otherwise in their contracts, the record label or independent producer would own the intellectual property (Ringer and Sanderson 1989: 662).

Matters have not been straightforward, however. Recording artists have not satisfied all of the criteria to be termed as employees: record companies and independent producers have not paid taxes on their behalf and have not provided them with employee benefits, such as sick leave or pensions. Recording artists have also grown increasingly independent of company stewardship. With reference to the system of advances and recoupment, music industry lawyers Jay Cooper and Kenneth Burry have noted how, 'Starting in the early 1960's... the financial responsibility for the artistic process shifted from the record company to the artist' (2001: 7). In addition, recording artists have taken greater control of their working practices, in some cases assuming responsibility for setting deadlines for studio work, selecting studio personnel and hiring session musicians. This autonomy has nevertheless rarely been complete. Labels and independent producers have continued to have significant oversight of recording projects and have contracted their artists for considerable periods. Therefore, from one perspective it has been possible to regard recording artists as employees; from another they could be viewed as independent contractors undertaking commissioned work (Stahl 2013: 186).

The American recording industry has tended towards the latter view. However, while this has helped it clarify to working relationships, it has not resolved ownership of rights. Commissioned works were not addressed by the 1909 Act, but case law gradually established that they qualified as work made for hire. This would have secured most sound recordings under this banner when first protected via the 1971 Law, thus providing one reason why the Senate Judiciary Committee could point to the employment relationship in determining authorship. The 1976 Act has nevertheless queried this notion. Its framers wished to place restrictions on corporate control and provide greater protection for individual creative authors (Hamilton 1987: 1290–91). One means of doing so was to grant the rights in commissioned works to independent contractors rather than the companies for whom they worked.

This idea was contested by the motion picture and book publishing industries, resulting in a compromise solution. The 1976 Act outlines two categories of work made for hire. First, there is the original concept of 'work prepared by an employee within the scope of his or her employment' (1976: §101). In addition, there are nine specific categories of 'specially ordered or commissioned' works, whereby authorship can be granted to the commissioner rather than the contractor: a contribution to a collective work, a part of a motion picture or other audio-visual work, a translation, a supplementary work, a compilation, an instructional text, a test, answer material for a test, and an atlas (1976: §101). These commissioned works can only qualify as work made for hire if the commissioner and contractor agree to this status via contract.

Sound recordings are not among the nine categories. This absence has been excused on the grounds that the lobbying took place in the 1960s, at which point recordings were not a feature of copyright legislation (HJC 2000: 196–7, 227). It has also been suggested that during this period recording artists and studio personnel were still primarily viewed as employees; therefore, record companies and independent producers did not need to classify recordings as commissioned works (HJC 2000: 88). Cooper and Burry have argued, nonetheless, that if 'Congress intended sound recordings to qualify, it would have expressly included sound recordings on the list in 1976 when the definition was last modified' (2001: 2). There has been further debate about whether sound recordings can be classified under the headings of 'compilation' or 'contribution to a collective work' (HJC 2000: 227, 269). Although record companies have frequently made these claims, they have not been entirely secure in them. Hence, American recording contracts have defined sound recordings as 'work made for hire' but have also stated that 'should they not turn out to be works for hire' the artist's copyright will be assigned to the contracting company for the full duration of the term (Stahl 2013: 224).

Given the recording industry's dominance in setting contractual terms, the categorization of rights ownership might be considered of little significance. The companies would ultimately secure control of the recordings, whether through works made for hire classification or via assignment. There are two reasons why record companies preferred the former methodology, however. First, the work made for hire route could be more effective administratively. Awarding copyright to the commissioning party foreclosed arguments over creative authorship and which shares of the work the creators should be accredited. Second, it allowed the companies to secure longer-lasting rights.

At first appearance, creative authorship would appear to offer rights of greater duration. In its original incarnation, the 1976 Act set a period of seventy-five years from publication for work made for hire, compared with life plus fifty years for authored works (1976: §302(a), §302(c)). The assignment or licensing of rights can nevertheless be 'terminated' after a period of thirty-five years, at which point the original author can reclaim ownership (1976: § 203). Abandoned in many other territories, the idea of rights renewal or reversion has provided one of the balancing measures of American law.[2] A thirty-five-year period has been granted so the party acquiring the rights has time to recoup its risk investment; the termination right has protected authors from unfair deals, a position that has been reinforced due to the fact it cannot be waived.

Work made for hire has provided the only exception to these rules. This is because the employer is regarded as the original author and consequently there is no reason to protect them from contractual malpractice. The copyright is therefore exempt from termination and can run uncontested for the full duration of the term. It is this aspect of the legislation that has made work made for hire the record companies' preference. Moreover, they have been able to declare it as their choice. In contrast to the laws of most Berne Convention countries, US legislation includes a registration system. Authors deposit their works with the Copyright Office and outline which category they fall under. Record companies have consistently selected work made for hire, classifying their recordings as 'compilations' or 'collective works'.

Work made for hire has also been the preference of recording artists. Although American musicians have commonly been cast as being employed or contracted by record companies, there have been instances where they have been able to declare their independence and secure ownership of sound recording rights. In doing so, they have been able to choose whether to register their recordings as creative works or as work made for hire. The latter designation has been opted for, as it has enabled recording artists to stem the rival interests of studio personnel and session musicians, who could otherwise seek co-authorship if the works were registered on creative grounds. It has also helped them to secure rights that run for the full period of copyright, rather than be subject to termination claims that could be raised by other creative contributors to the work.

In order to make these work made for hire claims, recording artists have had to cast themselves as independent producers or as record labels, demonstrating sufficient financial independence from any associated record companies and evidencing a guiding hand in the organization of their

---

[2] The UK had a policy of rights renewal in the 1710 Statute of Anne: an initial term of fourteen years, which could be renewed for another fourteen years. This was abandoned in the 1814 Copyright Act, which established a continuous term of twenty-eight years or life of the author. The 1911 Copyright Act introduced a reversion right. For literary, dramatic and musical works, the term of copyright was life of the author plus fifty years, but assigned rights would revert to the estate of the author twenty-five years after the author's death (CA 1911: §5(2)). There is no such measure in the 1956 Act or the CDPA.

recording projects. Among the earliest to do so were Led Zeppelin and the Rolling Stones, each of whom entered into licensing agreements with Atlantic Records at the cusp of the 1960s and 1970s, the former via their production company and the latter through a distribution agreement for their own record label. Other major artists of the 1970s, including Stevie Wonder, Van Morrison, Bob Dylan, Neil Sedaka and Paul McCartney, negotiated American recording contracts that granted them work made for hire ownership. They constituted an elite, however, with the vast majority of recording artists residing on the other side of the work made for hire divide. Studio personnel have meanwhile been denied the opportunity to claim a share of copyright as creative co-authors of sound recordings and have been cast as employees and contractors instead. They have also been encouraged to agree to this status in writing. As such, their principal means of assuming ownership of copyright has been to take on the responsibilities of organizational producers, initiating recording sessions and signing recording artists who in turn provide them with work made for hire.

Conclusion

The period from the 1950s to the 1970s witnessed a rethinking of sound recording copyright in response to the introduction and expansion of tape recording technologies. In its domestic recording format incarnation, tape resulted in an expansion of unauthorized manufacture, which in turn prompted more countries to enact and harmonize sound recording copyright laws. In its studio incarnation, tape opened up sound recording copyright to new concepts of creativity. It also helped to foster compartmentalization in the recording industry, leading to a situation whereby some record companies and independent producers created master tape recordings, but were not responsible for pressing vinyl records or duplicating cartridges and cassettes.

The recording industry nevertheless sought continuity through change. It had once been expedient to associate ownership of sound recording copyright with the manufacture of recordings. The record companies now believed their rights would be best protected if ownership were concentrated on recording sessions instead. This was achieved under a number of different rights regimes. In the United States, the record companies gained ownership of copyright via work made for hire legislation, casting themselves as the employers and contractors of the creators of recordings. In Britain, the 1956 Act was flexible enough for ownership to be granted to the makers of master tapes. The language of the Rome and Phonograms Conventions was similarly pliable, enabling its 'fixation of sounds' definition to transfer from the creation of master discs to the finalization of tape recordings.

There is an irony at the heart of sound recording legislation, however. It is when the recording industry moves away from manufacture that copyright assumes increasing importance: the less control it has over the means of production, the more control it requires over rights. Yet it is from strength in manufacture that its strength in copyright has been derived. The companies' authorial claims were most comprehensive in the period when they were all manufacturers and when ownership was granted for this aspect of their work. The move towards organizational, financial and employment definitions of authorship would enable a wider ray of participants to make authorial demands.

In the United States, it was possible for recording artists and studio personnel to claim copyright on creative grounds. The more common route towards ownership, however, was for them to register recordings as work made for hire. This option was additionally available to any composer, publisher, studio owner and artist manager who could demonstrate they employed or commissioned others in the creation of recordings. The situation was similar under the 'new' copyright methodology employed in the UK and other common law countries, as well as under the neighbouring rights policies of civil law territories. The principal means by which these parties could claim ownership was by presenting themselves as independent producers or by setting up record companies of their own.

It should be noted, nevertheless, that the recording industry was only moving away from manufacture in terms of having direct control of duplicative processes. Although some record companies and independent producers now hired third parties to undertake this aspect of production, the creation of physical products remained their primary concern. In fact, throughout the recording industry, the focus remained on the reproduction of records for sale. While this was the case, the record companies continued to enjoy the long-term control of copyright in the majority of recordings, as most artists had to partner with them – and do so from a position of weakness – in order to get their recorded work to market. This orientation would shift in the coming decades, as the industry expanded beyond the manufacture of goods towards increased licensing of rights. With this change, the ownership of copyright would assume even greater importance. In parallel, the record companies' hold over it would be loosened. This begs the question: when did this occur?

4

Expanding

By the late twentieth century, the recording industry could begin to be thought of as a copyright industry. Among academics, Simon Frith was forward-thinking in this respect. As early as 1988, he was arguing that 'the age of manufacture is now over. Companies (and company profits) are no longer organized around making *things* but depend on the creation of *rights*' (1988: 57. Emphasis in original).[1] Frith was not suggesting the era of mass reproduction of recordings was at an end, but that record companies were thinking of these recordings in a different manner. Rather than focusing on them as physical products, they were conceiving them as a 'basket of rights' (1988: 57). He maintained that the job of a contemporary record company was 'to exploit as many of these rights as possible, not just those realised when it is sold in recorded form to the public, but also those realised when it is broadcast on radio or television, used on a film, commercial or video soundtrack' (1988: 57).

As Frith indicates, it is with the elevation of licensing activities that the interests of copyright owners shift from the manufacture of goods towards the wider exploitation of rights. In order to assess the recording industry's outlook, this chapter therefore assesses its licensing and sales activities from the 1970s to the early 2000s. Its initial focus is blanket licensing, the main means by which broadcast and public performance have been monetized. After this, it turns to direct licensing, looking at the industry's interests in inter-company licensing, digital sampling and the synchronization of images with sound. The final section of the chapter addresses physical sales.

---

[1] Although Frith was referring to the music industries broadly, incorporating the music publishing and live music sectors, the recording industry was his main concern. Live music had never had an age of manufacture and it was not turning to the creation of rights (rather than being licensors, venue owners were licensees, paying for the use copyrighted music). Music publishing, on the other hand, had moved away from manufacture before this period. This sector's preoccupation with rights began in the early twentieth century with developments in mechanical rights and broadcast licensing.

The picture that emerges is not one of radical transformation. Although record companies increased their licensing practices, their revenues from broadcast, public performance, synchronization and sampling remained less important than those from retail. In fact, this proved to be a golden period for manufacture. The recording industry prospered as it transitioned from analogue formats to compact discs. Correspondingly, rather than exploiting a full basket of rights, its main interest was in securing control of reproduction rights and using them restrictively. The elimination of unauthorized manufacture and the limitation of competition remained the core concerns.

Licensing

1. Blanket licensing

Performing rights have long held importance for the record business but, as we have seen, the approach to them has varied. The UK granted exclusive performing rights to sound recordings in 1934, but elsewhere these rights were rarely in the industry's basket. Some territories, such as the United States, had no performing rights for recordings. Others granted record companies a share of equitable remuneration rather than exclusive controls. There was nevertheless commonality between territories when it came to licensing methods. Where agreements were in place, these tended to be negotiated by collecting societies rather than by record companies. They were also usually subject to oversight by governmental boards. In addition, rather than negotiating for the use of individual tracks, copyright users obtained blanket licences to access a whole repertoire of recordings. There was no differential pricing: one recording could only make more money than another if it gained greater exposure. The accord in performing rights practices also grew stronger over time. The following sub-sections address overlapping development of legislation in Britain, Europe and the United States.

a) Britain

By the late 1980s, the MU's practice of utilizing its PPL revenue for collective purposes was felt, by some, to be an antiquated. The immediate period witnessed the growing influence of neoliberalism and its attacks upon trade unions. The collective distribution of revenue was also rooted in a bygone era of the music industries. It emerged at a time when sound recording could be considered a disruptive technology. Recording was also secondary to music publishing and live music in both maturity and status. By the late twentieth century, recordings were central within musical life. Music publishing derived the majority of its revenues from uses of recorded music. Live music and recorded music had evolved a symbiotic relationship, whereby the majority of popular music tours were undertaken to promote album releases and the repertoire of amateur performers relied heavily on interpretations of hit recordings. In these circumstances, it could feel rational that the revenues for the broadcast and public performance of recordings should be distributed to artists who made the records, rather than a threatened coterie of live performers.

Against this background, the British government's Monopolies and Mergers Commission (MMC) undertook an investigation into PPL's practices. Its 1988 *Collective Licensing* report concludes, 'So far as performers' interests are concerned we do not think the existing arrangements are a satisfactory discharge of the United Kingdom's obligations under Article 12 of the Rome Convention' (MMC 1988: §7.37). Arguments about performing rights revenues had previously bifurcated between the remuneration of recording artists and the compensation of live musicians. The MMC drew its line in a different place, distinguishing between 'named' and 'unidentified' performers. The former are now more commonly referred to as featured artists: musicians with exclusive recording contracts who receive payments via advances and royalties. The PPL agreement had granted these performers 20 per cent of licensing revenues but the collecting society did little to track usage: money was collected for public performance with no tally of the recordings employed, and broadcast revenues were calibrated via a sample of the output of a limited number of radio stations. PPL were also 'unable to trace the present whereabouts of some of the named performers or their beneficiaries' and consequently much licensing revenue went unclaimed (MMC 1988: §7.36(a)). The 'unidentified' performer was a new concern. Now more commonly referred to as non-featured performers, these are the session musicians, orchestral musicians and backing singers who are paid set fees for their hired contributions to recordings. The MMC maintained it was these performers, rather than a collective of live musicians, who should be in receipt of the 12.5 per cent share of PPL revenue distributed to the MU (1988: §7.36(b)). It stipulated that 'all performers should receive equitable remuneration, directly paid by PPL, specific to each recording's use in broadcasting or public performance' (1988: §7.38).

Despite the protestations of the MMC, the MU had not broken with the Rome Convention, which permitted the collective use of funds. The *Collective Licensing* report upheld the individualistic ethos of the Thatcherite era, however, and led to the termination of the agreement between the Union and PPL. The MU's general secretary Dennis Scard recalled how 'controls over needletime, employment quotas and the policy of not allowing records to accompany live performance, all disappeared overnight' (Williamson 2015: 183). In 1994, the Union regained some influence, when it successfully contested PPL's control of the non-featured performers' share and began to distribute money to these musicians for performance uses of their recorded work ('Timeline' n.d.). This control was nevertheless short-lived. By 1996, Britain was enshrining legislation that followed European Community guidelines for performing rights.

b) Britain in Europe

Britain was formerly a member of the European Economic Community (EEC), which was founded in 1957 and was one of the precursor organizations to the European Union (EU). In the run-up to the signing of the Maastricht Treaty in 1993, which effectively created the EU, the EEC conducted a programme to harmonize the legislation of member states, including a 1992 directive on the 'Rental Right and Lending Right and on Certain Rights Related to Copyright' (EEC 1992). In respect of the performing rights, this Directive is indebted to the Rome Convention. Rather than granting exclusive controls for performers or producers, it states that they should receive equitable remuneration (1992: art. 8(2)). The mandate is nevertheless stronger than laid down in Rome. Remuneration is compulsory and payments must be 'shared between the relevant performers and phonogram producers' (1992: art. 8(2)).

Britain followed this instruction with regard to its own practices. In 1988, it enacted the CDPA, the legislation that continues to provide the basis of its intellectual property laws. This Act evidences some appreciation for the art of recording. It is influenced by the Whitford Committee report of 1977, which condemned the separation of sound recordings into part II of the 1956 Copyright Act (1977: §634). Consequently, recordings are included in part I of the CDPA, where they are given authorial recognition and classified as 'works'. According to the Committee, the 1956 Act was 'unjustified' in classifying sound recording lower than the 'original' copyright in musical compositions, as there is no 'distinction in the quality' between the two forms (1977: §634). The Gregory Report of 1951 had suggested shortening the duration of sound recording copyright to a period of twenty-five years (1952: §89). In contrast, Whitford believed there was 'much to be said' for giving sound recordings 'the same period of protection' as musical works (1977: §634).

The CDPA nevertheless distinguishes between the two types of copyright. The copyright in musical works is awarded to composers in respect of their creativity. In contrast, the copyright for sound recordings is grouped with film production and given to 'the person by whom the arrangements necessary for the making of the recording or film are undertaken' (1988: §9(2)(a)). This designation is indicative of the manner in which legislators prioritized tape recording's transformations: the focus is on economic upheaval rather than any aesthetic re-evaluation. It also reflects the need of the recording industry to confirm its authorial role. Whereas the 'maker' criteria of the 1956 Act could provide opportunities for pressing plants and independent studio owners to claim ownership, this definition awards control to the organizers and financers of recording sessions. It is taken from the previous Act's terminology for the ownership of films (1956: §13(10)). Reflecting the corporate nature of such ownership, the CDPA bases the duration of sound recording copyright on the date of publication, rather than the lifetime of the author. Moreover, while compositions have to be original to be worthy of copyright, the Act has no such requirement for sound recordings. The copyright remains physicalist in nature: there is freedom to mimic recordings; what you cannot do without permission is utilize the recordings themselves.

The CDPA also incorporates performers' rights, albeit that they are sequestered in part II of the Act, which is 'studiously (and, in places, cumbersomely) drafted so as to avoid use of the word "copyright"' (Arnold 2015: §1.86). Moreover, although the CDPA overhauls the Dramatic and Musical Performers' Protection Act of 1958, it initially retained the focus of this earlier legislation. Performers' rights were concentrated on the unauthorized recording of live performances and were accompanied by similar measures for record companies, who were offered protection in respect of the bootleg trade (1988: §185).

There was considerable expansion of performers' rights in 1996, when the CDPA was updated to incorporate the instructions of the EEC's Directive. At this point, performers gained exclusive reproduction, distribution and rental rights for the 'fixation' of their performances in recordings (EEC 1992: arts 2(1), 7(1), 9(1)).

However, while this represented an advance on the Rome Convention, which only offered them the 'possibility' of preventing such fixation, these measures have been described as 'an inefficient tool' (AEPO-ARTIS 2018: 145). This is because musicians have been expected to assign them when contracting with record companies. In addition, these fixation rights are separate to the rights that subsist in the sound recording, which the Directive grants to phonograph 'producers' (1992: arts 2(1), 7(1), 9(1)). This term was incorporated in the CDPA in 1996, using the phrasing of the original Act: the producer is the person who undertakes the arrangements for the making of the sound recording or film (1988: §178).

From the point of view of British performers, the most substantial consequence of the 1996 update is its grant of equitable remuneration for the public performance and broadcast of recordings, albeit that these measures were added to the CDPA in an idiosyncratic manner. The EEC Directive provided enough flexibility for Britain to continue its practice of granting exclusive performing rights for sound recordings, owned solely by phonograph producers. Moreover, whereas the Directive suggests that remuneration should be paid by licensees to performers and phonograph producers, the updated CDPA stipulates that performers receive these payments 'from the owner of the copyright in the sound recording' (1988: §182D(1)). Thus, in the same instance as it gives legislative recognition for the equitable remuneration of performers, the CDPA places them in an inferior position to phonograph producers, who are given control of the funds and regarded as owners of the rights. The 1996 update does provide performers with some protective measures, however. Their equitable remuneration cannot be recouped from record company advances and is safeguarded from assignment. Performers can only transfer these rights to collecting societies, which will 'enforce' them on their behalf (1988: §182D(2)).

In Britain, this responsibility has been accorded to PPL, with the result that equitable remuneration for performers is handled by a collecting society owned by record companies. The society adopted a fifty/fifty division of revenue between phonograph producers and recording artists, which it claims was arrived at in a 'voluntary' manner (PPL 2004: 28). This split also resulted from negotiations with the MU, however, and was guided by practice in Europe (Hanley 2017: 24). Denmark, France, Greece, Italy, the Netherlands, Portugal and Spain had already adopted an equal division of remuneration; Germany had meanwhile decided to give its performers 64 per cent of public performance revenues (Arnold 2015: §3.41; HJC 1978: 197–8).

A further division has been made within the performers' allocation. In Britain, the International Managers Forum (IMF) campaigned on behalf of featured artists, while the MU looked after non-featured performers' interests. These two representative bodies 'argued over the splits', but eventually agreed that the performers' share of equitable remuneration should be allocated 65:35 in the featured artists' favour (Williamson 2015: 185). Other countries have come up with different ratios (AEPO-ARTIS 2018: 28–9). However, while the split between performers and producers has occasionally been outlined in legislation, the split between featured artists and non-featured performers has rarely been detailed there. It has instead been established through organizational agreements.

c) The United States

By the early 1990s, over sixty countries had established public performance and broadcast rights for sound recordings and this number was expected to rise. The United States remained an exception. Therefore, despite the fact that its repertoire made up more than half of the music broadcast globally, American record companies and performers were frequently denied any performing rights revenue from abroad. Most countries withheld remuneration until offered reciprocal terms (HJC 1994: 46).

The 1971 Sound Recording Act had suggested further consideration of performing rights, but this subject was dropped from the reform agenda in 1974. The 1976 Copyright Act, in turn, did not include these rights, suggesting instead that investigative study was required. This was undertaken by the Copyright Office, who issued the 1,000-page report *Performance Rights in Sound Recordings* in 1978. By this time authors' collecting societies no longer objected to these rights, but the broadcasters remained intransigent. The NAB maintained that any imposition of licensing fees would be disastrous for their business and stressed again that broadcasting served to publicize recordings (HJC 1978: 436–40). They even proposed a reversal: record companies should pay broadcasters for the promotional work radio was undertaking (HJC 1978: 5). Although the report ultimately came down on the side of record companies and performers, concluding that sound recordings 'fully warrant a right of public performance', there was no immediate legislative response (HJC 1978: 177). Opposition from the broadcast industry remained 'too strong' (Ringer and Sandison 1989: 675). A further substantive push would not be made until the early 1990s, when the RIAA renewed its campaign for these rights. It was a key player in the development of the WPPT, which WIPO was formulating in this period in response to the digitalization of intellectual property. The RIAA argued to the American government that its ability to influence this international agreement was hampered by the limitations of domestic law (HJC 1994: 46).

In the 1970s, the RIAA had sought performing rights for sound recordings that would encompass all forms of broadcast. The organization now realized its best chance of securing legislation was to restrict its demands to new forms of digital transmission, including developments in Digital Audio Broadcasting (DAB), cable networks and digital satellite broadcasting. Having witnessed the implacable force of the established broadcasting industry, it wanted to gain rights in these services before powerful vested interests emerged (HJC 1994: 43, 46–7). However, despite the fact that analogue broadcasting was ring-fenced from these proposals, the RIAA still faced resistance from the NAB, which was aware that many commercial broadcasters would eventually go digital. The NAB therefore insisted that terrestrial digital broadcasting be exempted from any new measures. In doing so, it echoed claims that record companies made against the imposition of the mechanical right in the early twentieth century. The NAB argued that traditional broadcasters should not be made subject to performing rights because 'the highly complex economic and contractual relationships between and among record producers and performers, music composers and publishers, and broadcasters date back some sixty years' (HJC 1996: 105–6). It did note, however, that it was 'amenable to negotiating over the terms of legislation that would create a limited performance right that could be applied only to... subscription services' (HJC 1994: 78). In its opinion, a subscription service could 'hardly make the claim that a performance right would fundamentally, and unexpectedly, alter the way it has done business for decades' (HJC 1996: 106).

It was in this form that performing rights legislation eventually emerged. The 'narrowly crafted' Digital Performance Right in Sound Recordings Act of 1995 addresses subscription and interactive services only (HJC 1995: 13). These services pointed to the inequity of this situation. Rather than hampering terrestrial broadcasters, the performing rights legislation would strengthen their hand. They would operate in a rights-free environment, whereas the new digital providers would be subject to licence payments and broadcasting restrictions

(HJC 1996: 124). Record companies were not satisfied with this legislation either. They gained a performing right but it was limited in nature. The 1995 Act includes statutory licensing and remuneration rules similar to those of the Rome Convention. Revenue has been split so that 50 per cent goes to copyright owners and 50 per cent to performers.

There are nevertheless some differences. The Rome Convention grants equitable remuneration as a means of protecting the economic interests of record companies and of compensating performers for the use of recordings in performance contexts. The American Act awards its remuneration in respect of creative work. There is also legal recognition of the non-featured performers' share: they are granted 5 per cent of the overall revenue (Copyright Act 1976: §114).

Although featured artists appear to have been satisfied with this division, they had a separate cause for complaint. In 2000, the RIAA established SoundExchange as the collecting society that would distribute performing rights revenues. Its first payments were held up, as featured artists disputed the record companies' decision that the money should be recouped from their advances. Following the resolution of this dispute in the artists' favour, an initial distribution of US$5.2 million was made in October 2001 (Leeds 2001). By 2003, SoundExchange had become an independent not-for-profit corporation.

The creation of American legislation and the harmonization of European copyright law had a significant effect on sound recording's performing rights. These rights had long been considered important, but previously this importance had led either to their enactment being denied (as in the United States) or to them being used restrictively (as represented by the British MU's policy to keep music live). The focus now was on licensing their use. Revenues that had once been regarded as 'icing on the cake' were taken more seriously (PPL 2014: 20). At the beginning of the 1990s, performing rights were worth just 0.5 per cent of global recording industry revenues (PPL 2014: 20; HJC 1994: 29). This share increased by the decade's end, at which point the recording societies in some territories generated licensing revenues similar to those of parallel societies for composers and publishers. The British recording industry witnessed a notable increase. PPL collections grew from a total of £118 million in the 1980s to £430 million in the 1990s, with a significant amount of this money coming from reciprocal agreements with collecting societies abroad (PPL 2014: 5–6).

2. Direct licensing

a) Inter-company

The direct licensing of sound recordings has a longer history than their blanket licensing, but its development has been occluded. It was first manifest in the licensing of records between record companies, which can be traced back to agreements drawn up between companies in the early 1900s. The American company Victor Records, for example, had a contract with the Gramophone Company in Britain, whereby they issued one another's master recordings in their respective territories in exchange for percentage licensing fees (Jones 1985: 81, 91–2). A similar agreement was in existence between the Anglo-Italian Commerce Company and the French recording company Pathé Frères (Gelatt 1977: 104). Inter-record company licensing remained in evidence in the mid-twentieth century, notably among international companies seeking access to the repertoire of American labels. It also took place within countries, with smaller companies licensing their repertoire to larger labels for wider distribution. In addition, the majority of agreements between production companies and record labels took the form of licensing deals.

This practice has peaked and troughed. In the 1960s there was a desire among major record companies to increase their global presence. Consequently, they established branches in territories they had previously reached via licensing deals. This was particularly noticeable in Britain, where American companies such as CBS, MGM and RCA, and the German company Polydor all set up label divisions. The practice was reflective of the wider popularity of British repertoire abroad: the companies hoped to sign domestic artists and gain profits from having a local base (Gillett 1983: 381). Relationships between small labels and major companies also changed. In Britain, there was some abandonment of licensing deals in the early 1980s, following the establishment of the independent distribution network, the Cartel. In other instances, there was an increase in licensing activity. As well as licensing whole catalogues of recordings, record companies conducted deals for the use of individual titles. The practice of sanctioning recordings for use on compilation albums took off in the early 1970s, with originating companies agreeing terms with budget labels such as K-Tel and Ronco. It expanded in the 1980s and 1990s, with exchanges taking place between all types of record company, as well as the introduction of a wider variety of compilations.

Although this inter-company activity has taken the form of licensing deals, it has been reported by the recording industry under the heading of physical sales. Reflecting this, the recording industry has not demarcated it separately in its annual accounting yearbooks, thus it has been difficult to quantify its contribution to revenue. The same methodology is true of another practice that developed in this period: the licensing of digital sampling.

b) Sampling

It was in the late 1970s that the first digital samplers were brought to market. These machines had the ability to record any sound source, but their deployment was soon influenced by the contemporary hip-hop practice of looping and 'scratching' passages of vinyl records to highlight their percussive breaks, instrumental riffs and vocal refrains. Original recordings could be sampled and edited. They could then be embedded in new recordings. This form of borrowing originally appeared to operate at the fringes of copyright law but record companies quickly clamped down on the most obvious and extensive sampling cases. Their exclusive reproduction rights gave them power to veto any unauthorized use of recordings. This right of veto also gave them a strong hand in granting permission to employ sampled material. They could directly license and set fees as they wished.

This is a power that could have been withheld, as evidenced by the 1971 report that accompanied the introduction of the sound recording copyright in the United States. The Senate Judiciary Committee made a distinction between musical compositions and sound recordings. In its opinion, compositions were 'raw material' that could be adapted in the process of recording (1971: 6). This is why compulsory licensing of compositions was justified: access to this material should not be restricted, as it would foreclose the creative activity of making recordings. In contrast, the Committee viewed sound recordings as a 'finished product'; therefore, it saw 'no justification' in subjecting them to similar compulsory licensing measures (1971: 6). Sampling has questioned this idea. Recordings are not finished: they can be looped, reversed and remixed. Yet despite the demand from some quarters for the introduction of compulsory licensing for sampling, the owners of sound recording copyright have been free to establish their own licensing rates (Demers 2006: 142).

Sampling practice has highlighted further differences between the licensing of sound recordings and musical works. Usage of the master rights has been agreed by payment of negotiated fees. Prices have varied widely, dependent on the indebtedness of the new recording to the sampled source, the willingness of the licensor to sample the recording, the eagerness of the licensee to use it, the stature of the sampling artist and the market success of the sampled track. In some instances, copyright owners have also demanded additional fees when sales thresholds have been reached (Victoroff 2017: 53–4). Usage of sampled compositions, in contrast, has sometimes been calculated via compulsory licensing rates (this has been most common in the United States). In instances where this method has been employed, the sampled composers have tended to gain between 10 per cent and 25 per cent of the mechanical royalties (Victoroff 2017: 52). Elsewhere, there has been more flexibility, but general practice with sampled compositions has been that the composer (or more commonly their publisher or collecting society) will bargain for a percentage share of the licensee's composition rather than a fee.

Compositions and sound recordings have also been treated differently in respect of their exclusive rights. Regardless of the extent to which the original sound source has been manipulated, sampling has been transformative in nature: it places the original work in a new situation. As a general means of protection, musical compositions have been granted adaptation or derivative rights for transformative uses. This reflects the formalist nature of the copyright. It is not just the finished creation that is safeguarded; the author also has protection against arrangements of their work. In comparison, few countries have introduced adaptation rights for sound recordings. The copyright is physicalist in nature and therefore the concentration is on recordings themselves. The United States has provided an exception. It first granted a 'derivative' right for recordings in 1976. This right has operated in a physicalist manner, however, being limited to the creation of works in which 'the actual sounds fixed in the sound recording are rearranged, remixed, or otherwise altered in sequence or quality' (HJC 1976: 106). In practice, it has been hard to distinguish from the right of reproduction.

Physicalist copyright has been viewed as offering a narrow form of protection. It does not address the expressivity of artists; instead, all that is protected is the physical manifestation of their work. As such, in contrast to the 'thick' protection for musical works, the copyright for sound recordings has been labelled 'thin' (Barron 2016: 105). Sampling has nevertheless revealed just how extensive a physicalist copyright can be. The control of musical works may well be thick, but it is also loose. Composers have some latitude in respect of incorporating rhythms, timbres and chord changes from previous works. It has even been possible to borrow melodies or lyrics if shown to be commonplace. Sound recording copyright, in contrast, has been thin but rigid. In the early years of sampling, licensees placed some faith in fair use provisions, believing that shorter samples might escape copyright infringement. The accepted duration diminished over time. In 1991, the landmark case of *Grand Upright Music Ltd v Warner Brothers Records* held that a twenty-second sample was infringing. Subsequently, users were advised to 'get a license or do not sample' (Gowers 2006: 67). By 1999, the British case of *Produce v BMG* was indicating that a seven-second sample could be considered 'substantial' (Greenfield and Osborn 2004: 94).

This physicalist copyright has nevertheless provided some loopholes of its own. One result of the expense of clearing master rights is that some licensees have chosen to replace their samples with 'interpolated' soundalike performances of recordings. This practice first rose to prominence in the early 1990s, when hip-hop artists began to utilize it as a way of avoiding master licensing fees (in contrast, the licensing of the musical work could not be escaped and so in most instances the artists had to grant compositional shares to the writers of the interpolated works). Interpolating is also indicative of how important the finances of sampling had become. By the 1990s, hip-hop had developed into one of the most popular music genres. Its sample-based nature meant that the licensing of this music could be lucrative. This was also an era in which other sample-indebted genres, including a variety of forms of electronic dance music, were popular. By the end of the decade, the minimum cost of clearing a sampled master recording was between US$2,000 and US$7,000, while the costs for a star artist to sample a famous track could be considerably higher (Demers 2006: 118).

c) Synchronization

Synchronization is another area of recording industry licensing that witnessed an increase in revenue in the final decades of the century. This practice dates back to the advent of talking pictures in the inter-war period and was originally facilitated in the United States in the absence of sound recording copyright. Following an early period of blanket licensing in the 1920s (Shafter 1939: 353), the fees for synchronization have generally been bargained for on an individual basis, with licensees 'sometimes paying considerable sums' (Nimmer 1963: 440). It has been common to negotiate 'all-in licences', granting permission to use both the composition and the recording, with the fee split equally between the two (Blume 2014). There has been a temporal logic to this practice. If the recording has been issued at the same time as the film, television programme or advertisement, the copyright owner has been restricted in their negotiating demands, as usage has been viewed as driving publicity for the recording. If the licensee has sought use of a recording after it has been a success, it has been possible to command higher payments. In respect of the resultant revenues, recording artists have generally been in receipt of 50 per cent of the sound recording payments for this use of their work (Cooke 2015: 35).

During the 1960s, the recording industry was reluctant to license its back catalogue for audio-visual use. The IFPI and FIM laid down joint principles in 1962, which stated that the 'use of commercial records for the provision of music on film sound-tracks is not in the best interests of the Industry and should be discouraged' (HJC 1978: 397). A decade later, this practice was beginning to take off. *American Graffiti* and *Mean Streets*, both from 1973, were two of the earliest American films to make extensive use of pre-existing recordings for their soundtracks. Subsequently, this use of licensed material would become a common way of providing music for films and television programmes. As Frith indicates, it was in the 1980s that synchronization licensing began to be more actively pursued. As well as employing hit recordings for their soundtracks, films such as *Pretty in Pink* (1986), *Stand by Me* (1986), *Soul Man* (1986) and *Pretty Woman* (1990) utilized them for their titles. Hit recordings were also more frequently employed in adverts. Record companies began to work in tandem with companies such as Levi's, whose use of vintage recordings had a considerable effect on record sales.[2] There was also an increased willingness among recording artists to participate in commercials, with the adverts that Michael Jackson and Lionel Ritchie made for Pepsi marking a turning point.

Frith was also correct in predicting that this activity would increase. The 1990s witnessed the rise of music supervisors: intermediaries who have been hired for their skill in placing recordings with visual media. This period also saw some of the earliest licensing of sound recordings for use in video games, as well as increased revenues from adverts. In 1995, the Rolling Stones authorized the use of 'Start Me Up' in a Microsoft commercial for a reported US$3 million fee (McNamara 2011). Blur's recording 'Song 2', released two years later, would accumulate more than £2 million from various licensing deals. From the band's

---

[2] In a similar manner to the replacement of samples with interpolations, there are instances when advertisers have saved money by commissioning soundalike versions of recordings rather than using originals. This includes Levi's for its use of 'I Heard It through the Grapevine' in 1985 (Frith 2004: 185 (note)).

perspective, the uses of this one recording 'made more of a difference financially than anything else' (Maconie 1999: 245). Its promotional activity would nevertheless be exceeded by Moby's *Play*. This album was released in 1999 and has been documented as being the first to have each of its tracks licensed for commercial use (Osborne 2019: 177). It has been estimated that Moby earned £10 million from exploiting this basket of rights (*Sharon Osbourne* 2017).

Physical sales

1. Revenue

Although the 1980s and 1990s witnessed advances in equitable remuneration, inter-company licensing, sample clearance and synchronization licensing, these practices remained dwarfed by physical sales. It was in this period that the compact disc was launched and rose to prominence. The record companies regarded this format as being of such importance that they utilized some of their new exclusive rights in support of it. This was the case with the rental right, which was established for American sound recording copyright in 1984, and for members of European Union via the 1992 Directive. Record companies had fretted that an audio equivalent of the rental market for video recordings might emerge and sought an exclusive right that would give them control over any such activity undertaken for 'commercial advantage' (Copyright Act 1976: §109). Their concerns became more pronounced following the development of digital home recording formats, as they feared that consumers would rent and record copies of CDs rather than purchase them outright. In countries that did not introduce this right, such as Japan, a rental trade emerged (HJC 1994: 22). In America and Europe, in contrast, the concentration remained firmly on sales. There was similar activity in relation to the making available right, which was granted in respect of online music. As we shall see in chapter six, the recording industry employed this right to protect its trade in compact discs, as well as to orient the online market in a manner that echoed the sale of physical goods.

This prioritization can be witnessed in the global reports issued by the IFPI. Throughout the 1990s, retail sales were the only revenue stream that the organization bothered to document. Performing rights revenue would not be included until 2001, at which point it totalled US$600 million globally (IFPI 2022: 11). This represented a considerable increase on the revenue of the early

1990s, but these rights still constituted only 2.5 per cent of the industry's reported finances. Synchronization licensing remained absent from the IFPI's reports until 2010, when it was calculated as being worth 2 per cent of the market (IFPI 2022: 11). Although there may have been some underreporting here, this figure is nevertheless indicative of the unevenness of this practice: large payments were being paid to a minority of recordings. The revenue from digital sampling might possibly have been more diffuse, but was presumably of lesser significance. The IFPI has still not seen fit to delineate it in its reports.

2. Protection

The Commission of the European Communities reported in 1988 that 'Piracy in respect of compact discs is so rare as to be unheard of, probably because the manufacture of CDs is too costly and technically complicated for pirates' (1988: §2.35). Parallel with the rise of compact discs, Europe witnessed a decline in 'the market share of pirate products' (1988: §2.27). Record companies nevertheless feared that the compact disc could betray them. When it was first introduced to company bosses at a conference in Athens in 1981, the format aroused concern that it could be perfectly reproduced (Barfe 2004: 295). By the mid-1990s, these fears were being realized. The IFPI reported that Western retail markets were being 'systematically penetrated' by illegitimate recordings from abroad (HJC 1994: 29).

The recording industry responded in a number of ways, including diverting increased funds to anti-piracy units, lobbying governments more intensively and running media campaigns about the levels of unauthorized manufacture. There were also efforts to reinforce and harmonize international copyright laws. Most of the unauthorized copying of compact discs was taking place 'through the back door of legitimate factories', many of which were located in Eastern European and Asian countries that offered scant copyright protection for foreign recordings (Kernfeld 2011: 180). To help combat such activity, Western copyright-holding industries campaigned to bring intellectual property rights under the auspices of the World Trade Organization. This was achieved with the 1993 Agreement on Trade-Related Aspects of Intellectual Property Rights (TRIPs), which requires signatory countries to implement minimum standards of copyright enforcement. Another feature of TRIPs is its facilitation of 'cross-sectorial retaliation', enabling countries to reinforce their intellectual property interests by imposing trade restrictions on other areas of economic activity (Marshall 2005: 109).

The recording industry's concerns did not end here. As well as targeting international 'pirates', it sought to correct the habits of consumers. Fear of home recording had been growing for some time. During the 1971 debates relating to the American federalization of sound recording copyright, Senator Edward Biester had worried, saying, 'I must have a small pirate in my own home. My son has a cassette tape recorder, and as a particular record becomes a hit, he will retrieve it onto his little set' (HJC 1971: 22). He asked if the new measures would render his child liable to prosecution. Barbara Ringer replied they 'would not' (HJC 1971: 22). She could not envision 'anybody going into anyone's home and preventing this sort of thing, or forcing legislation that would engineer a piece of equipment not to allow home taping' (HJC 1971: 23).

Attitudes began to harden. During the late 1970s and early 1980s, many Western markets suffered a downturn in revenues from recorded music. This coincided with a rise in sales of blank cassettes, as well as of tape recorders, many of which were linked to record players in hi-fi systems or with second recorders in dual cassette decks. The recording industry pointed towards home taping as affecting its trade. In America, the RIAA urged the government to enact legislation to prevent such recording. Congress failed to deliver for them, deciding it would be 'impractical and impolitic' to outlaw this practice (Johns 2009: 447). The idea of a tape levy – imposing a copyright tax on blank cassettes – was also denied (Frith 1993: 4). Some record companies retaliated by attempting to add high-pitched signals to vinyl records so they could not be taped effectively. This too resulted in failure, as it 'aimed to secure intellectual property at the expense of degrading the content itself' (Johns 2009: 505). In Britain, the recording industry followed its own failed attempt to secure a tape levy by launching a notorious scaremongering campaign. The record companies' trade body, the British Phonographic Industry (BPI), decided to stamp vinyl records and pre-recorded tapes with the message 'home taping is killing music: and it's illegal'. Elsewhere the recording industry did make some gains. Tape levies were introduced in Argentina, Australia, Austria, the Congo, Germany, Finland, France, Gabon, Hungary, Iceland, the Netherlands, Norway, Portugal, Spain, Sweden, Turkey and Zaire (Oman 1991: vii).

The industry achieved greater levels of compensation against digital recording. Digital Audio Tape (DAT) was introduced in 1987 with the promise (and threat) it would allow consumers to make home recordings of equivalent quality to their original sound sources. It was followed in 1992 by the launch of the MiniDisc and the Digital Compact Cassette (DCC), which also promised perfect reproduction. In America, the Audio Home Recording Act (AHRA) of 1992 imposed levies on sales of hardware for these formats, with much of the revenue being diverted to record companies. It also stipulated that manufacturers of digital recording technologies incorporate the Serial Copy Management System (SCMS), which restricts the number of times that compact discs can be duplicated on these formats.

3. Profits

There are two main reasons why the recording industry protected and prioritized physical sales. First, the amount of money that was coming from this source. The IFPI calculated the global retail value of recorded music as being worth US$20 billion in 1988. At this time, tape cassettes were the leading format, followed by vinyl albums and then compact discs. By 1999, retail revenues amounted to US$39 billion, with the compact disc constituting three-quarters of units sold.[3] A second reason for the prioritization is because the majority of this money was going into the record companies' accounts. In contrast to public performance and broadcast, where the publishing industry received a large share of revenues, the money from sales was divided in the record companies' favour. In the UK, as a result of a 1991 agreement by the copyright tribunal, it was decided that the 'mechanical' right for compositions would be accorded 8.5 per cent of published dealer price revenues.[4] In the United States, the compulsory licensing rate in 1999 was 7.1 cents for each recording. Artist royalties had a similar orientation. The revenues for synchronization licensing, sample licensing and blanket licensing were split fairly evenly between artist and record company, with blanket licensing also being safeguarded from recoupment. In respect of physical sales, in contrast, it was rare for an artist with an exclusive recording contract to receive more than a fifth of the money generated, with the remainder going to the record label and/or the production company. Moreover, this share would only be paid to artists once their advances had been recouped.

[3] This data comes from the IFPI's *Recording Industry in Numbers* reports, as documented by David Arditi of the University of Texas (2021: 74–89), who kindly has shared his compiled figures for this book.

[4] This has not always resulted in a 91.5:8.5 division of the money, as the publishing revenue is based on the published dealer price, whereas the record companies' revenues from that dealer price can be reduced due to trade discounts. In addition, for smaller record companies, the publisher revenues are based on records pressed, while the recording revenues are based on records sold. Consequently, the publishing share can more realistically be evaluated as being worth 8 per cent of the retail price (Hesmondhalgh et al. 2021: 61–2).

The different payment methodologies were the result of historical legacies and the relative bargaining powers of the parties involved. They were also shaped by the manner in which the recording industry divided its revenues into a 'primary' sales source and 'ancillary' licensing sources. It accepted lower shares from broadcast and public performance because these activities promoted sales; it demanded less from synchronization licensing and sample clearance because these activities followed on the back of those sales. The revenue splits were also reflective of costs. The record companies expected the lion's share of physical sales revenue because they bore the expenditure of manufacture, distribution, packaging, marketing and promotion. Broadcast, synchronization and sampling revenue, on the other hand, did not generate similar expense.

Record company profits were nevertheless increasing. At the cusp of the 1980s and 1990s, the retail price of compact discs was approximately 50 per cent higher than cassettes and vinyl records, yet this was not a true reflection of their differing costs. By 1994, British record companies were admitting they set 'prices according to the consumers' willingness to pay rather than according to the costs of production' and that they could charge premium prices for the CD because of the 'perception' it was 'a higher-quality product' (MMC 1994: §7.27, §7.26). Recording artists could feel cheated in this environment. Rather than receiving equivalent higher rates of pay, they were often on reduced royalties. *Billboard* reported in 1992 that artists were receiving between 35 per cent and 85 per cent of their contracted royalties in respect of compact discs, as they were still being expected to account for the 'manufacturing costs incurred' when this format was introduced (HJC 1994: 76).

The recording industry was also benefiting from greater sales of back catalogue. Older recordings could be priced similarly to contemporary releases, but cost considerably less to market and promote. The increased activity in this area was due, in part, to an expanded audience for popular music. The market had previously been concentrated on the fifteen to twenty-four age group, but consumers were now being engaged throughout their lives (Negus 1992: 67–8). It was also because consumers were encouraged to purchase digitized versions of recordings they already owned on vinyl or cassette, which in turn prompted a climate in which music of the recent past was explored. Against this background, rather than prioritizing any new rights it had received, the recording industry looked for ways that its control of reproduction rights could be extended. One of these was to campaign for longer copyright terms. Another was to expand the notion of 'piracy' and become more stringent against it.

Conclusion

Simon Frith's prognosis was not wrong. The late twentieth century witnessed an expansion in the recording industry's licensing activities and it began to self-identify as a copyright industry. However, this should not belie the fact that physical sales remained the central concern of the majority of record companies. The 1990s witnessed their greatest revenues, which came primarily from the reproduction of goods. Consequently, interest in the progressive, licensing aspects of copyright was outweighed by a desire to thwart unauthorized manufacture. In fact, the digital environment increased the industry's urge towards punitive action, as the quick, inexpensive, widely distributed and perfect reproduction of recordings had become a reality.

The environment was changing in other ways too. An increasing number of record companies were pulling out of the direct manufacture of goods, employing third parties to undertake this function for them. As we have seen, the recording industry gained or adapted legislative criteria in accordance with this transition, with the award going to producers and employers, rather than manufacturers. Yet even with these legislative designations, the record companies could not be certain they would retain hold of the rights. In an increasing number of cases, it was recording artists who could be regarded as the financers and organizers of recording sessions. Many of them also had responsibility for hiring non-featured performers and studio staff. As a result, the recording industry had to develop new ways to justify its ownership of the masters.

5

Justifying

As the twentieth century drew to a close, there was a growing belief among British and American recording artists that ownership of sound recording copyright was rightfully theirs. They were paying for their recordings via recoupment of advances and many of them were making key decisions about the development of their work. Record companies also sensed that artists might have grounds for these claims. As a result, they relied on a safeguard. If artists were to be regarded as authors, the companies would ensure assignment of copyright through contractual terms.

Ownership through assignment has been weaker than authorial ownership, however. Although record companies commonly sought transfer of rights for the life of copyright, they could not be certain this full term would be achieved. Moreover, as the duration of copyright expanded and sales of back catalogue increased, there was greater cause for artists to question lifetime transfer. They would have plenty to gain if ownership were returned to them after a set period, most notably in respect of their contractual dealings. If their recordings had been successful, they would be able to bargain for them to be accorded improved royalty rates on expiry of the assignment, either by renegotiating with their existing record company or through signing with a new label.

Record companies found themselves in an unfamiliar position. Until this period they rarely had to justify their ownership of copyright. They now faced challenges, both at the level of individual contractual dealings and in wider policy contexts. This took different forms in different territories. The first section of this chapter addresses the situation in Britain in the early 1990s, when the recording industry faced a governmental investigation into its activities. This inquiry noted the importance of copyright to record company practice, and looked at the authorial terms of the CDPA as well as the contractual transfer of rights. The companies propounded a financial risk theory as they sought to underpin their control, which was backed with legislative, statistical, causative and benevolent claims. The chapter then turns to tensions in the market as the decade progressed. It concludes by looking at the situation in the United States at the turn of the millennium. Here, the shoring up of copyright ownership took legislative form. The recording industry effected a change to the law, with the aim of avoiding assignment of rights by classifying sound recordings as commissioned works made for hire. This amendment was contested by recording artists, who argued they were the creators, financiers and organizers of recordings. In response, the record companies promoted a form of chaos theory, suggesting there would be administrative turmoil unless master rights were under their central control.

Risk theory

In the early 1990s, the MMC undertook an investigation into the record business in the UK, prompted by concerns that monopolistic practices had led to the high costs of compact discs. Its findings are summarized in *The Supply of Recorded Music*, which has been described as 'the most detailed analysis… undertaken by a government body' on how the music industries work (Cloonan 2007: 70). This report is centred on the activities of major and independent labels. From the outset it underlines their financial core, noting that 'Copyright is central to the operations of the record industry' (MMC 1994: §1.4).

In spite of its depth, *The Supply of Recorded Music* does have lacuna. The MMC agreed with the industry's argument that 'Under the 1988 Act the copyright would normally be owned by the record company' (1994: §2.139). Upholding this status was a complex process, however, and the record companies' claims warranted further probing than given by the MMC. They were questionable legislatively, they rested on debatable statistics and the causes of the statistical argument could have been investigated, as could the rhetoric that underpinned it. The MMC failed to explore these avenues, offering little time for the counter arguments of artists' representatives and even less for artists themselves. Instead, the Commission tended to endorse the record companies' self-selected norms.

1. The legislative claim

As detailed in the preceding chapter, the CDPA originally classified sound recordings alongside films. Rather than being awarded to the 'maker', as had been the case with the 1956 Act, copyright was granted to 'the person by whom the arrangements necessary for the making of the recording or film are undertaken' (1988: §9(2)(a)). This designation had benefits for the recording industry. By moving towards an organizational definition of production, the legislation could encompass a broad array of companies, including those who did not manufacture their own discs. Their ownership of rights was not assured, however, as an 'arranger' and their 'undertakings' are ambiguous terms. The legal guide *Copinger and Skone James on Copyright* indicates that 'many permutations are possible' (Garnett et al. 2011: 249). Therefore, in outlining industry practice to the MMC, the British companies found it necessary to explain their rationale for claiming ownership. Their first argument was to maintain the legislation pointed towards them:

> The courts had held that the word 'undertake' meant 'be responsible for', especially in the financial sense but also generally. It could therefore be assumed that in using the same formula for sound recordings as for films in the 1988 Copyright Act, Parliament had intended that copyright should vest in the person who had undertaken the financial responsibility for making the recording. The ownership of that copyright was the reward for the risk they had undertaken.
>
> (1994: §108)

Claims about financial risk were not new. As far back as debates for the 1911 Act, British record companies had argued that, unless they were granted exclusive legislative control, their businesses would be usurped by free-riding rivals (Gorrell Committee 1910: 229). The originating company would have the expense of creating the recordings and testing them in the market; a rival company could then undercut their costs by copying only proven hits.

Nevertheless, while financial risk was a significant aspect in determining ownership, it was not the sole priority of British legislation. One difficulty with the record companies' argument is that they alluded to a suggestion that was not incorporated in the CDPA. Debating the proposed legislation in parliament, Lord Williams of Elvel suggested that the section on authorship was unclear. As a result, he proposed that the copyright owner should be defined as the person 'who commissions that recording and pays or agrees to pay for it in money or money's worth' (Lord Kilbracken 1987: 886). Lord Beaverbrook's response was quoted by the MMC: 'The Bill deals with copyright in sound recordings in the same way that the present [1956] law treats films; namely, that the first owner is the person who makes the necessary arrangements for the recording' (MMC 1994: §4.15). After further discussion, Lord Williams withdrew his amendment, with the result that the section was published as drafted and contained no specific mention of payment for the work.

A further difficulty with the companies' argument is that case law had been reluctant to promote financial input above other organizational concerns. *Century Communications v Mayfair Entertainment* (1993) held that copyright ownership of a production should go the party who 'initiated its making and organised the activity necessary for its making and paid for it' (336). In *Beggars Banquet v Carlton Television* (1993), ownership was determined in relation to the control of finances, rather than their provision.[1] The record companies nevertheless promoted financial risk as being the most important determinant of copyright ownership. In doing so, they gained the support of the MMC, which stated that the CDPA 'intended to put sound recordings on the same footing as films, where the established practice was that copyright lies with the person who takes the financial risks of investing in its production' (1994: §2.149). What the Commission failed to point out, however, is that this practice had been established by custom as much as through law.

The MMC also suggested that a recording artist or studio producer would only be able to gain ownership if they made a recording 'at their own expense rather than with advances from a record company' (1994: §2.150). This was another debatable claim. It could have been argued instead that these advances were the artist's expense. Although other creative industries have utilized advance payments, these have commonly been restricted to an author's personal expenses (Marshall 2013: 585). The recording industry has in addition contracted its artists to pay back costs of production. As a result, recording artists have become embroiled in the financial risks of record making. According to the record companies' own logic, they could therefore be regarded as being at least the co-owners of copyright in recordings they have made. In respect of fully recouped artists, this argument could be taken further still. They have cleared their debts and could thus be viewed as having borne the overall financial

---

[1] Later cases were decided similarly. In *Slater v Wimmer* (2012), Judge Birss QC regarded Wimmer as the copyright owner because he 'was not merely the banker, the project was his project' (85). It should be noted, however, that this case and those addressed in the main text concern film production. The economics of record and film production are different: the job of a film producer is to secure financial backing; the job of a record company is usually to supply it. The 2015 case of *Henry Hadaway v Pickwick Group* did concern two record companies. Here, Judge Melissa Clark awarded authorship to the company who 'retained absolute control of the production process' (85), going against the company who co-financed and commissioned the recordings' (85). In reviewing the previous cases she noted how they 'make it clear that "the person by whom the arrangements necessary for the making of the film are undertaken", is a question of fact in each case', meaning that each should be decided on its own merits (49).

responsibility for the work. Providing a critical voice on behalf of performers during the MMC investigation, the International Managers' Forum (IMF) made this argument, proposing that copyright should reside with artists upon 'recoupment of recording costs' (1994: §10.54). Moreover, by this period a larger number of performers were making their own decisions about their recording projects; they were sourcing independent studios and record producers, as well as selecting non-featured performers to play on the tracks. Consequently, as well as contributing to financial arrangements, they had assumed responsibility for the 'general' undertakings and could therefore satisfy each of the arranger criteria within British law.

There were, however, no legal cases in which British recording artists contested the recording industry's legislative claims. There were not likely to be any either, as the record companies shored up their ownership of copyright by contractual means. Although they were suggesting to the MMC that they were the legal authors of recordings, the companies were at the same time negotiating terms that acknowledged the performers' authorial roles, as indicated by their request for the assignment of sound recording copyright (Barr 2016: 145–8). This belt and braces approach was clearly contradictory: why were the companies asking for this transfer if they believed they were the original owners? It nevertheless satisfied some of the demands of British case law, which indicated that the best means of clarifying the uncertain terms of copyright legislation was through contractual agreements (*Robin Ray v Classic FM* 1998: 627).

2. The statistical claim

The record companies sought control for the life of copyright. This could be assured if they gained legislative recognition as authors, but was less certain when they gained rights through the transfer of ownership. Recording artists might wish to negotiate for the transfer to be for a shorter term and they might request licence rather than assignment of rights. Moreover, the transfer could be subject to a termination clause. The IMF proposed that British copyright law should include 'reversion' measures, granting the return of ownership to the original author after a set number of years (MMC 1994: §10.54).

In order to negate claims such as these, the record companies offered statistical evidence to the MMC that they bore the ultimate financial responsibility for bringing sound recordings to market. While acknowledging that artists' advances would be recouped from royalties, the companies emphasized an aspect of these payments that differentiated them from loans. In the event that an artist's recording project was not a success and they were consequently dropped from a company's roster for failing to clear their costs, the artist would not be expected to pay back any outstanding debts. This financial risk would instead be borne by the record company.

The major companies indicated that failure was predominant, informing the MMC that 'only one in ten of the pop artists with whom they sign contracts turns out to be successful' (1994: §2.102). They claimed that, as a result, they should enjoy copyright ownership of the successes to make up for the losses of failures. The labels maintained 'It was only by concluding contracts which embodied such terms as retention of copyright, exclusivity and a reasonable length of contract term' that they could reap 'the necessary long-term benefits for those few artists who succeeded' (1994: §12.99). The MMC endorsed this idea, seeing nothing 'inherently inequitable' in these contacts; it was convinced that 'Ownership and control of copyright for a significant period is essential to a record company that has made a large initial investment in recordings and in an artist's career' (1994: §1.14).

The record companies' formula was questionable nonetheless. The IMF pointed out that the one-in-ten success ratio was based on short-term analysis. It failed to take into account the fact that record companies would retain copyright in sound recordings for fifty years, regardless of whether artists remained signed with them throughout this period. Therefore, copyrights could accrue revenue long after signees had been dropped on account of non-profitability. The IMF also noted that, whereas the losses from 'unsuccessful' artists would be detailed in company balance sheets, the value of their copyright catalogues would not appear there (1994: §8.35). It believed a reversion right would provide artists with greater bargaining power, as it would reduce the need to 'obtain capital… on disadvantageous terms' (1994: §10.50).

Doubts could also have been raised about the statistic's provenance. The recording industry had employed it in different ways at different times. On some occasions it referenced the number of releases that made the charts. On others it detailed the number of records that were profitable. It had also been cited in relation to the number of artists who were dropped for providing insufficient returns. The record companies did not outline which of these measures they were employing for the MMC. Their calculation of profitability had also been variable. It had sometimes been based on the recoupment of recording artists' advances, but at other times had been applied to the overall expenditure on a release, adding in costs of manufacture, distribution, marketing and promotion. In addition, the use of the statistic occluded the fact that artists and record companies had different breakeven points. A failed record for an artist may well have been profitable for their record company, even in situations where the latter had borne more of the costs.

The one-in-ten statistic had also been curiously long-lived. The recording industry appears to have first employed it in the 1950s, after which its use was perennial despite significant changes to business practice (Osborne 2021c: 58). Three factors in particular should have affected its consistency. First, the recording industry had been through peaks and troughs. The usual reaction of record companies during leaner times was to cut the size of their artist rosters and introduce more cautious signing policies. As a result, there should have been a higher ratio of hits to releases during these hard times, at least if measured in relation to chart entries. Second, the major record companies had moved from an industry model whereby they manufactured their own records, to one where much of this activity was undertaken by outside companies. The majors' manufacturing interests had been one of the causes of overproduction, as they needed to generate sufficient product to keep their pressing plants busy (Denisoff 1975: 97–8). Manufacture also provided a platform from which to experiment. The majors duplicated product for smaller companies, thus gaining a steady stream of revenue that safeguarded them against the 'adverse financial impact resulting from the considerable risk involved in speculative investment in new recording artists' (Hill 1978: 32). Some commentators believe they took greater artistic chances when they were manufacturers (Harrison 2011: 171). The third factor is that record companies had become increasingly sophisticated in respect of consumer data. Having neglected detailed audience analysis, they were by the 1990s undertaking extensive market research (Frith 2001: 34).

Although use of the one-in-ten statistic remained consistent, academic accounts of it changed. In the 1970s and 1980s it was used as evidence of a 'mud against the wall' approach to releasing music (Chapple and Garofalo 1977: 14). Paul Hirsch documented a record company belief that 'There are no formulas for producing a hit record' (Hirsch 1971/2: 55). Labels would therefore issue an array of titles, hoping some would stick. Bernard Miège drew pessimistic conclusions from this scenario, arguing that it resulted in job insecurity and impecuniosity for artists (1989: 89–90). In contrast, Frith saw it as evidence of consumer sovereignty (1978: 97). David Hesmondhalgh has added a further view, arguing that the signing policies of these decades resulted in 'a substantial degree of artistic innovation and experimentation' (2013: 249). From the record companies' perspective, this approach was not entirely cavalier. They worked on the assumption that once their own breakeven points had been cleared, the 'accumulation of profit is very rapid' (Frith 1978: 118). It was on this basis that their revenues from successes commonly outweighed their losses from failures.

By the 1990s, the costs of recording, promoting and marketing records had increased considerably (Negus 1992: 40). This was also the era in which sophisticated methods of audience and sales analysis took hold. Keith Negus claimed that this resulted in 'a straightforward reluctance to experiment, a reduction in risk-taking and a propensity towards a partial view of the world' (1999: 52). Michael Jones argued that record companies were no longer involved in 'overproduction'; they were instead 'over-signing' new acts (1997: 313). This policy was considered more cost-effective. Although the companies would 'initiate the commodification of a number of commodities', they would 'choose to concentrate marketing and promotional resources on only a proportion of these on the basis of "intelligence" garnered from the market place' (Jones 1997: 149). The point of analysis was no longer what happened once a record was in the market, but the system of prioritization before it was released.

Building on these studies, it would eventually be suggested that record companies had a systematic approach to failure. Frith came to view success ratios in a new light, asking, 'What if a record's failure reflects not the irrational activities of musicians and consumers but the perfectly rational activities of record companies themselves?' (2001: 47). In contemplating why a record company would choose not to promote some of its artists, he outlined the following areas of policy: 'the development of the portfolio management structure; the carefully orchestrated programme of global release and promotion; the calculation of what budgets are available for what products when; a sense at any one moment of to which project it makes most sense to devote energy' (2001: 48). Lee Marshall would go further, stating that failure could have 'beneficial aspects for labels' (2013: 584). He noted that it served 'important rhetorical purposes in relation to governments, policy makers, and consumers, and... in contractual negotiations with... artists' (2013: 584).

The Supply of Recorded Music is demonstrative of this rhetoric. It upholds a tradition of allowing the industry to cite its one-in-ten ratio while failing to outline the methodology by which it reached this result. There are nevertheless indications that the record companies were alluding to the recoupment of artist advances (1994: §5.106). The report offers an examination of the accounts of the major labels operating in the UK, albeit that this is of little use for gauging the ratio's accuracy. The data is revelatory, however, in indicating the consistency of losses. Rather than being unpredictable, the record companies' costs from unrecouped advances remained fairly stable. In the five years from 1989 to 1993 they ranged from 15.2 per cent to 18.3 per cent of gross revenues (1994: Table 8.6). Thus, they could be considered as evidential of a systematic approach to failure. Moreover, while the one-in-ten statistic suggested an overall climate of loss, it appears to have been measured against the recoupment of royalties, rather than the full revenues of recordings. The major labels were consistently profitable during the period in question. Their profit margin on revenues was 8.6 per cent in 1989, and was projected to be 7.9 per cent in 1993 (1994: Table 8.6).

3. The causative claim

The Supply of Recorded Music upholds another tradition. It portrays recording artists as being responsible for the scale of advance payments. As previously indicated, there have been two main expenses for artists to recoup: recording advances (for the costs of creating masters) and personal advances (for living costs). These costs have sometimes been combined as 'all-in' payments.

According to Nigel Parker, recording costs were first devolved to performers because of an increase in studio expenditure. This escalation occurred in the 1960s and 1970s, when the division of creative input became increasingly blurred. Recording artists were no longer restricted to providing performances that were 'captured' by studio technicians and instead became increasingly involved in developing the 'aggregation of sounds' (SJC 1971: 5). As artists began to create recordings of greater 'scope and ambition', one response of record companies in Britain and America, 'but generally not elsewhere', was to 'recoup the entire cost of making recordings from the royalties payable to contracted featured performers' (Parker 2006: 163).[2] In respect of copyright law, these developments could have helped performers to claim sound recording copyright on creative grounds. In comparison to the early years of recording practice they were now more evidently the authors of original works. What happened instead is that the costs of recording were employed by record companies in support of their own economic rationale for claiming ownership. The companies grouped these costs with their expenditure on personal advances

---

[2] In France, it is still contracting practice that record companies do not recoup the cost of advances. In many other countries these costs are now recouped.

and used them as evidence of the investment most artists would fail to recoup. As a result, the companies suggested that the long-term ownership of sound recording rights was rightfully theirs.

In respect of personal advances, *The Supply of Recorded Music* presents the scale of this expenditure as being the artists' desire:

> The record companies say that they are not as inflexible over copyright as has been suggested. They have sometimes negotiated contracts where they hold copyright only for a period but in such contracts they would expect to adjust the other terms so as to ensure that the payback period was commensurate with the period for which they owned the copyright. Although contracts in this form had been negotiated in the past, in general new artists currently preferred to secure larger advances and royalties rather than ownership of copyright. The same normally applied at the point where a contract was being renegotiated. In such cases an artist would often willingly agree to extend the term of an agreement in return for larger advances and royalties.
>
> (1994: §2.136)

These claims could have been queried. Artists were not solely responsible for the escalation of advance payments. The increase in these costs was also due to the companies' bidding wars. Speaking to the MMC, one label spoke of setting advances at a level 'necessary to persuade the artist to accept the offer in preference to a rival record company' (1994: §11.5). This practice cemented the power of the richest companies. Jerry Moss of A&M noted how by this period 'Big advances were starting to be more of a key fix in this game' (Knopper 2009: 61). According to Steve Knopper, 'it was getting harder for anybody to compete with major labels… who were spending tens of millions of their massive CD profits to turn talented new artists into Michael Jackson-style hit machines' (2009: 61). The result was an environment in which most artists failed to breakeven.

There could also have been closer examination of causes and effects. The record companies suggested to the MMC that, in comparison to securing a high advance, an artist 'may have relatively smaller interest in the details of other contract terms and, if his recording career does not prove successful, they are unlikely ever to assume significance' (1994: §2.132). It may have been the case, however, that recording artists felt the pull of high advances because of the industry's low success rate and its deployment by record companies to secure ownership of copyright.

The companies were nevertheless correct in indicating that alternative practices had emerged. In the 1970s, many recording artists had been fixated on advances. For example, the Sex Pistols' film *The Great Rock 'n' Roll Swindle* is centred on the group gaining a series of advance payments from record companies in both Britain and America; they are not seeking ownership of the masters (*Great Rock 'n' Roll Swindle* 1980). This was also a period in which high signing fees were publicized. It was this money, rather than ownership of recording rights, that provided the illustration of having 'made it'. This outlook was beginning to be challenged, nonetheless. In the same era as the Sex Pistols vaunted their high advances, the Police signed a deal with A&M that contained no personal advance fees and no provision for recording costs. The band's manager Miles Copeland reasoned, 'we asked for less from them and we also demanded that they take less from us' (*Sharon Osbourne* 2017). As a result, the Police gained a royalty rate of 18 per cent, which tripled the average for newly signed artists at this time (Hill 1978: 35). The band's singer Sting has noted that 'because we didn't start off with this sort of feudal relationship where they gave us money and expected us to lay the golden egg every time, they didn't own us' (*Reel Stories* 2021). However, the group do not appear to have been granted control of the master rights.

Elsewhere, the punk movement occasioned a proliferation of independent labels, some of which operated on a profit-share basis: revenues would be split equally between artists and record companies once all expenses had been mutually recouped. There was also a tendency among these labels to share copyright ownership with artists or hand it over entirely. The most notorious example is Factory Records, whose standard contract read in full, 'The company owns nothing, the musicians own their music and everything they do, and all artists have the freedom to fuck off' (Harris 2004: 8). This provides sharp contrast to the earlier practice of independent labels. Robert Wyatt, for example, was the only artist on Virgin in the early 1970s who achieved ownership of his master rights (O'Dair 2014: 209). It also contributed to Factory's demise. When the label encountered financial difficulties in the 1990s, it was unable to attract backers because it did not own any recordings (Hesmondhalgh 1998: 261).

Speaking to the MMC in 1994, representatives of the recording industry claimed that 'An artist's only avenue for protecting and exploiting his copyright was to license it to a record company and this was achieved by auctioning it to the highest bidder' (1994: §12.101). This was not necessarily true. An increasing number of artists were setting up record labels of their own. The DIY ethos of punk and electronic dance music spurred this movement, with bands such as the Buzzcocks, Crass, A Boat and the KLF creating their own imprints. Other artists were questioning the justness of recoupment, assignment and contractual options. In the same year as *The Supply of Recorded Music* was published, George Michael made an attempt to extricate himself from his record contract with Sony Music but was defeated in court. His press statement read, 'even though I both created and paid for my work, I will never own it or have any rights over it. I have no control or say in the way that my work is exploited. In fact I have no guarantee that my work will be released at all' (Greenfield and Osborn 1998: 59). George Harrison complained similarly that it was 'immoral' that the Beatles did not own their recording rights and the opportunity to purchase them had been denied (Kordosh 1987).

4. The benevolent claim

The recording industry's policy of failure could have been regarded as inappropriate practice. It was resulting in a situation whereby the majority of artists fell by the wayside, while those who did succeed could be subject to unfavourable terms. The record companies were meanwhile systematically achieving profits of their own. Given this background, it is understandable that the companies felt it necessary to employ a further rhetorical argument when giving evidence to the MCC. They wished to portray themselves as being benevolent. As a result, they claimed they were utilizing the profits from their few successes to make investments in music that might not otherwise be heard. This argument was useful in two respects. It helped to justify the success rate and at the same time supported their claims for copyright ownership.

In employing the one-in-ten ratio in this manner, the companies were again operating in accordance with previous practice. An earlier use of this rhetoric had occurred in 1965, when American labels hoped to resist a proposed increase to compulsory licensing fees. They reported that 60 per cent of their popular music albums and 87 per cent of their classical music releases failed to break even (HJC 1965: 797). It was their argument that any squeeze on margins would force smaller labels out of business and would drive the rest to increase the prices of their records. The remaining major companies would be forced into restrictive policies, such as issuing 'fewer recordings of serious and classical music' (HJC 1965: 824).

Success ratios made similar appearances in subsequent American debates. The RIAA quoted them during the 1971 hearings that established sound recording copyright. In this instance they were employed as a means of illustrating the threat of free-riding tape manufacturers. The trade body suggested, 'The pirate skims the cream of what artists and record companies offer – except for one particular ingredient, which he avoids like the plague… our risks' (HJC 1971: 25). It warned that without copyright protection there would be catastrophic results: 'If the profits in hit recordings continue to be taken from the industry, the economic foundation of the whole industry will be in serious danger' (HJC 1971: 29). The RIAA noted this would 'further reduce the ability of such manufacturers to produce new recordings of classical music' (HJC 1971: 29). By the time of the 1978 hearings on performing rights, classical music was offering even fewer financially successful returns. It was calculated that 95 per cent of all classical long-playing records failed to earn a profit, while for classical cassettes the figure rose to 99 per cent (HJC 1978: 475–6). These statistics were utilized by the RIAA in its campaign for these rights. It argued, 'With performance fees, the record producing companies might be encouraged to make more classical and experimental recordings, for which the sales outlook is uncertain' (HJC 1978: 477).

This rhetoric was in keeping with the general tendency of sound recording copyright debates, which were traditionally oriented towards classical music. In America, the majority decision in the 1937 *Waring* case held that common law copyright could apply to sound recordings where performers had been able to 'elevate [their] interpretations to the realm of independent works of art', and in doing so ruled out protection for the 'ordinary musician [who] does nothing more than render articulate the silent composition of the author' (Ringer [1957] 1961: 13). Evidencing a similar outlook, the US Congress believed that 'serious music' should not come under the banner of work made for hire (HJC 2000: 108). This appreciation for the performative skills of classical musicians was mirrored by a lack of respect for the art of recording. Within classical music, the techniques of record production were deemed passive at best and interfering at worst. The ideal was to unobtrusively recreate the ambiance of the concert hall (Symes 2004: 83–7). In Britain in the early 1950s, members of Gregory Committee assessed the legislation for sound recording copyright by attending the recording of a Mozart symphony (Sterling 1992: 220 (note)). Witnessing no overt phonographic artistry, they argued there is 'a great measure of what is only technical and industrial in [a record's] manufacture' (Gregory 1952: §86). This thinking fed into the 1956 Copyright Act, which reduced the status of sound recordings to 'ancillary' works.

By the time of the 1994 MMC inquiry there was less willingness to distinguish between high and low art forms. This was due partly to an increased appreciation for the creativity of popular music recording. It was also in keeping with the post-modern tenor of the times. In addition, this was an occasion when classical music was not useful for securing the record companies' needs. They were justifying their practice of gaining assignment of sound recording copyright for the full duration of its term. This idea appeared to go against the beliefs of Anglo-American copyright legislation, which was founded on the belief that copyright ownership should be of limited duration, particularly when corporately controlled. The record companies were therefore in need of an activity that would make their success rate appear noble, as well as be in keeping with the impulse of copyright to 'act as a stimulus to creativity and innovation' (Kretschmer 2008: 5). Their support for classical music would not help here. Rather than inspiring the development of original works, it was an endorsement of repertoire from the past.

As a result, the British record companies turned to the creative future rather than the classical heritage. They argued that a record company's main role was to invest the profits from its successes in the development of new music. Furthermore, this risk-taking required protection. The companies proclaimed to the MMC:

> If material modifications were made to the key provisions in recording contracts, dealing in particular with the extent of copyright acquired by the record company, the length of the contract and the exclusivity provisions imposed on the artist, then the companies would be forced to take a much more short-term view of their relationship with artists, which would not only be detrimental to the longterm development of those artists, but which would inevitably mean that the companies would not be able to invest as widely in new UK artists as they did at present.
>
> (1994: §12.103)

This line of reasoning had been developed as dialogue between British record companies and government increased. Martin Cloonan has noted how, during the early 1990s, 'key people in the popular music industries came to realize that politicians needed to be lobbied' (2007: 21). One reason for this engagement was their need of support for their copyright claims. Another was that their industries were being scrutinized: *The Supply of Recorded Music* was one of a number of official investigations. Government was also keen to open discussions. Its interest was reflective of an era in which the profits of heavy industry had declined while those of the cultural industries had grown.

According to Cloonan, 'at a time when cultural policy was increasingly becoming part of economic policy and when the music industries seemingly felt some unease about stressing pop's cultural value, the pragmatic response was to make the economic case' (2007: 75). The record companies' argument was nevertheless split between the two. Although the companies promoted their economic worth, they also sought protection. In doing so, their talk of new music leant more towards its artistic qualities than to financial policy. There was no mention of portfolio management or budget calculations. Instead, the emphasis was on the risk-taking nature of supporting the new. Similarly, rather than foregrounding their search for the next blockbuster acts, the companies talked of supporting the marginal, the challenging and the forward-looking. They stressed they were signing 'creative' artists, issuing 'innovative music' and sponsoring acts with 'minority appeal' (1994: §11.29, §12.79, §12.105).

The philanthropic nature of this activity could have been queried. In a competitive business, in which only a small proportion of artists were being signed and even fewer were successful, prospective artists had little bargaining power. Those who managed to secure record company interest would generally be on lower royalty rates than established artists and their contracts would contain a greater number of restrictive clauses (Dannen 2003: 79; Negus 1992: 149–50). Writing in the 1970s, Leslie F. Hill of EMI conceded that it was newly signed artists who had 'the greatest profit potential for the company' (1978: 35).

The record companies downplayed these profit margins and instead ensured that their 'commonsense view of the world' began to permeate British government (Cloonan 2007: 41). Research undertaken by Negus and Jones in the 1990s documented a system of tight financial control and restricted musical innovation. It was in this same period, however, that the companies placed increasing stress on their risk-taking deeds. This tactic was employed in one of the first investigations into the record business in this era, the National Heritage Committee's 1993 Inquiry into CD Prices. Nevertheless, while the major labels suggested they were involved in 'a high risk business', the Committee only noted that they 'can be' (Cloonan 2007: 70). *The Supply of Recorded Music* was published the following year and evidences a new level of accord. The MMC agreed this 'high-risk business' was driven by the search for new artists (1994: §1.13).

The companies had much to gain by highlighting their poor chances of success. Risk-taking was used in defence of their long-term ownership of sound recording copyright: the MMC conceded that 'since the record companies take the risk of investing in artists when they are unknown, they should not have the rewards taken away on those occasions when their investment turns out to be successful' (1994: §2.140). It supported the system of exclusive, long-term contracts: the major labels successfully persuaded the MMC that their agreements provided the platform from which 'to take the very significant risks in investing in new artists' (1994: §12.99). It even justified the high prices of CDs: the companies maintained that by controlling these costs they could 'generate sufficient funds to invest in … new music and artists' (1994: §11.29).

Anglo-American copyright philosophy was being turned on its head. The MMC endorsed the record companies' argument that long-term corporate ownership would encourage, rather than undermine, the development of new work. Moreover, they did so without verifying the one-in-ten statistic or by probing the nurturing claims that were being made. Artists who were not prioritized for promotion would not have been likely to recommend their companies' virtues, while those who did succeed could find themselves paying for the losers, not least through being deprived of copyright ownership. Other factors could have been questioned as well. Although the record companies may have been signing new artists quantitatively, this did not mean their music was new qualitatively. In order to fulfil the task of generating copyright revenues to support future generations, their signings tended to fit into established grooves.

This is not to say that the recording industry's rhetoric was baseless. The careers of most artists would end in failure and the record companies would write off those artists' losses. It should be noted too that the system of advances was not wholly iniquitous. Some recording artists appear to have been happy to sustain their careers on advance funds rather than royalty payments (Marshall 2005: 73–4). Others would not be dropped, despite 'failing' and being in debt. There is also evidence of artists being supported by their labels on artistic merit alone. Andrew Leyshon has argued, in addition, that the system of advances could be advantageous for performers from poorer backgrounds, suggesting that if all artists had to provide their own recording finances, this would lead to an environment favouring those with 'plentiful reserves of social, cultural, *and* financial capital' (2014: 168. Emphasis in original).

It was a system that was of benefit to record companies, nonetheless. Copyright revenues may have provided funds for new music, but new music also underpinned the companies' system of ownership and control. In fact, the rhetoric of newness was so successful that the recording industry returned to it repeatedly. By the late 1990s, British politicians could be heard echoing claims that '80–90 per cent of artists signed to record companies will not succeed' and stating that the record companies' voice was one they heard 'loud and clear' (DCMS 2000: 3; Smith 1997: 81). This rhetoric would not be confined to Britain either. It was employed by the recording industry across the European Union and would be utilized by the IFPI for its global campaigns (IFPI 2010: 6–7; MMC 1994: §10.35).

Extensions and recoupment

As well as aiming to secure ownership of rights for the life of copyright, record companies were aligned with other creative industries in wanting to extend copyright terms. The increasing popularity of older catalogue items spurred these claims, as did the desire to gain parity with increasing terms that were achieved elsewhere. Some of the campaigns were successful. In 1993, a European Union Directive instructed member states to grant copyright periods of life plus seventy years for authorial works and fifty years from 'fixation' for sound recordings and films (EEC 1993: art. 3). When implemented in Britain in 1995, this extended the term for musical compositions, but did not represent an increase for sound recordings, which had been protected for fifty years since 1911. It did entail an increase for some other European countries, however, and was a considerable advance on the Rome Convention's minimum duration of twenty years (1961: art. 14). This Directive provided inspiration for the American Copyright Term Extension Act of 1998, which resulted in twenty year increases to the country's copyright periods. Authorial rights now lasted for the life of the creator plus seventy years; work made for hire copyright lasted for ninety-five years from publication.[3] The scope of this work made for hire legislation would, in turn, encourage European record companies to campaign for a further extension to their own sound recording rights.

There was a sense, nevertheless, that with each extension of ownership, the record companies' position became more tenuous. Their rhetoric of supporting

---

[3] The duration of rights was even more extensive for pre-1972 recordings. In 1973, the decision in *Goldstein v California* clarified that they could continue to receive protection via state law. During the copyright revision process, record companies had requested that these recordings receive federal protection, but they subsequently developed a dual attitude. When it came to the reproduction, distribution, derivative and rental rights the companies preferred the status quo, as there were advantages to maintaining state law provisions (HJC 1967: 519). First, it had been determined that state protection for all pre-1972 recordings would last until 2067, at which point these early works would finally enter the public domain (Copyright Act 1976: §301(c)). Second, it had become established practice that record companies owned the rights to these recordings. Third, state law does not include termination rights. Thus, the companies' ownership could continue unabated. Their attitude towards performing rights was different. State law left them in an ambiguous position regarding the statutory licensing of digital radio. Although a number of cases went to trial, it was not confirmed whether pre-1972 recordings were entitled to remuneration. As a result, the record companies campaigned for federal protection for their performing rights only. This was secured via the CLASSICs Act of 2018, albeit that this legislation does not let the companies have things entirely their own way. While it provides them with remuneration for the digital broadcasting of these early recordings, it truncates the duration of the rights. The copyright for recordings made prior to 1923 now expires within three years of this Act coming into force; those made between 1923 and 1946 expire five years later; recordings from 1947 to 1956 expire after a further fifteen years; post-1956 recordings continue to have copyright protection until 2067 (Copyright Act 1976: §1401).

new music could only be stretched so far. With each increase it warranted closer inspection from legislators and governmental authorities. More fundamentally, it would be called into question by recording artists, for whom lifetime assignment looked increasingly punitive. During the 1950s and 1960s, the majority of popular music performers expected to have short recording careers. Against this background it is understandable that many of them focused on the scale of their advance payments rather than the durational aspects of their contracts. By the 1990s, there was a climate of longevity: some popular music recording artists had now enjoyed long-lasting success; sales of back catalogue had grown; the duration of copyright was increasing. This prompted a greater desire among artists to campaign for ownership of rights.

Prince was one of the first American musicians to speak out against his contractual situation. In 1977, he signed a deal with Warner Brothers that offered him a considerable amount of creative control. It did not, however, keep pace with the contractual situation of Michael Jackson, an artist with whom Prince was 'fiercely competitive' (Newman 2016). In the wake of the success of his 1982 album *Thriller*, Jackson had negotiated a deal with Sony whereby his recordings would be owned by his production company MJJ Productions and distributed by the major label. By 1993 Prince was declaring himself a 'slave'. He regarded it as 'completely abhorrent' that he had recouped his advances, yet his record company 'masters' still owned his work (Newman 2016). In response to these complaints, a member of staff at Warner said 'It felt like getting punched in the solar plexus… Especially all the racial connotations' (Newman 2016). The record company was nevertheless reluctant to lose hold of the recordings. Prince would eventually extricate himself from Warner in 1996, at which point he released the pointedly titled *Emancipation* on his own NPG label, an album for which he owned the rights and which he registered as a work made for hire.

At the time of his campaign, Prince received little support from other musicians. REM, another Warner act, slighted on his obsessiveness, stating the only thing he had to say was 'Do you own your masters?' (Doyle 2014: 75). Mike Mills of the band additionally compared laws to sausages, maintaining that 'you don't want to see how they get made' (Belam 2016). There had been similar reluctance among performers to provide support for George Michael's case. This may be accounted for on fear of speaking out against their labels. There was also concern among artists that, should legal decisions go against Michael or Prince, this would cement the poor contractual position of performers generally (Maconie 1999: 64).

Less confrontationally, an increasing number of recording artists were gaining improved terms. This was the case with some of the successful American rock acts of the 1990s, including Metallica and Mötley Crüe, both of whom successfully negotiated ownership of their masters; the latter purchased their back catalogue for US$10 million in 1998 (Banas 2020). It also included REM, who 'waited for their contract to expire' at the end of the 1990s, at which point they quietly negotiated copyright ownership (including rights to their earlier recordings) in exchange for lower advances (HJC 2000: 131). Meanwhile, Bruce Springsteen became 'one of the few artists' who made recordings in the 1970s and was able to repurchase ownership of their master rights (Springsteen 2016: 258). There were in addition artists with sufficient power to claim high advances, high royalty rates and ownership of copyright. Janet Jackson signed a contract with Virgin Records in 1996 that granted her a US$80 million advance and a licensing agreement for her masters, which would return to her seven years after the release of the last album covered by the deal (Eggertsen 2019).

Artist lawyers became more influential as the decade wore on and were in some instances able to demand contractual reversion of rights. This could occur either after a set period of time (based either on the release date or an agreed number of years after the conclusion of the deal options), after a certain number of albums were released (after which the artists would gain back their earlier albums, in chronological order, in return for partnering with their record companies for each new album issued) and/or with the recoupment of advances (Forde 2019: 95; Ingham 2015; Wells 2017: 196). Conversely, record companies would sometimes request longer periods of licence or assignment if records achieved particular levels of sales (Wells 2017: 196). Artists could also contract for the opportunity to buy back their recordings. However, if they had not recouped their advances this expense could reach 'prohibitive and unaffordable heights' (AWAL 2018). David Bowie hit upon a method of establishing the necessary funds, having reportedly suffered 'a mental breakdown of sorts' on discovering that his former manager Tony DeFries owned up to 50 per cent of his back catalogue (Espiner 2016). This was one of the prompts for the launch of 'Bowie Bonds' in 1997. Bowie was able to raise US$55 million by offering investors a share in his future royalties, an alleged US$27 million of which was used to purchase DeFries' share of the rights (Espiner 2016). Once he had full ownership of his catalogue, Bowie started touring his hits 'because he was now making for himself, rather than anyone else' (Jones 2017: 408).

The majority of artists nevertheless remained powerless in respect of owning copyright. This was particularly galling in instances where they had paid off their advances but remained obliged to their companies' contractual terms. Into the late 1990s, Prince continued to campaign on other artists' behalf, asking rhetorically 'How many musicians own their masters?... Not a lot. And very, very few of African-American descent' (Segal 2014: 92). He was now supported by other performers who were finding critical voices of their own. Courtney Love compared this recording industry practice to 'sharecropping' (Love 2000). Tom Waits described it as a 'plantation system' (D'Alton 2012: 81). For Chuck D, the record companies' whip-hand made it feel as though he was 'a black man in 1866' (Allbritton 1999). The analogy that was most frequently deployed, however, was that the record company still owned the artist's house even though the mortgage had been repaid (*The Disrupters* 2016; HJC 2000: 169, 269; Love 2000; Napier-Bell 2014: 262).

Chaos theory

American recording artists did have an additional possibility of regaining their rights. It remained uncertain whether sound recordings could be classified as commissioned works made for hire. If this classification was successfully contested, the record companies' rights in recordings would be subject to termination rules. The late 1990s was therefore a crucial period for record labels in the United States. On the one hand, their term of copyright increased. On the other, the first works registered under the 1976 Act were reaching the point when authors could terminate assignment of rights. This had the potential to reduce the companies' period of ownership from ninety-five years to thirty-five years, and was regarded as the 'time bomb' in their 'vaults' (Holland 2000: 103).

The RIAA campaigned for an amendment to legislation, becoming 'heavy political contributors' in the process (Stahl 2013: 199). In 1999, the organization appeared to have achieved its aim. An update was made to the 1976 Act, adding sound recordings to the list of commissioned works made for hire. Recording artists quickly contested this manoeuvre, arguing that it represented a substantive change to their position in United States law. As a result, the House Judiciary Committee held hearings in May 2000, gauging the arguments of both sides. The record companies' case was fronted by Hilary Rosen, president and CEO of the RIAA, with backing from Paul Goldstein, professor of law at Stanford. In opposition, Sheryl Crow spoke on behalf of the Recording Artists' Coalition, a hastily assembled organization for featured artists. She was supported by several other musicians and legal authorities, including her attorney Jay Cooper and Marci Hamilton of the Cardozo School of Law.

Rosen argued that gaining work made for hire status was only a technical amendment: it was 'intended to clarify the law, not change it' (HJC 2000: 128). She maintained this status was 'ingrained in industry practice', noting that 'From the earliest days of our industry, sound recordings were agreed to be works for hire in contract after contract after contract' (2000: 128). Matt Stahl has noted, however, that this practice only became ingrained because of 'the unequal bargaining power of performers and companies' (2013: 197). In mounting a defence for this practice, Rosen employed the rhetoric of risk that had been witnessed in British copyright debates. She detailed how record companies were paying 'multi-million dollar advances' and 'several times that amount of money spent on marketing and promotion', but their chances of 'real profit or success are statistically so low' (2000: 121). The RIAA's main line of argument was different to that employed in Britain, however. As Michael Greene, president of the National Academy of Recording Arts and Sciences, noted, they were promoting a form of 'chaos theory', arguing there would be administrative bedlam if record companies were not granted control (2000: 171). Rosen claimed that centralized ownership '*benefits everyone involved in the creation and distribution of recorded music – including artists and producers, as well as record labels – because work for hire status is essential to preserve the marketability of highly collaborative works like sound recordings*' (2000: 129. Emphasis in original). Giving ownership to one party (which would normally be the record company) rather than the many (the recording artists and other creative contributors) would provide the best means of facilitating licensing processes.

As with arguments put forth by British record companies to the MMC, this rationale had considerable history. American record companies used it in relation to the copyright bills of the 1940s and 1950s (Ringer [1957] 1961: 36). British record labels had employed it in their own pursuit of copyright ownership (Gregory 1952: §176; Whitford 1977: §409). Rosen placed it within a work made for hire context, arguing that 'If highly collaborative works were subject to the termination right, they would get tied up in endless disputes and negotiations over copyright ownership' (2000: 129). She highlighted problems that would be caused if copyright were owned by the creators of sound recordings rather than those responsible for hiring the creators, outlining how 'almost *everybody* who participates in the creation of a sound recording would have a bona fide claim of authorship under U.S. copyright law' (2000: 129. Emphasis in original). The competing parties would include 'the producer, the engineers, the mixers, the background vocalists, the owners of samples used in the recording, and others – along with each member of the group of featured recording artists' (2000: 129).

In response, the recording artists argued that work made for hire classification had long been a core industry concern. As a measure of its importance, Cooper outlined how record companies insisted on classifying recordings as work made for hire in their deals with new artists and that it was extremely difficult to renegotiate this designation in subsequent contractual agreements (2000: 213–17). He nevertheless maintained that these contractual claims were not legally 'effective' (2000: 216). Hamilton backed this suggestion, stating that prior to the work made for hire amendment 'such contractual provisions would have been void' (2000: 148). Consequently, recording artists had some chance of enforcing termination rights (2000: 271). Hamilton argued that if sound recordings gained confirmation as commissioned works, this would alter the balance of power. Recording artists would suffer in the same manner as photographers and freelance writers had done when their activities were classified in this way under the 1976 Act. They would lose any 'small leverage' they may have had in their negotiations with record companies, who would thereafter be able to insist upon ownership of copyright via 'take-it-or-leave-it work made for hire status' (2000: 153).

In making their case, the recording artists posited themselves as solitary geniuses. Sheryl Crow pursued this Romantic line, stating that a sound recording 'is the final result of the creative vision, expression and execution of *one person – the featured artist*'; the record label, in comparison, was 'by no means, involved in the process of defining the music' (2000: 166. Emphasis in original). She also noted that 'any claims to the authorship by producers, hired musicians, background singers, engineers would be false' (2000: 166). In addition, Crow indicated a difference between recording artists and other creative workers, such as journalists and film actors, whose output was already subject to commissioned status under work made for hire rules. Recording artists had greater artistic control. Crow stated, 'I am basically left to my devices in creating a work' (2000: 161).

There were also differences when it came to financial responsibility. Crow explained how the creative contributors to films 'receive fees from the studio' and noted that the costs of production are 'never charged back' to them (2000: 166). In contrast:

> *As a recording artist, I do not receive a fee for making an album.* I may receive an advance to cover the costs of the recording process, which I am responsible for paying back in full. The costs are deducted from and or recouped from my share of royalties. *I do not receive a dime from the sale of my albums until I have paid for all costs incurred during production. I pay for the record – not the label.*
>
> (2000: 167. Emphasis in original)

Crow stood the employment relationship on its head, suggesting that the record company does not hire the recording artist: it is the artist who hires the investment of the record company (Stahl 2013: 204).

The introduction of financial arguments led to a tactical move. Although its rhetoric was Romantic in nature, the Recording Artists Coalition did not seek ownership on creative grounds. It instead sought the maintenance of work made for hire criteria. However, rather being oriented towards record companies, it believed featured artists should be regarded as the hiring parties. Crow stated:

> Because I produce my own records, I am basically the captain of the ship and ultimately, the decision-maker, I must also decide what musicians I want to perform on each song, given the desired sound I want to attain, what engineering staff to implement my sonic vision, what studio will be appropriate... and how much money I want to spend.
>
> (2000: 165)

Cooper outlined the contractual nature of this arrangement:

> We have to go to the contract that Ms. Crow and most artists sign. And in that contract, it says to Ms. Crow, 'You will deliver this album. We are going to pay you in advance. You pay for all the recording costs. If you exceed the advance, it comes out of your pocket. You will hire the producer. You will hire the musicians. You will hire the studio. You will hire the engineer. You will hire the mixer. You will hire all these people'.[4]
>
> (2000: 190–91)

Seeking ownership of sound recording copyright, the members of the Recording Artists' Coalition chose to cast themselves as employer-authors rather than creative-authors.

---

[4] Practice varies between countries. In Britain, for example, it has traditionally been the record company that hires the studio and staff.

The RIAA countered that they had already made this argument on the artists' behalf. Rosen and Goldstein had pointed out that employer status not only was applicable to the labels but was available to featured artists as well. They noted how musicians such as Dave Matthews, Quincy Jones, the Rolling Stones and Trent Reznor had ownership of their master recording rights and registered them as work made for hire (2000: 130). There was nevertheless a difference between the positions of the record companies and artists. The Coalition was not aiming to get sound recordings classified as commissioned works. It believed recording artists could instead claim ownership under the first work made for hire condition in the 1976 Act: they were the authors because they had the responsibility for hiring contributors to work for them 'within the scope' of their employment (1976: §101).

Altruism appeared to be in short supply. Just as the companies used work made for hire status to trump the creative claims of recording artists, the featured artists were using similar criteria to deny any claims of non-featured performers or recording personnel. They also mirrored their record companies in suggesting that work made for hire status had been contractually established: the artists indicated that they contracted non-featured performers as employees, thus giving 'work made for hire ownership rights to the [featured] artist as employer' (Cooper and Burry 2001: 11). The agreements of studio producers also stipulated that their 'contributions to the Masters… shall be works made for hire for Artist or, alternatively, shall be deemed assigned to Artist by this agreement' (Stuart 2017: 208).

There had been question marks over the legal effectiveness of the work made for hire provisions in record company contracts. Similarly, there were doubts whether artists were contracting non-featured performers and studio producers as employees. Non-featured performers may have been supervised and were working according to deadlines, but they were also in receipt of royalties (in the form of performing rights payments) in addition to their one-off fees. Studio producers were even more akin to independent contractors. American copyright law acknowledges their creativity and many of them were being employed on terms that included royalty payments. This situation prompted a further correspondence between the cases made by the record companies and featured artists. Both parties were aware that their claims for work made for hire status could be refuted. And so, just as the companies made a legislative attempt to get sound recordings added to the list of commissioned works, the featured artists recognized the need for the employee status of non-featured performers and studio producers to be 'resolved by legislation' (Cooper and Burry 2001: 11).

Neither position prevailed. The hearings concluded with the removal of sound recordings from the list of commissioned works for hire, but the copyright office did not use this as an opportunity to clarify the authorship of sound recording copyright. The legislation remained ambiguous: the record companies did not gain the amendment they sought, but were not denied authorship either; featured artists did not clarify their employer position, but could resist the counter-claims of non-featured performers and studio personnel to be co-authors of recordings.

Conclusion

Ambiguity was, for the time being, a good result for record companies. In Britain, there was governmental approval of their dual policy. The MMC endorsed their suggestion that they were the authors of sound recordings. The record companies' desire to gain life of copyright assignment was also supported, even though this latter request would appear to contradict the authorial claim. In America, the companies could proceed with their practice of registering recordings as work made for hire. They also maintained their own safeguard policy of demanding contractual assignment of recording artists' rights. In both territories, an increasing number of recording artists were attempting to restrict this assignment, but were doing so in a manner that did not challenge copyright orthodoxy. Rather than claiming rights on artistic grounds – an action that was possible in America and could have been campaigned for elsewhere – the artists claimed authorship by positing themselves as the arrangers of recording sessions or the employers of studio personnel. In short, they gained ownership of the masters by casting themselves as phonograph producers.

Stahl has argued that any creative contest regarding authorship would have 'opened a Pandora's box' (2013: 42–3). Escaping this fate, record companies and featured artists benefited from claiming rights ownership on economic grounds. Yet the continuation of this practice favoured one party more than the other. Featured artists were endorsing the record companies' preferred system rather than questioning it. They were content to be the deprivers of rights as long as they were not being deprived. Moreover, the numbers were on the record companies' side. In addition to denying authorship to non-featured performers, studio producers and engineers, this methodology was only of benefit to a restricted number of featured artists. During the work made for hire hearings it was revealed that Sheryl Crow did not have ownership of her sound recording rights, despite the attempts of Cooper to renegotiate her contract (2000: 216). There was also a letter of support from Billy Joel, stating he too was subject to work made for hire provisions (2000: 255). Meanwhile, performers including Jon Bon Jovi, Coolio and Michael McDonald complained to the press that 'Artists have been cheated out of their works just about ever since the record business began' ('Artists, Representatives' 2000: 123). It was still only the most 'powerful' who could turn things around and position themselves as hirers (HJC 2000: 271). In the meantime, the majority of artists would continue to work on their companies' behalf. The situation in the United States corresponded with the situation elsewhere. Artists remained restricted in their ownership of copyright. Although British record companies suggested that their desire to hold rights for life of copyright was 'not always achieved', it remained the case that they would 'normally' gain ownership and this would 'normally' be for the full term (MMC 1994: §2.18, §2.42, §5.128).

The main reason why most recording artists remained adrift in terms of ownership was the industry's continued focus on sales. Counterintuitively, it was the financial risks involved in creating and marketing physical products that provided the record companies with security. It was these risks that led to the corporate ownership of sound recording copyright and it was this manufacturing basis that gave them control of the market. In the majority of instances, a recording artist would need to partner with a label to access the processes of reproduction, distribution and retail. As long as this system remained pervasive, the companies would be dominant in contractual negotiations, including the transfer of rights. Yet it was a system of ownership that was underpinned by rhetoric, rather than cemented in law. It would be tested as the distribution of music moved online.

6

Networking

In the same period as the RIAA was negotiating a change to work made for hire legislation, it was defending the American recording industry on a separate front. In December 1999, it filed for a copyright infringement lawsuit against Napster, the peer-to-peer software provider that signalled the impact that MP3 file-sharing could have on the sale of physical products. Rather than license Napster, the RIAA aimed to shut it down.

This action has provided the lasting impression of the industry at the turn of the millennium. In the 1990s it was so awash with the sales of compact discs it ignored the development of online music; then, when it belatedly acknowledged file-sharing, its response was reactionary, short-sighted and futile. This belief is caught in two industry-related books that address this period. Louis Barfe argued that record companies were 'caught Napstering' (2004: 324); Steve Knopper claimed they had an 'appetite for self-destruction' (2009). Industry professionals have acknowledged they were ill-equipped to deal with the situation. Doug Morris, who was CEO of the largest major company, the Universal Music Group, confessed in 2007 that the recording industry 'just didn't know what to do' (Mnookin 2007).

However, these claims are not entirely accurate. The industry was also quick off the mark in respect of digital distribution. As early as 1993, the RIAA was noting that computerized networking 'may soon become the means of making music accessible to the public, thus... eroding and perhaps even one day eliminating the sale of recorded music' (HJC 1994: 40). A year later, the American government was arguing on the industry's behalf that 'distinctions among the rights of authors, producers and performers that are the basis for the separation of copyright and neighboring rights are rapidly becoming irrelevant' (WIPO 1994b: 270: 71). The recording industry nevertheless sought parity on its own terms. Its trade bodies did not believe that sound recording copyright should be awarded on creative grounds, as was the case with the authorship of literary and artistic works, nor did they seek a realignment of revenues that would see the record companies' share diminish so that performers, composers and publishers could gain an equivalent rise. Rather, they sought an international system of copyright for sound recordings that would parallel the agreements secured for authors via the Berne Convention. This would engender a concordance of exclusive rights: although most countries had enacted reproduction rights for recordings, there were many that still had no distribution or rental controls. It would also prompt wider adoption of performing rights and the establishment of national treatment for the exchange of revenues. Most importantly, the recording industry desired legislation that would be broad enough to cope with changes wrought by digital services. It sought the implementation of online copyright protection systems, as well as measures to outlaw attempts to circumvent their code. It also wanted clarification and supplementation of exclusive rights so that record companies would be assured of control of the interactive use of recordings online.

Against this backdrop, Simon Frith reiterated the 'straightforward' position that the recording industry 'is not a manufacturing industry, it is a rights industry' (2000: 388). In one respect, he was not only correct but could have gone further. What is notable about the industry's initial reaction to digital distribution is its overwhelming focus on intellectual property. The major record companies abandoned their role as the developers of new recording formats and were instead preoccupied with protecting their rights. We can witness this orientation in the remarks of label bosses. While Edgar Bronfman, who was CEO at Universal at the turn of the millennium, spoke of 'Roman legions' of lawyers he would unleash against copyright transgressors (Alderman 2001: 24), Doug Morris confessed there was no one at his company he could call a 'technologist' (Mnookin 2007).

Yet there continued to be ways in which this analysis could be questioned. In the first instance, the recording industry's orientation towards 'making *things*' remained much in evidence (Frith 1988: 57. Emphasis in original). The primary objective of its legal manoeuvres was to preserve the market for compact discs. Second, as downloading and streaming successively rose to prominence there were ways in which the recording industry was reversing Frith's prognosis. It should have been relatively straightforward for record companies to look at these means of delivering content and view their recordings as intellectual property rather than manufactured goods: streaming and downloading are not 'physical' and they are not formats per se; they are also multifaceted in respect of the exclusive rights they can trigger. However, rather than viewing these media as baskets of rights, the recording industry preferred to equate them with physical products.

This could be witnessed at a number of levels. Despite the fact that online services lend themselves to the access of individual tracks, the recording industry retained a focus on albums, a format that has made most sense in the physical domain. The industry also preserved a physical rationale for its popularity charts and its award certifications: the access model of streaming, paid for by subscription and advertising, was made equivalent to 'sales' (Osborne 2021a: 28–35; Osborne 2021b: 47–51). This physical orientation was also in evidence in legislative practice. The advent of downloading and streaming resulted in the creation of the making available right, an exclusive control that addresses interactive services in the digital domain. For the recording industry, this right has served two purposes. It has ensured that all activities relating to online access are encompassed within legislation, thus giving copyright holders the ability to restrict them and exploit them. In addition, it has enabled the industry to avoid plurality. The making available right was designed so it would sit alongside and operate in a similar manner to the reproduction right. Manufacture provided the foundations for the industry's legislative and contractual strength. Correspondingly, just as the record companies sought to prolong the trade for physical recordings in the face of digital developments, they aimed to extend the copyright and contracting methodology for these products to the online domain.

This chapter looks at three phases in the digitalization of the recording industry. Its first section addresses the preparedness of record companies for the arrival of online music, focusing on the development of the making available right. The second section examines the prohibitive actions of the industry as the online market expanded. It sought to stamp out peer-to-peer services, originally targeting the companies behind file-sharing applications before turning to the prosecution of individual consumers. The third section addresses the industry's preservative attitude. It desired the same levels of control over 'legitimate' digital services as it had over physical retail. It also believed that online revenues should be divided in the same manner as those for physical formats.

Pre-emptive

The early 1990s witnessed advances in the field of 'digital transmissions' (HJC 1994: 1). DAB was expanding its reach, and the capacities of digital cable networks and digital satellite broadcasting were also increasing (HJC 1994: 30–3). These developments posed a new problem for the recording industry: consumers might not need to buy physical products at all. They could instead use DAT players to record digital transmissions. Record companies complained that 'such taping would displace sales for prerecorded works and harm copyright owners' (Oman 1991: iii). They were also alert to the threat of computerized networking. The IFPI flagged the development of 'on-line electronic delivery services' in 1993 (HJC 1994: 45). By this time, two types of delivery were already envisioned: music could be made available for download and it could be streamed (Witt 2015: 13). The IFPI were particularly concerned about the latter usage, worrying that the resultant 'celestial jukebox' would enable 'consumers to select music to listen to at their convenience without ever making an actual copy' (HJC 1994: 45).

The record companies requested further protection. They argued that levies would be insufficient to make up for losses caused by digital copying, and that the SCMS might be irrelevant in the face of online services, as consumers would not need to preserve music files by recording them onto digital tape (Commission of the European Communities 1988: 133; HJC 1994: 47). It was against this background that the recording industry in the United States renewed its campaign for statutory performing rights. The RIAA argued that digital transmissions might 'erode' and 'eliminate' the sale of recorded music (HJC 1994: 40). Thus, it was essential they gained appropriate copyright protection for any means of delivery that might threaten to take the place of those sales. There was also a move towards international harmonization. Within the European Economic Area (EEA) there was awareness of the ability of new technologies to entail 'the *de facto* abolition of national frontiers and increasingly make the territorial application of national copyright law obsolete' (Commission of the European Communities 1988: 5). The United States' response to this situation was to seek national treatment for recording's performing rights. What was required in the face of this 'rapidly emerging digital world' was coordinated protection (WIPO 1995: 377).

The recording industry's agenda overlapped with the interests of WIPO. Since 1970, this organization had been responsible for administrating the major international copyright treaties, including the Berne, Rome and Phonograms Conventions. In 1991, it gathered delegates at Geneva for the first meeting of a committee of experts, who would discuss a possible new 'Protocol' to Berne (Ficsor 1997: 199–200). These discussions had two main aims. First, in respect of authors of works, they would look at the effects of contemporary 'technological developments' on copyright law (WIPO 1992: 42). Second, WIPO would address the same technological impact in respect of the 'protection of producers of sound recordings' (WIPO 1992: 32). The organization was cognizant of the possible effects of digital transmission and digital recording, believing their impact could render the protection accorded by the Rome and Phonograms Conventions as 'no longer high enough' (1992: 39). Consequently, it proposed that recordings should be addressed in the Protocol 'as if such inclusion would be made in the Berne Convention itself' (1992: 39). This would entail 'the strict application of national treatment and the recognition not only of the exclusive right of reproduction... but... also the other rights protected under the Berne Convention... in particular the rights of public performance, broadcasting, rental and importation' (1992: 39).

There was still discrimination against sound recordings, however. WIPO did not believe the producers of phonogram recordings should receive these rights on creative grounds. It maintained that sound recordings 'are not works and their producers are not authors' (1992: 32). The organization went as far as saying that producers are responsible for a 'non-existent artistic contribution' to sound recordings (1992: 39). Therefore, rather than granting ownership in respect of originality or artistry, WIPO stated that its 'purpose' was 'to have the producer of the sound recording to be the person or legal entity in whom or in which the protection vests' (1992: 39).

There were objections that a Berne Protocol would facilitate corporate interests. Representatives from civil law countries were accompanied by a delegate from CISAC in proposing that sound recordings should instead be studied under the banner of neighbouring rights. Broadcasting organizations such as the NAB and the European Broadcasting Union argued that recordings should be removed from discussions entirely (WIPO 1992: 41–8). Other parties noted the absence of performers in the Protocol. This could be attributed to WIPO's beliefs. It maintained that performers are no more creative than phonogram producers, and suggested that engineers are the only contributors to recordings who demonstrate any degree of artistry, albeit that it was 'very doubtful whether such a contribution exists in respect of all sound recordings and, even if it does, whether it is of sufficient importance and of a sufficient degree of artistic originality to render the sound engineer an author and the sound recording a work' (1992: 32). The International Federation of Actors nevertheless argued that 'performers should be recognized as creators of artistic works' (WIPO 1992: 5). In addition, the representative from FIM and delegates from Germany, Finland, the Netherlands, Italy and Sweden demanded that the interests of performers be grouped with those of phonogram producers (WIPO 1992: 41–8). WIPO bowed to majority opinion. Rather than attempting to reconcile different rights interests in a single Protocol, it proceeded with two separate committees of experts. Literary and artistic works would be explored via the 'Possible Berne Protocol'; record companies and performers would see their interests represented in a 'Possible Instrument on the Protection of the Rights of Performers and Producers of Phonograms'.

Recording industry trade bodies seized upon the latter forum to promote their views about digital services. The RIAA argued that phonogram producers should have exclusive rights in 'the new technological environment of digital audio transmissions, whether via broadcast, cable, telephone, satellite, or other means' (HJC 1994: 44). The IFPI objected to the ancillary nature that the Rome Convention accorded to performing rights and was scornful that this status had recently been upheld by the EEC, whose 1992 Rental and Lending Rights directive made equitable remuneration compulsory for 'broadcasting and communication to the public' in all member states (1992: art. 8(2)). According to Nicholas Garnett, the IFPI's director general and chief executive, 'The proposition that broadcasting and other communication to the public represent merely "secondary" uses of phonograms, if it was ever valid – which is doubtful – is now somewhat outmoded' (HJC 1994: 36). He argued that protection for electronic delivery should 'less closely track existing performance right concepts and have more in common with provisions relating to reproduction and distribution rights' (HJC 1994: 30). Exclusive controls were required so that phonograph producers could 'control the ways in which individual phonograms are released into the market', 'correct distortion of the market from unauthorised diffusion', 'establish price structures for the phonogram' and 'coordinate releases of phonograms between different markets around the world' (HJC 1994: 36–7).

WIPO endorsed these arguments. In 1993, it presented draft provisions for the Instrument for Performers and Producers, which contained a performing rights proposal that was 'virtually identical' to Garnett's (HJC 1994: 49). Equitable remuneration would be retained for analogue broadcasting, but would not apply 'in the case of digital communication to the public of phonograms' (WIPO 1993: 20). WIPO stated that digital transmission rights must be exclusive; 'otherwise, the necessary control over this means of exploitation may not be guaranteed' (1993: 15). This view received considerable support in the United States, where the RIAA, the AFM and the Copyright Office were campaigning for the recognition of exclusive performing rights at home and abroad (HJC 1994: 10, 44, 55). It also had the support of Bruce Lehman, who led the US delegation at the WIPO conferences and acted as chair of President Bill Clinton's working group on intellectual property rights. He feared the 'potential mischief' of equitable remuneration, suggesting that if it were imposed on digital transmissions many European countries would fail in their duty to remunerate American record companies for this use of their work (HJC 1996: 194). He also complained about the manner in which Rome adherents used the lack of reciprocal performing rights in the United States as a means of withholding royalties, and how they 'siphoned off' remuneration to subsidize their local music communities (HJC 1996: 194). Other countries had different views. WIPO found that 'opinions on whether an exclusive right was warranted for digital broadcasting were divided' (WIPO 1994a: 48). There was also debate among delegates about whether a digital transmission right might combine exclusivity with equitable remuneration (WIPO 1994b: 252; WIPO 1995: 375-6). The Commission of the EEC stated that 'In responding to the challenges posed by technology, the best of existing traditions should be kept to find an adequate solution' (WIPO 1994a: 46).

The line was eventually drawn in a different place. At first there had been talk about the need to control all forms of digital transmission, but as discussions progressed this was honed to the 'on-demand, interactive digital delivery of phonograms' (WIPO 1994b: 252). These would be complicated services to account for nonetheless. Interactive delivery operates across copyright boundaries. In addition to activating the 'non-copy-related' performing rights, which address situations where consumers have 'live' experiences with copyright works, they involve the 'copy-related' rights of reproduction and distribution, whereby intellectual property is 'made available to the public, typically for "deferred" use' (Ficsor 1997: 208). Although delegates agreed that various rights were involved, there was lack of consensus about how they should be combined.

There are a number of reasons why countries proposed different solutions, but what was probably most decisive were the separate contractual practices that had evolved in relation to their copyright laws (Ficsor 1997: 207; USCO 2016b: 80). Until the 1990s, many European countries did not have distribution rights; therefore, their preferred way of categorizing interactive services was to house them under a combination of the reproduction and communication to the public rights (Samuelson 1997: 393-4). The United States was still formulating its plans for sound recording's performing rights at this time. Consequently, its preference was to couple the reproduction and distribution rights. Its distribution right could only be employed for downloading, however, as it addresses activities 'that enable a member of the public to obtain possession of a copy of a work' (USCO 2016b: 28). In respect of on-demand streaming, the reproduction right would need to be accompanied by the American equivalent of communication to the public: its public performance right (USCO 2016b: 28).

Whatever the categorization, the record companies wanted the rights to be clarified so they could have their desired protection for online activity. At the WIPO conferences, it was the European Commission who made the decisive move, proposing a 'making available right' for digital transmissions that would make 'a clear distinction... between the traditional right of communication to the public and the interactive parts of the right' (WIPO 1999: 677). This right was enshrined in the WPPT, which realized the objectives of the New Instrument and was agreed in Geneva in 1996. It is also an aspect of the WCT, which concurrently fulfilled the Berne Protocol for authors' rights.

The WPPT provides phonogram producers with 'the exclusive right of authorizing the making available to the public of their phonograms, by wire or wireless means, in such a way that members of the public may access them from a place and at a time individually chosen by them' (WPPT 1996: art. 14). As a result, the right for interactive online services operates similarly to the reproduction right for physical formats. Compulsory access to recordings is denied; phonogram producers can withhold licences from online services if they wish. The services are not subject to equitable remuneration; record companies instead have the authority to set their own royalty rates and ensure that artist payments are recoupable from advances. The right is also global in scope, as it is accompanied by national treatment rules (WPPT 1996: art. 4).

Although the making available right represented a pre-emptive response to digital technologies, it was established with little controversy. There was general agreement that it should be an exclusive right, as well as satisfaction with the way it was outlined (Ficsor 1997: 210; Samuelson 1997: 17). Musicians' unions do not appear to have complained about its creation, despite the fact it could deny non-featured performers a tranche of communication to the public revenues. This might, however, be due to the fact that it was addressing a nascent technology and the original impulse was preventative rather than exploitative. That said, the new right also appears to have escaped censure from advocacy groups such as the Digital Future Coalition, who otherwise objected to the expansions of copyright that were formulated in this era (Carson 2010: 144). This acceptance can be accounted for on two grounds. First, it was envisaged that the making available right would work in conjunction with the reproduction right, which was already an exclusive right and was free of compulsory licensing. Second, there is the subtle way that the right was enacted. An 'umbrella solution' was conceived for its incorporation within national laws (Ficsor 1997: 210). Contracting parties were entitled to create a distinct making available right but they could also house it under their communication to the public or distribution rights.

The European Union implemented the WIPO Treaties via the Information Society Directive of 2001, which instructs member states to grant phonogram producers an interactive right (EC 2001: art. 3(b)). Although they were given latitude in how they undertook this, most territories introduced the making available right as a sub-set of communication to the public.[1] The United States implemented the WIPO Treaties via its Digital Millennium Copyright Act of 1998, which outlines how this will entail only 'technical amendments' to domestic law (USCO 2016b: 15–16). It was held that the distribution right did not need to be reworded in order to encompass the downloading of recordings (Ficsor 1997: 209). Meanwhile, the Digital Performance Right in Sound Recordings Act of 1995 had been developed with WIPO's discussions in mind (HJC 1995: 15). It incorporates interactive streaming under the public performance right, exempting it from the compulsory licensing measures it introduced for other digital communications to the public (1995: §2A). The American embrace of the making available right was not wholly tacit, however. It rested on the Charming Betsy doctrine, which holds that US statutes should be 'construed so as not to conflict with international law or with an international agreement of the United States' (Carson 2010: 161). Therefore, the fact that the United States said it had implemented the WIPO Treaties was taken as evidence it had implemented them.

These quiet beginnings should not belie the making available right's importance. In respect of interactive services, it has had a more decisive impact than the reproduction right. It is the making available right that addresses the 'offer' of files, rendering it fundamental in the persecution of file-sharing. It also underpins the on-demand streaming of music, an activity that has replaced rather than mirrored the retail of recordings in stores. Legal professor Jane Ginsburg has proclaimed the making available right as the great 'innovation' of the WIPO

---

[1] This includes Britain (CDPA 1988: §20(2)(b)). Section 182(D) of the CDPA indicates that the making available is the one aspect of communication to the public free from equitable remuneration. Acting several years ahead of this, the record company owners of PPL decided in 1995 that on-demand digital services were 'analogous to the distribution of sound recordings' and therefore should not come under their collecting society's purview (PPL 2012: 18).

Treaties (USCO 2016b: 62). The IFPI regards it as an 'important achievement', praising the 'international community' because it 'unanimously acknowledged that record producers in particular needed this exclusive right' (2003: 1).

Although there is no mention of performers in the IFPI's statement, they are also addressed by the WPPT. The Treaty grants them equitable remuneration for broadcasting, public performance and transmissions by wire. It also includes moral rights in respect of their live and recorded work. In addition, performers are provided with exclusive rights in respect of the reproduction, distribution, rental and making available of their recordings. There is a difference, however, in the object of protection. The Treaty grants its rights to phonogram producers in respect of 'their phonograms' (WPPT 1996: arts 2(d), 11–14). In doing so it accords with WIPO's beliefs. Ownership is not awarded for creativity: producers are granted rights on economic or organizational grounds. The award goes to organizer-producers rather than manufacturer-producers, with the owner defined as 'the person, or the legal entity, who or which takes the initiative and has the responsibility for the first fixation of the sounds of a performance or other sounds, or the representations of sounds' (WPPT 1996: arts 2(d), 11–14). The rights of performers, in contrast, address 'their performances fixed in phonograms' (WPPT 1996: arts 7–10). They are not granted ownership of rights in the actual recordings.

In addition to controlling their own rights, phonograph producers have used contractual agreements to oversee the exclusive rights of performers. In respect of contacts signed after the implementation of the WPPT, the making available right has been one of a number of exclusive rights that performers will be expected to transfer through assignment. Performers whose contracts were drawn up before the enactment of the making available right are also regarded as having passed it on. This is because of expansive contractual clauses, which enable record companies to stake a claim for 'all rights existing now or that come into existence in the future in all territories of the world, the universe and its satellites' (Trubridge 2015).

Prohibitive

During the period the WPPT was being formulated, the use of interactive services was largely restricted to amateur recordings (Alderman 2001: 15). The internet was also a minority interest. Only 3 per cent of American classrooms had access to it in 1993 (Alderman 2001: 15); 82 per cent of British consumers still had no access by 1997 (Scaping 1998: 11). Against this background, the recording industry can be regarded as prescient in seeking out new legislative measures. It was, however, wayward in its imaginings of the form these services would take. The industry was fixated on compact discs: it feared that the content of this format would be perfectly reproduced in other digital forms. The online market eventually emerged with a technology that promised inferior sound quality to the CD. MP3 files have compressed the data of compact discs to around a tenth of their original size. They were first published by the Moving Picture Experts Group in 1993, but did not rise to prominence until Nullsoft's Winamp player was released in 1997, bringing with it the increased use of copyrighted recordings online. Thereafter, rather than seeking to license any new services, the recording industry used its full panoply of legal measures to suppress them. This orientation is perhaps understandable, given that its reproduction-based revenues were continuing to expand. In addition, the industry had recently had successes in thwarting digitization, having instigated a clampdown on DAT machines and stunted the rental market for CDs.

It was in the United States that the online market first appeared and here too that retaliation was initiated. In 1998, Diamond Multimedia introduced the Rio PMP300, the first handheld MP3 player to be commercially successful. Within six months the company was being sued by the RIAA, which alleged that because the Rio did not include the SCMS it violated the terms of the AHRA (*RIAA v Diamond Multimedia* 1999). The US Court of Appeals for the Ninth Circuit ruled in Diamond Multimedia's favour, determining that the Rio did not qualify under the AHRA as it could not directly record transmissions. It also suggested that the noncommercial transfer of recordings from a computer to an MP3 player constituted fair use of copyright material under American law. Undaunted by this defeat, the RIAA launched a suit against MP3.com in April 2000 (*UMG Recordings v MP3.com*). This website had been founded in 1997 as a hosting site for the MP3 files of independent musicians. It expanded its reach in 2000, launching the MyMP3.com service, which enabled subscribers to stream compact discs on condition they proved they had purchased them. This was achieved by placing their own discs in their CD-Rom drives for a few seconds or by purchasing them from one of MP3. com's cooperating online retailers. It was MP3.com, however, who uploaded the corresponding digitized files onto their website. They too made a fair use defence but this was defeated in court. Judge Jed S. Rakoff held that they violated the American record companies' reproduction rights. The music industry also emerged triumphant in the case it launched against Napster (*A&M Records v Napster* 2000). Although it was users of this service who were responsible for exchanging copyrighted MP3 files online, it was found that Napster could be liable for vicarious infringement of the plaintiffs' intellectual property rights. This was on the grounds that it hosted the users' files on its servers and knowingly facilitated their exchange.

Further preventative measures were pursued. Record companies had endorsed the No Electronic Theft Act of 1995, which overturned previous US law. Previously, copyright could not be infringed in situations where the user received no 'commercial advantage or private financial gain', but this Act facilitated prosecution of the uploading and downloading of digital files (Copyright Act 1976: §506(a)). The recording industry also led the Secure Digital Music Initiative (SDMI), which sought (and failed) to create a rival compression system to the MP3 that would include a digital watermarking scheme as a means 'to protect the playing, storing, and distributing of digital music' (Giblin 2011: 13).

These actions appeared to run counter to the logic of computer networking. For advocates such as the Electronic Frontier Foundation, the Free Software Foundation and the Access to Knowledge movement, the internet was a forum for the sharing of ideas: its logic was that 'information wants to be free' (Lainer 2010: 28). In its liaison with the internet, the recording industry was violating this imperative. It was aligned with other copyright holding industries in seeking to maintain control over content. It also looked to ways that this control could be extended, exploring the potential to copy-protect its product and monitor the digital activities of users.

The introduction of these measures prompted a raft of critiques. Within academia one complaint was that anti-circumvention legislation placed 'the power to regulate copying in the hands of engineers and the companies that employ them' (Vaidhyanathan 2001: 174). Another was that it created an environment in which '*code* becomes *law*' (Lessig 2004: 160. Emphasis in original). According to Frith and Marshall:

> while the corporate argument is framed as 'bringing copyright law into line with the new environment'... from an academic perspective what has actually happened is that the original principles of copyright have been surreptitiously put aside. A system that was originally framed by reference to the public good – it involved restrictions on the monopoly power of rights owners – has become a

means of ensuring private interests. What was once a system for ensuring public access to knowledge has now become a system, at least in the digital sphere, to prevent it.

(2004: 4)

The recording industry was one of the progenitors of anti-circumvention technologies and was widely criticized for its role. More generally, it was held guilty of narrowing the fair use and fair dealing provisions for copyright users and encroaching upon the public domain. What really ignited the 'copyright wars', however, was the second phase of the industry's campaign. In 2003, the RIAA decided to pursue individual file-sharers, an action described by Lawrence Lessig as the 'battle that got [the] whole war going' (2004: 179, 296). In addition to negating the promise of the internet to provide an information-rich society, the recording industry was now viewed as affronting the civil liberties of consumers.

The RIAA's campaign has been branded as an attack upon unauthorized downloading, but rather than targeting the reproduction of files it addressed their distribution between consumers. Thus, the making available right was brought into play. The organization's policy was arrived at due to two developments in the market. First, following the legal demise of Napster, new peer-to-peer services such as Grokster, Morpheus and Kazaa had emerged. Rather than hosting files on their own servers, they facilitated the direct exchange of MP3s between users, thus hoping to avoid charges of vicarious infringement. This stance would be effectively challenged by the RIAA and the Motion Picture Association of America in 2005, but in April 2003 a Los Angeles federal judge held for Grokster, suggesting it was not responsible for the activities of its users. The second factor was the launch of Apple's iTunes store the same month. The American recording industry had been susceptible to accusations it was violating anti-trust laws: it was thwarting online music and therefore consumers had little choice other than to use 'illegal' peer-to-peer services (*A&M Records v Napster* 2000: 923). The licensing of this service freed it from such claims.

The result for the recording industry cannot be regarded as a success, however. Although it gained legal permission to prosecute individual file-sharers, it did not win the public relations war. Moreover, the campaign appeared to increase rather than decrease unauthorized activity. It was directly responsible for the creation of The Pirate Bay, an openly provocative file-sharing index. It also led to the formation of the Pirate Party, a political group that was founded in Sweden in 2006, and which soon had chapters in other countries. Campaigning for 'a rollback of copyright laws and total amnesty for Internet file-sharers', the Party made electoral gains in countries with proportional representation systems and held seats in the European parliament following the 2009, 2014 and 2019 elections (Witt 2015: 242).

The recording industry attempted to portray its activities as being of benefit to recording artists, yet here it was hoisted by its own petard (Cloonan 2007: 84; Sun 2019: 143). It was defending a copyright system that granted ownership to employers and administrators, rather than one that recognized the creative authors of works. As such, it became a target for those who wished to claim that copyright was only of advantage to commercial entities. Introducing their 2004 collection *Music and Copyright*, Frith and Marshall found a common belief that 'the legislative response to digital technology has not only vastly increased the scope of copyright but has also done so in a way which benefits corporate interests at the expense of both artists and consumers' (2004: 4).

The recording industry may have anticipated some of these responses but probably did not expect any of its recording artists to come out in support of unauthorized file-sharing. This practice was nevertheless endorsed by a number of performers, including The Offspring, Alex Kapranos of Franz Ferdinand and Chuck D of Public Enemy. There were also artists who decried it, including Dr Dre and Metallica, but this was the minority position. Metallica were vilified for taking Napster to court and threatening to confiscate the hard drives of fans who exchanged files of their material online (Brannigan and Winwood 2014: 117).

What has tended to be glossed over in respect of this situation is that opinions were divided along sound recording copyright lines. In general, artists who supported peer-to-peer file-sharing did not own their master rights. Rather than profiting from the compact disc boom, they had grown frustrated at their share of the spoils. Dave Stewart of the Eurythmics noted that 'anything anarchistic like Napster is good – it makes artists ask why they are not in control of what they are doing' (Barfe 2004: 327). Thom Yorke stated, 'The idea that they [record companies] are the victims of an immoral act is incredible to me. They claim to have the best interests of the artists at heart. Oh, really? They haven't had the best interests of the artists in mind for fifty years' (Kot 2009: 228). His band Radiohead would not own the copyright in any of their recordings until their seventh album *In Rainbows* was released in 2007. Courtney Love was in a similar situation and was equally critical: 'What is piracy? Piracy is the act of stealing an artist's work without any intention of paying for it. I'm not talking about Napster-type software. I'm talking about major label recording contracts' (2000).

In contrast, Dr Dre had owned his recording rights since 1996, when he set up his own label, Aftermath Records. Metallica had been copyright owners since embarking on a joint venture with Elektra Records in 1994. The group wished to challenge the idea that 'People have this relationship with the Internet and think that if something is on it they have a right to it' (Winwood and Brannigan 2014: 124). Their campaign against Napster was also one of asserting their agency. According to the band's drummer Lars Ulrich, 'It's really about controlling what you own: we clearly own our own songs; we own the master recordings to those, and we want to be the ones that control the use of those on the Internet' (*Charlie Rose* 2000). Responding to this statement, Chuck D noted that Metallica 'own their masters and they control their realm… but they're the exception to the rules' (*Charlie Rose* 2000).

Chuck D depicted the furore over file-sharing as being 'the industry versus the people' and portrayed himself as being on the people's side (*Charlie Rose* 2000). He bemoaned that until the advent of Napster, 'the industry had control of technology and therefore the people were subservient to that technology and whatever price range that the people would have to pay for it' (*Charlie Rose* 2000). Iggy Pop also sympathized with consumers, stating that 'prosecuting some college kid because she shared a file is a lot like sending somebody to Australia 200 years ago for poaching his lordship's rabbit' (Pop 2014). In turn, there were consumers who used the ill-treatment of recording artists to validate their file-sharing activities (Sun 2019: 137). Alison Wenham, former chairman of the British Association of Independent Music (AIM), believes that:

> consumers were justifying their attitude by reference to the behaviour of the major record companies. It's easy not to like the music industry. 'You (the music industry) have ripped off your artists, you have not treated your artists well, you ripped me off during the '80s and '90s with inflated CD prices, so you deserve it'. There was a certain, some would say justifiable anger in the way the public perceived us.
>
> (Sun 2019: 137–8)

Some members of the industry had foreseen that the campaign would cause problems. The most notable objector was Hilary Rosen, former head of the RIAA. She argued that 'suing the file-sharers was a disastrous policy' that was 'guaranteed to alienate fans and leave a stain on the industry's reputation that could last for decades' (Witt 2015: 159). Rather than pursue it, she resigned her post.

Rosen was correct in her predictions. Prior to the advent of digital services, the recording industry's ownership of rights had for the most part been endorsed. The record companies had also been reaping their highest rewards. Their CD-inspired golden period of the 1990s was followed by a decade that can be considered their nadir. Profits were in decline; their power was called into question. Yet this was the context in which the British recording industry launched a campaign to extend the term of sound recording copyright. PPL raised the issue with the British government in 2002, and by 2006 the record companies' case was being heard as part of Andrew Gowers' *Review of Intellectual Property*. Although out of step with the sentiment of the period, there was some logic to launching the campaign at this time. Repertoire-wise, the fifty-year term of copyright meant that the earliest records of the rock 'n' roll era were due to enter the public domain. Economically, term extension could provide a means to claw back profits lost to peer-to-peer file-sharing. These circumstances required a new outlook, however. Previously, the recording industry had shown few qualms in assuming ownership of sound recording copyright or demanding control for the full duration of the term. It was now aware of a 'backlash against copyright owners in general' and realized it would need the support of recording artists to achieve its goal ('Campaign Stirs' 2004: 7).

This posed problems. There was a need to prove that artists would profit from longer lasting copyright. In doing so, the campaigners made much of performers' rights, indicating that recording artists and record companies would benefit mutually from any extension to the period of equitable remuneration. At this time PPL money only constituted around 11 per cent of total British recording industry revenues, however, with almost the entirety of the remainder falling under the reproduction right (Green 2017: 9). In respect of reproduction revenues, the industry journal *Music Week* outlined how it was becoming more common for performers to 'win or retain control of their copyrights' and consequently they had 'more to gain – and lose' ('Why it's Time' 2004: 7). There was truth to this statement. The first tranche of artists to support the campaign included U2, Billy Bragg and Feargal Sharkey of the Undertones. A common feature among them was their ownership of master rights.

This was nevertheless still a minority position. To receive wider backing from performers, concessions were required. British performers made a number of demands, including the implementation a reversion/termination right, as was potentially enjoyed by recording artists in the United States. John Smith, who was then general secretary of the Musicians' Union, pointed to difficulties with this proposal, noting that reversion would in many instances be a 'misnomer' as sound recording copyright had 'always belonged' to record companies (2006: 8). There was also a request for a 'use it or lose it' clause, which would witness the transfer of copyright to recording artists in the event their recordings were not actively promoted. In addition, performers sought 'clean slate' provisions for any period of extension beyond fifty years. This would entail the waiving of recoupment and the chance to bargain for improved royalty rates.

Although these requirements ran counter to the companies' interests, they still had plenty to gain from securing the artists' support. One benefit was that artists could be 'more hard-line than any record label would dare be' (Talbot 2006: 14). As the focus shifted from corporate interests towards those of performers, the requested period of extension began to increase. Record companies had argued for a duration of ninety-five years, seeking equivalence with work made for hire legislation in the United States. The recording artists wanted life plus seventy years, giving them parity with European songwriters ('Government Must' 2006: 8). In response, the IFPI reported happily that 'what has been perceived by some as a record company campaign has been taken over by the artists' ('A United Voice' 2006: 1).

The industry's utilization of these voices was inconsistent, however. On the one hand, it deployed its rhetoric of newness, arguing that record companies were in need of long and secure ownership of back catalogue to finance the music of tomorrow ('Copyright Issue' 2004: 6). On the other, it claimed it was safeguarding the 'pensions' of older performers. As a result, early British rock 'n' roll stars, such as Cliff Richard and Joe Brown, were placed at the forefront of the campaign. The *Gowers Review* did not believe these two objectives could be reconciled. In seeking evidence that a longer term 'would increase the incentives for record companies to invest in new acts', it found that any extra money generated would be 'negligible' (Gowers 2006: §4.31). The Review poured scorn on the idea that longer-lasting copyright would provide younger musicians with 'incentives to make music' and argued it would instead be of most benefit to established stars (2006: §4.29, §4.32). Gowers provided a reminder that 'Eighty per cent of albums never recoup costs and so no royalties are paid to the creator', and added that 'If the purpose of extension is to increase revenue to artists, given the low number of recordings still making money 50 years after release, it seems that a more sensible starting point would be to review the contractual arrangements for the percentages artists receive' (2006: box 4.2). His report concluded that extending the term 'would not increase the number of works created or made available, and would negatively impact upon consumers and industry' (2006: §4.40).

Facing this rejection, the pro-extension campaigners turned their focus to the European Parliament. There were five more years of debating and lobbying before matters were eventually decided in their favour. The resultant Directive 'on the term of protection of copyright' grants EU phonogram producers their desired extension to copyright, but also betrays an orientation towards performers. There is increased respect for the artistry of recording. The Directive states that the 'socially recognised importance of the creative contribution of performers should be reflected in a level of protection that acknowledges their creative and artistic contribution' (EC 2011: §4). It also grants recordings artists some special measures, albeit that they fall short of their original demands. The term is set at seventy years from publication (EC 2011: art 1(2)(a)). Featured artists receive clean slate provisions, but these are restricted to waiving unrecouped balances after fifty years of copyright (EC 2011: art. 1(2)(c)). Rather than gaining reversion rights, they are granted the opportunity to terminate ownership of copyright completely, but only after a period of fifty years. At this point, if the phonogram producer 'does not offer copies of the phonogram for sale in sufficient quantity or does not make it available to the public', artists can rescind their contracts and their recordings can enter the public domain (EC 2011: §8). The Directive also has provisions for non-featured performers. In addition to gaining a longer term for their performing rights, they are for the first time given a share of other revenue streams. During the final twenty years of a sound recording's copyright life, non-featured performers are granted 20 per cent of the revenues 'from the exclusive rights of distribution, reproduction and making available of phonograms' (EC 2011: §11).

By the time this Directive was issued, the recording industry's campaign against file-sharing had foundered. As well as bringing bad publicity, it was unsuccessful in reducing this activity. Ultimately, it was this failure, rather than poor public relations, that resulted in the industry turning against it. Edgar Bronfman, who took control of the Warner Music Group in 2004, stated:

> We expected our business would remain blissfully unaffected even as the world of interactivity, constant connection, and file sharing was exploding. And

of course, we were wrong. How were we wrong? By standing still or moving at a glacial pace, we inadvertently went to war with consumers by denying them what they wanted and could otherwise find. And as a result, of course, consumers won.

(Kot 2009: 56)

Moreover, it was market forces rather than anti-piracy projects that did most to diminish the unauthorized sharing of files. In 2016, the recording industry's global revenues from on-demand streaming exceeded its revenues from downloading (IFPI 2022: 11). In its advertising-supported models, streaming offered consumers access to music that was more efficient and comprehensive than that offered by unauthorized downloading sites, but which could also be accessed for free. In this respect, the recording industry might rue that it did not listen to Lessig, who predicted this eventuality in 2004:

The 'problem' with file sharing – to the extent there is a real problem – is a problem that will increasingly disappear as it becomes easier to connect to the Internet. And thus it is an extraordinary mistake for policy makers today to be 'solving' this problem in light of a technology that will be gone tomorrow. The question should not be how to regulate the Internet to eliminate file sharing (the Net will evolve that problem away). The question instead should be how to assure that artists get paid.

(2004: 298)

Preservative

Although the recording industry can be accused of being short-sighted in respect of digital distribution, it did have a plan for the resultant payments: traditional practices should be maintained. When Nicholas Garnett wrote in 1993 of wanting to 'control the ways in which individual phonograms are released' there were three aspects of the physical market he wished to see mirrored online (HJC 1994: 36–7). First, similar to the manner in which record companies were able to set prices for their physical goods, they should have a free hand in negotiating online licensing agreements. Second, the division of digital revenue between recording rights and publishing rights should be similar to that for physical products. Third, the physical market should provide the model for artists' royalty rates, particularly once online services had matured and become 'primary'.

Recording artists have gained some benefits from the first of these measures. If interactive services had received the same legislative terms as extant performing rights, the licensing would most likely have been undertaken by collecting societies and in many territories would have been subject to governmental oversight. This could have resulted in inferior licensing deals. Recording artists have also gained from the second measure. When it comes to revenue splits between recording rights and publishing rights, online services have had more in common with physical products (where the split is approximately 90:10 in the recording rights' favour) than with licensing revenues for broadcasts (which in Britain have been split fairly evenly between recordings and songs, and in the United States have been oriented towards the publishing sector, most notably in respect of analogue broadcasting for which the recording rights receive no royalties) (Cooke 2015: 36). The benefits of the third measure have been more debatable. Broadcast revenues have been subject to equitable remuneration, with the result that royalties are split roughly equally between performers and record companies. The making available right has been made akin to the reproduction right. Therefore, as with physical products, the royalties for interactive services have been dependent on contractual negotiation. Theoretically, featured artists have had the ability to bargain for percentages higher than those of equitable remuneration. This has rarely happened in relation to traditional exclusive contracts with record companies, however. For non-featured performers the difference has been wider still. In most countries it has become established practice for them to receive royalty payments for broadcasts and public performance. The making available right has been established in a different manner to other performing rights, with the result that royalties for interactive services have commonly been denied.

The record companies' approach to digital revenues can be traced back to the early 2000s, when the major labels made attempts to counteract file-sharing by offering online services of their own. In 2001, Universal and Sony launched Pressplay, a service that granted its users access to 500 streams and fifty downloads each month, ten of which they could burn to compact discs. The subscription fee was US$14.95, equivalent to the price of a CD. The download files were subject to Digital Rights Management (DRM), which in this instance meant they expired after thirty days and could not be transferred to portable players. This service was followed by MusicNet, which was developed by the remaining majors: Warner, BMG and EMI. For a fee of US$9.95, subscribers were offered 100 streams and 100 downloads per month. The DRM for this service was even more restrictive than Pressplay's. Downloads could not be burned to CDs; the user was instead directed via a link to Amazon.com, where they were encouraged to purchase full-priced versions of the physical recordings.

Given the fact that unlicensed, free-to-use peer-to-peer services continued to proliferate in the wake of the Napster verdict, the failure of these business-to-consumer ventures should not come as a surprise. In addition to arousing little interest from the public, they were not welcomed by artist managers, who complained about the payment methodology. Although recording contracts have rarely mentioned specific exclusive rights by name, they have distinguished between different types of revenue. Most commonly there has been a demarcation between 'sales' (offering standard royalty rates, which in this period approximated between 15 per cent and 20 per cent of dealer price revenues) and 'licences' (addressing synchronization, sampling and broadcast uses, for which a 50 per cent share of revenue has regularly been applied). The managers noted that Pressplay and MusicNet 'license the music' and argued that their clients should receive half the licence fees (Strauss 2002). The artists were nevertheless paid sales percentages, including various deductions for packaging and promotional copies, despite their lack of relevance to the online world. This led to another issue that was raised by the managers: the meagre transactional rates of pay. It was calculated that recording artists were receiving just US$0.0023 per downloaded song (Strauss 2002).

These complaints would be echoed in relation to the record companies' contracts with Apple. Recordings were first licensed to the iTunes store in 2003, via deals that have remained largely intact and which have been emulated for other online services. Apple have kept around 30 per cent of revenue to 'cover running costs' and paid the remaining 70 per cent to copyright owners (Forde 2012: 30). In the United States, this money has been handled in the same manner as revenue for physical sales. It has been paid to the recording rights-holders, who have kept 90.9c in every dollar and distributed the remaining 9.1c to music publishers and composers for their mechanical royalties. This methodology has been reflective of the American position on downloads: they have not been regarded as activating the public performance right and have instead been categorized under the reproduction and distribution rights. Other countries have developed different practices. In Britain, for example, rather than receiving 70 per cent of the revenue, the recording licensors have been given a 62 per cent share, while the remaining 8 per cent has been distributed directly from Apple to publishers and composers. The publishing sector has split its revenue

75 per cent to the reproduction right and 25 per cent to the making available right, thus indicating a communication to the public element but also suggesting that downloading is more akin to physical sales than broadcasts. The British recording industry, in contrast, has regarded downloading as being wholly 'analogous to the distribution of sound recordings', which it has described as being 'a traditional record company function' (PPL 2012: 18). Therefore, a sales model has been applied.

As with Pressplay and MusicNet, objections have been raised about artist royalties. Record companies originally provided higher rates for downloads than for physical sales, but moved towards equivalence as the market matured. There was some justification for doing so, as download sites have had much in common with and provided a replacement for traditional record shops. The agreements have nevertheless taken the form of licensing deals. In 2010, F.B.T productions successfully sued Dr Dre's Aftermath Records on this point and secured a licensing rate for downloads (*F.B.T Productions v Aftermath* 2010). Several class actions followed this landmark case, but in most instances artists settled for nominal increases, with their royalties remaining 'a long way off' 50 per cent (Cooke 2016a).

On-demand streaming has been more difficult to equate with sales. It has at least as much in common with radio broadcasting as it does with reproduction. To a certain extent this has been reflected in revenue shares. After an early period in which record companies received between 55 and 60 per cent of licensing revenues, their average shares had been reduced to 52 per cent by 2017 (Hesmondhalgh et al. 2021: 114). In response, publishers gained higher payments, although these remained considerably lower than their proportionate revenues for radio broadcasting. In Europe, they optioned to circumvent some aspects of collective licensing, including oversight by governmental tribunals. This helped the publishing sector to increase revenue shares from an average of 8 per cent in 2008 to approximately 15 per cent by 2016 (Hesmondhalgh et al. 2017: 114). In the United States, the Copyright Royalty Board determined that the publishing share should rise from 11.4 per cent of the revenue in 2018 to 15.1 per cent in 2022. The difference from physical sales has also been reflected in the publishing sector's division of its revenues. In Britain, it has elected to split the money equally between the reproduction and making available rights. Practice has been similar in the United States.

The recording industry has betrayed some awareness that the access model of on-demand streaming is qualitatively different to retail. In Britain, the

Beggars Group originally offered its artists an ex gratia 50 per cent royalty rate, announcing in 2012 that they 'couldn't justify it as a "sale"' (Ingham 2012: 1). Similar policies were adopted by other labels, including the Universal Music Group for 'some' of its artists (Ingham 2013: 2). At this time, however, on-demand streaming was only worth 6.7 per cent of the recording industry's total global revenues (IFPI 2022: 11). Within two years this figure had doubled and it was apparent it would continue to multiply. The Beggars Group backtracked on its policy in 2014, stating that because streaming was now 'core income' it would have to 'bear its share of all our costs' (Smirke 2014). As a result, physical royalty rates were implemented.

This approach chimed with views the RIAA expressed in 1993, when it argued that record companies could tolerate a lower share of online revenues if the services were 'ancillary to a sale', but this would not 'be sufficient' if they were to become a primary medium for recorded music (HJC 1994: 50). By 2015, this primacy had been achieved. It was in this year that the global recording industry's combined revenues for downloads and streams overtook those for compact discs and vinyl (IFPI 2022: 11). Coinciding with this development, it became common practice for record companies to offer the same rates for streaming as for sales, with most contemporary artists receiving in the region of 15 to 20 per cent of the recording rights revenues for their work (Cooke 2015: 11).

Conclusion

The recording industry has been described as being the 'canary in the digital mine' (Page 2021: 5). It was the first of the creative industries to encounter file-sharing, and it made a series of mistakes when battling online services and attempting to retain its traditional ways of doing business. Thereafter, as it 'pivoted' towards on-demand streaming, it became an exemplar for how to embrace the new methodologies of the digital environment (Page 2021: 11–12). Yet there is an additional story to be told. Another reason why the industry prospered is because it refused to let go of the past. Although computer networking led to a questioning of the justness of copyright legislation, the recording industry defended its intellectual property rights. It was prescient in campaigning for online legislation that would operate in the same manner as the rights that underpinned physical sales. Consequently, the industry came to enjoy the benefits of interactive technologies (reduced costs, greater reach, greater availability of catalogue) while preserving advantageous aspects of its industrial past (exclusive ownership of rights, a division of revenue with the publishing sector weighted in its favour, a balance of revenue with recording artists also to its benefit). This has provided the major companies, in particular, with considerable rewards.

The remaining question is whether this balance can be maintained. Regardless of its preservative attitude, the recording industry cannot ignore the fact that online services have been transformational. The majority of its revenues are now derived from licensing. With this transition, it has assuredly become a copyright industry. Looked at from one perspective, this places record companies in a position of power. They can use their rights as bargaining chips in negotiations with online services, each of which requires access to the same wide repertoire of recordings to compete effectively. Because the rights are exclusive, the companies have the ability to withdraw access to their material. This enables them to gain favourable terms, as well as insist the services do not develop musical copyright holdings of their own. The recording industry faces challenges, nonetheless. As has been noted throughout this book, its strength in rights has been derived from its strength in manufacture. Although it has modelled the digital environment on its industrial past, it still has to deal with consequences of manufacture's decline.

7

Owning

The recording industry is following the footsteps of the music publishing industry. In the early twentieth century, publishing was dominated by manufacture, with its central focus being the publication of sheet music. It then witnessed a turn to licensing, as the mechanical right, radio broadcasting and public performance transformed its trade. As this happened, the relationship between creators and copyright owners changed. Songwriters and composers were able to request higher royalty shares. They were also able to secure shorter transfers of copyright. By the end of the century, it was common for American writers to have 50 per cent royalty rates, and the most successful could secure the return of their rights within five to fifteen years of the conclusion of their deals (Passman 2009: 262, 285). In Britain, songwriters could bargain for around 75 per cent of the publishing revenues for most uses of their music, with the rights being assigned for the term of their contracts plus an average twelve to fifteen years (Harrison 2011: 137).

Record companies are, to a certain extent, echoing this. Until 2012, the majority of their revenues were derived from manufactured goods (IFPI 2022: 11). The rise of on-demand streaming turned things around. By 2021, only 19 per cent of the industry's global trade revenues were derived from physical sales (IFPI 2022: 11). Although copyright has never been more important to record companies, artists have never had a better chance of improving their royalty rates or owning master rights. The nature of ownership has also changed. It used to be the case that, even if an artist acquired recording rights, they would have to assign them to a company for a set number of years. There are now alternatives. Rather than engaging a record label, an artist can keep hold of copyright and still get their recordings to market. They can take home the majority of the proceeds and oversee uses of their work.

This could be portrayed as the culmination of a prolonged fight against the powers that be. Finally, after decades of surrendering their material to corporate enterprises, recording artists have claimed substantial ownership of intellectual property. Some of them are promoting this fact and have become advocates for the independence of rights. It should not be forgotten, however, that prior to this period the idea of artists owning their master rights was not particularly common or vaunted. Sound recording copyright was in existence for many decades before there were concerted attempts by performers to posit themselves as its proper owners. In addition, when artists such as Prince and George Michael campaigned against their record companies, they garnered little public support from their contemporaries. While it is arguable that music makers have long deserved ownership of sound recording copyright, it is the distinct conditions of the online environment that has made this more plausible.

These conditions have led some authorities to suggest that, as well as being followed by an age of copyright, the recording industry's manufacturing era has been succeeded by the 'age of the artist' (Mulligan 2020). There is a new generation of performers who 'are helping forge a reshaped industry built upon new, more-equitably balanced contracts and deal structures' (Mulligan 2020). The situation is somewhat uneven, however. The openness of digital platforms has enabled some artists to carve out independent careers and thus raise their demands when and if they do engage with record companies. This openness has also led to more competition than before. Consequently, there are other artists who have great need for record company support to rise above this field. They therefore negotiate from a position of weakness. Moreover, while some artists have been able to 'pivot' in the online domain, there are others who remain bound by terms of the physical world. In most instances, non-featured performers gain no royalties for streaming, despite its similarity to broadcasting. Studio personnel might receive some royalties, but are unlikely to secure ownership of copyright unless doing so as labels. 'Heritage artists' with 'legacy contracts' are also experiencing difficulties (Cooke 2016b: 36–7). These terms have been coined in relation to older acts who have dedicated followings but remain tethered to their early contractual terms, most notably in respect of having low royalty rates and lacking ownership of copyright.

In response there have been campaigns to 'fix' this revenue source through copyright reform (Cooke 2020). A number of proposals have been suggested, including the implementation of reversion rights, the revision of contracts and an expansion of equitable remuneration to embrace on-demand streaming. These proposals are anathema to most record companies, the largest of whom have meanwhile been garnering substantial profits. In 2019, Sony Music CEO

Rob Stringer boasted of these returns, stating that 'The good news is that our margins are way better when compared to the last great era of profit 20 years ago; our margins are amazing now. Revenue, profit margin, market share, all of those things' (Ingham 2019b). Between 2020 and 2021, the copyright assets of the Warner Music Group increased in value by US$10 billion (Ingham 2021b). In 2021, Universal Music Group's CEO Lucian Grainge was reported to have earned more than US$150 million in wages and bonuses (Beaumont-Thomas 2021). This equalled the on-demand streaming revenue generated in the UK in 2020 for all featured artists combined (Hesmondhalgh et al. 2021: 132). In fact, rather than being threatened by a rising tide of independent performers, it is the major labels' own profitability that could provide the greatest challenge to their ways of doing business. Investment companies have seen the riches that can be derived from rights ownership and been keen to compete in this market.

This final chapter explores these tensions. Its first section addresses the move towards artist ownership; its second looks at reasons why artists are desiring and promoting this control. Following on from this, the third section details responses to this development by some sectors of the recording industry. The chapter then turns to the economics of ownership and proposals for reform. In doing so, it notes an area in which recording rights still do not mirror those for publishing. Few participants have expressed a desire to overhaul legislation so that ownership goes to the creative authors of works.

Making and buying

There are two main termination points in recording contracts: the duration of the deal (commonly decided by a series of 'options' clauses, which the record company rather than the recording artist has the right to exercise) and the duration of the transfer of rights in the recordings that have been made. Few recording artists have contracts that bind them in perpetuity. If they are not dropped by their record companies, they will reach a point when they will be able to exit or renegotiate their contracts, either after an agreed number of years or after having released an agreed number of recordings. Artists have been in a different position when it comes to ownership of the masters. Until fairly recently, nearly all new artists would have been expected to sign away copyright for the full duration of its term. The main opportunity they would have had for owning master rights would have been upon completion of their contracts.

If they had been successful, they might be in a position to sign new contracts that granted them a limited degree of ownership. Commonly, this would be future recordings only. It would also be with ownership deferred. The artists would be expected to assign their rights for a set period, after which they might finally have control of some of their recorded work.

Things have changed. Starting in the 1990s, the competitive bargaining for new acts resulted in some performers securing a limited transfer of master rights at the outset of their careers. These artists would still have encountered the power imbalance imposed by physical production, however, with their need for the manufacturing, distribution and promotional muscle of record companies resulting in contracts weighted in those companies' interests. Digitalization has occasioned greater change. Recording advances are no longer such a necessity, as it is possible to record with decent quality on digital audio workstations at home. Moreover, as industry analyst Mark Mulligan has pointed out, the 'combination of streaming, social media and artist distributors mean that artists can find global audiences without the need for a label' (Mulligan 2020). In fact, not only is it possible for artists to find audiences, this has become a necessity. Record companies will expect them to have built up fan bases before they offer them deals.

Will Page, the former chief economist for Spotify, has outlined the effects this has had on the relationship between the recording artist ('the principal') and the record company (the intermediary 'agent'), whose services the artist might want to 'buy':

> The appeal of buying into intermediaries was that they provided finance upfront and would exercise their gatekeeper power to draw a crowd in return for ownership of the resulting creation. Sign away your copyrights, receive a sizeable cheque in return and the wheels of the crowd-drawing machine would begin to turn, hopefully, in your favour. These days, the first question intermediaries ask is 'What audience are you bringing?' If the role of creating an audience has shifted back from the agent to the principal, this creates an inconvenient truth for the make-or-buy decision. Why, the principal might ask, should I cede control over my work to an agent, when the first question they ask is 'What audience can I bring to them?'
>
> (Page 2021: 134)

It is now fairly straightforward for unsigned artists to make their recordings available to the public. Some streaming services, such as YouTube and SoundCloud, are open to all users. Others, including Spotify, are closed to individual artists but it is possible to gain access by partnering with distributors. Various options can be pursued. A DIY distributor will deliver content to the streaming service and administer the revenue. An independent distributor will offer the same services as a DIY distributor, with the addition of providing some marketing support. Neither will request transfer of master rights. Rather, the independent artist will automatically assume the status of copyright owner, satisfying either the producer criteria of the WPPT or the United States' work made for hire rules. It should be noted, nonetheless, that ownership in these scenarios can be akin to that of record companies in the early twentieth century: control of the rights might make little difference to the artist's practice or revenue. It is only if another party is likely to make unauthorized use the material, license it or seek transfer of ownership that the importance of intellectual property will come into play.

If the artist is successful in gaining a following, they will arrive at the 'make or buy' decision detailed by Page: should they persist with the DIY route or is it better to contract with an intermediary? If they choose the latter option, they might wish to sign with a record company, but this is no longer the only option. Services companies provide an alternative means of getting music to market. Their agreements have some similarities to those of production companies, but are logically opposed to traditional recording contracts. Rather than receiving recording advances, the artists supply their own funds for the sessions. The input from the services company is limited to particular functions of the artists' choosing. These usually include digital distribution, marketing and royalty administration, but can also embrace synchronization licensing, manufacture of physical products, and public performance and broadcast rights management. In return for taking on an increased workload and greater financial risk, the artists gain higher royalty rates. They also retain underlying ownership of the master rights, which will be licensed to the services company, rather than assigned. The transfer will be for a fairly short period: two of the leading services companies have offered six- and twelve-year licensing deals. Some artists sign directly to services companies in what are known as 'artist services' deals; others set up their own record companies for their partnerships, and as a result come under the 'label services' banner.[1]

---

[1] The organization of artists' labels can complicate ownership of copyright. Much of the work can fall to artist managers. It has been suggested that in instances where these responsibilities include financial investment in the recordings, the managers have 'a case for shared ownership of intellectual property' (O'Riordan and Gillon 2021: 273).

As well as being available to performers at the outset of their careers, services deals have found favour with artists who have fulfilled the optional terms of their recording contracts. If they have built up large fan bases, these heritage artists will have considerable power in relation to make or buy decisions. They may have little need or desire for the personal advances, recording advances and marketing budgets of record companies, particularly when offset against the transfer of copyright and low royalty rates that tend to accompany them. While they may not be able to gain control of their earlier recordings, a services deal will give them the rights in their future work. This form of contract was initiated in 1993, when Billy Bragg entered into an agreement with the independent company Cooking Vinyl. It has since been utilized by seasoned artists such as Nick Cave, Noel Gallagher, Travis, Van Morrison, Björk, Marilyn Manson and Alice Cooper.

Meanwhile, when it comes to the most successful contemporary performers, it is now almost *de rigueur* to gain some autonomy from record labels. Speaking in 2018, a source at a leading company admitted 'the idea of a major [owning] a modern star's rights in perpetuity is pretty much dead' (Ingham 2018a). There are a number of means by which these artists are overseeing their careers. Some have set up production companies and entered into licensing agreements with major labels. Drake (in 2009), Beyoncé (in 2011), Kanye West (in 2016) and Rihanna (in 2016) have all taken this path. Star performers are not always partnering with traditional record companies, however. Roc Nation, a record label set up by Jay-Z in 2009, works with the live entertainment company, Live Nation. Other artists have partnered with online services. In 2016, Frank Ocean set up the production company Boys Don't Cry, which has been distributed by Apple Music. Chance the Rapper has remained independent of record company involvement, but granted Apple exclusive streaming rights for his 2016 album *Coloring Book.*

The desire for control

There is kudos in gaining ownership of the masters. It indicates the clawing back of control from the recording industry. In the physical era, the rejection of corporate influence could be signified by signing to an independent label. In the digital era, label names are less visible. Intellectual property has provided an alternative means for an artist to symbolize their independence. There is a difference between the two practices, nonetheless. Signing to an independent label could signal that a performer was prioritizing art and politics over financial returns. The copyright manoeuvres, in contrast, have usually been made with profits in mind. At the same time as declaring independence, ownership of copyright provides a symbol of having 'made it'.

Rights ownership has been of particular importance to artists of colour, among whom there is a sense of redressing the iniquitous deals of their predecessors. Having secured full ownership of his catalogue, Jay-Z celebrated this achievement in the recording 'We Made It', which declares, 'Hop off the slave ship… I own my own masters… I ain't missin' no royalty statements'. Chance the Rapper has been similarly vocal about his independence. His track 'No Problem' warns, 'If one more label try to stop me… it's gon' be some dread head niggas in ya lobby'. The British grime artist Wiley has meanwhile boasted in song of having '100 per cent' publishing and recording rights.[2]

Sound recording copyright has also been tactically employed. Cementing their status as master rights owners, Beyoncé, Rihanna and Kanye West were among the performers who joined with Jay-Z in 2015 to launch the artist-owned streaming service Tidal, claiming that with this action they would 'turn the tide' on previous industry practice (Popper 2015).[3] Demonstrating similar enterprise, Frank Ocean spoke of the 'seven-year-chess game' involved in buying back his master rights from Def Jam (Caramanica 2016). In order to secure his severance agreement, Ocean granted Def Jam distribution rights for his album *Endless*, which was issued 19 August 2016. Indicating his disdain for his former company, he used his own production company to release his next album the following day.

Artists have been aware of their status as role models. On winning Britain's Mercury Music Prize for his 2016 album *Konnichiwa*, Skepta stated it was his mission to encourage young Black artists to 'get out of' traditional deals, because 'DIY is the future' (Ellis-Peterson 2016). Speaking similarly of his own independent status, Chance the Rapper noted, 'I'm the first nigger to do this successfully, so I have to show a bunch of kids that they could do that shit'

---

[2] Jay Electronica ft. Jay-Z, 'We Made It (Freestyle)', written by Thedford, Carter and Rowe; Chance the Rapper ft. 2 Chainz and Lil Wayne, 'No Problem', written by Bennett, Carter, Cato, Epps, Hoard, Osteen, Rosenberg, Szymanski, Wilkins, Williams and Woods; Wiley, '100 per cent Publishing', written by Cowie.

[3] There has been a retreat from this position, albeit at a profit. Tidal was sold to the fintech firm Square in April 2021 for approximately US$300 million ('Square, Inc' 2021).

(*Joe Budden* 2018). Some distributors have sought to tap into these ideals. Sam Winwood of AWAL recalled Prince's terminology when advocating his services company, informing artists, 'you can be masters of your own destiny, you don't need to give away your rights' (*The Disrupters* 2016).

Aside from the rejection of corporate power, there has been a sense among performers that these rights are justly theirs to own. This is best evidenced by those who have sought and failed to gain control of the rights in their older recordings. The most prominent cases are provided by Taylor Swift (who was outraged when Scott Borchetta, the owner of her early masters, sold the rights to the Ithaca Holdings company in 2019) and Kanye West (who sought extrication from his contract with the Universal Music Group in 2020, demanding they give him rights to recordings made between 2004 and 2012). Both artists proclaimed their financial entitlement to have ownership of their earlier work. In doing so, West revived a familiar analogy, asking us to 'Imagine a bank lending you money to buy a house and then when you've repaid that mortgage, them telling you they still own it' (Stutz 2020). Swift argued that 'an artist should be able to earn back [their rights] over the course of their deal' (Ingham 2019a). The two performers also provided artistic justifications for ownership. Swift wrote of her sense of betrayal that music she 'dreamed up' was not hers to own (Ingham 2019a). West commented that 'we create their value' (Stutz 2020). This Romantic impulse is reflected in their suggestions that recording rights should be a legacy for artists to pass on to future generations. Swift complained of being stripped of her life's work (Ingham 2019a). West said he wanted to secure his masters for his children (Ingham 2020a).

Although Swift and West have thus far failed to gain control of the rights in their back catalogues, there is an alternative means by which artists can reclaim their early work. They can re-record it and own the rights in the new versions. Swift provides the most well-known example of doing so, but other musicians, including Jeff Lynne, Squeeze, Def Leppard and Simply Red, have also made re-recordings. They have been facilitated in this respect by the physicalist nature of sound recording copyright, as well as by the permissions that have been a feature of record contracts since the mid-twentieth century. Swift's success with her re-recordings has nevertheless prompted a re-think. Her current label, Universal Music, has doubled the length of its re-recording terms, so that artists now have to wait longer before they can remake their work (Malt 2021).

Universal has, however, granted Swift ownership of master rights in recordings made since signing with the company in 2018. She has stressed the importance of this, stating, 'I am now signed to a label that believes I should own anything I create' (Ingham 2019a). Similarly, Kanye West has rights ownership in recordings made subsequent to 2012. He has proposed a new form of music industry contract in which 'The artist owns the copyright in the recordings… and leases them to the record label/publisher for a limited term, 1 year deals' (Dredge 2020a). Mark Mulligan believes that the advocacy of these performers has led to an era of 'empowered artists' (2019a). Writing in 2019, he proclaimed, 'Any artist signing a deal now that finds themselves five years from now complaining about not having control of their masters will, to put it bluntly, only have themselves to blame' (2019a). Olivia Rodrigo provides one example of taking the idea on board, indicating that she was inspired by Swift to keep hold of the copyright in her recordings (Snapes 2021).

Artists have been campaigning for further improvements to their contractual terms. In 2016, it was estimated that musicians with exclusive recording contracts were gaining royalties for streaming services of between 15 per cent and 20 per cent of the recording rights revenue (Cooke 2016b: 35). Thus, many were getting the same rate as for physical sales. A significant issue with these payments, however, is that they had been calibrated in relation to the expenses of industrial manufacture and physical distribution. These costs are absent in the online world. To counter the claim that digital royalties should reflect this, record companies suggested that 'in the wider scheme of things… manufacture and distribution was a small part of the budget' (Cooke 2016b: 35). However, as late as 2013, it was calculated that these costs absorbed at least a quarter of record sales' revenues (Donovan 2013). Moreover, other expenses have been alleviated in the online environment. There is minimal expenditure on design and packaging, which in comparison has accounted for 5 per cent of physical sales revenues (Hesmondhalgh et al. 2021: 217). In addition, approximately 10 per cent of the dealer price for each physical record has gone to composers and publishers in respect of mechanical royalties. When it comes to on-demand streaming, it is service providers who bear this cost. The recording industry has therefore provided another justification for the continuance of physical royalty rates, arguing that its investments in A&R and marketing have 'gone up' (Cooke 2016b: 35). There is, however, little evidence of these payments increasing considerably. The BPI, for example, documented only a slight rise in the A&R expenditure of British labels between 2010 and 2019; in the same period costs of marketing went down (Hesmondhalgh et al. 2021: 126).

Against this background, traditional record companies have made some allowances. In 2018, it was reported that streaming royalties for artists signing with major labels had risen to an average 18 per cent rate (Ingham 2018b). In Britain, the Musicians' Union was nevertheless advising that 'Anyone who signs a deal for less than 30 points on streaming needs their head examined' (Sexton 2017: 12). By 2019, this figure appeared to be within reach. The major labels suggested that their average royalties for streaming were now at 25 per cent (Ingham 2019c). At the top end, for established artists with 'newly renegotiated' contracts, there was a possible 30 per cent rate (CC Young 2020).

These royalties have nevertheless paled in comparison to those gained by artists who have ownership of copyright. Rates for services companies vary, but an average royalty of 70 per cent has been 'assumed' (MMF n.d.). Artists with distribution deals have been able to gain a 90 per cent rate, while fully independent artists have been able to obtain 100 per cent of the recording rights revenues (Voogt 2019). Copyright-owning artists have been able to gain other benefits as well. It has been possible for them to access both halves of the equitable remuneration for the public performance and broadcast of their recordings: a percentage as rights owners and a percentage as performers. In addition, they have been able to oversee the repackaging of their back catalogues and have thus profited from lucrative sales of special editions and box sets.

Beyond this, some artists have gained what could be regarded as the ultimate financial benefit of having control of copyright. Rather than licensing or assigning their rights, they have sold ownership outright. This would appear to run counter to previous ambitions. Having sought high royalty rates and ownership of the masters, they have signed both away in perpetuity. These one-off payments have, however, spared artists from having to deal with the complexities and challenges of rights administration. A more fundamental reason for these sales is that the prices offered have reached disorienting amounts, particularly for those who are at the point in their careers to consider 'estate planning' (Hanley 2021: 37). A few examples from 2021 will suffice. David Guetta negotiated in excess of US$100 million for his recordings (Ingham 2021c); Mötley Crüe gained a tenfold return on their investment when selling their masters (Smith 2021); providing an indication of the long duration of American sound recording copyright, the Bing Crosby estate secured approximately US$50 million for his recordings (Stassen 2021b); Bruce Springsteen's master rights were valued at US$195 million (Christman 2021).[4] David Bowie's were speculated as being worth US$1 billion (Ingham 2021d).

---

[4] This figure was derived using a common methodology for calculating the value of master rights: the average gross yearly profits of the recordings were multiplied by twenty (Christman 2021).

Investing in music

Between 2010 and 2016, the IFPI released a biennial series of reports titled *Investing in Music*, which represent its thoughts on these new ways of doing business. When the series began, the compact disc was still the leading format in terms of global revenue. By the time it concluded, on-demand streaming had taken over. The reports have a consistency, nonetheless. They each state that new artists are the 'lifeblood' of the industry (2010: 6–7; 2012: 7, 9; 2014: 6; 2016: 10); they boast how record companies invest more money in 'research and development' than the pharmaceutical and biotechnology sector (2012: 9; 2014: 9); and they proclaim that in order to provide this nurturing environment, the companies need long and secure ownership of master rights: 'It is copyright that makes investment in music possible. It is copyright that allows the industry that helps artists gain a return on its investment' (2014: 4). During this period Placido Domingo was chairman of the IFPI. In his opinion, rather than calling the reports *Investing in Music*, they 'could also be titled *Investing in Copyright*' (2014: 4).

The IFPI's claims should not be wholly gainsaid. Throughout this period and beyond, traditional record labels have provided the launchpad for the majority of commercially successful new acts. They have also been best placed to afford this. The reports indicate how much money it would take to bring a new project to fruition. A spend of 'between $200,000 and $500,000' in 2012 had risen to 'between US$0.5 million and US$2 million' by 2016 (2012: 11; 2016: 6). Marketing is shown as the major component of these costs, reaching US$200,000–US$700,000 by the final report (2016: 6). The IFPI suggested this money would be spent regardless of the final outcome. Evidence is provided by Nick Raphael, president of Capitol Records UK, who states, 'We put just as much effort and money, if not more so, into the acts that don't succeed as with those that do' (IFPI 2014: 9). There is plenty that is glossed over, nonetheless. The reports do not mention the strategic prioritization of acts, nor do they address the major companies' role in establishing high rates of expenditure. In addition, copyright is not discussed as something that provides profit for the companies. The IFPI reiterate, instead, that revenues will be ploughed into the future. Labels will 'reinvest the proceeds of successful campaigns in the discovery and nurturing of the next generation of talent' (2012: 7).

New music is employed in service of tradition. According to the IFPI, there had been 'a mistaken belief among some that the role of labels would be diminished in the digital age' (IFPI 2014: 6). Downloading and streaming made audible a 'long tail' of musicians, many of whom were placing their recordings online without the help of traditional record companies (Anderson 2009). The IFPI's daunting expenditure figures belittle this activity. Few independent artists would have the requisite US$500,000 to compete for mainstream recognition, a sum the trade body suggested would be spent whether or not the project was a success. The IFPI were not advocating deals for all artists in the long tail; their message was that a recording contract was necessary for those who wished to reach the head.

Newness additionally provided a means of undermining rival businesses. Services companies were condemned by the IFPI for not having new music in their blood. One of the original critiques of their agreements was that they were the preserve of heritage acts; it was suggested these companies could only afford to forgo ownership of copyright because they did not invest in young artists ('Years of Service' 2015: 9). The IFPI employed this thinking to argue for the reverse: the record labels' own 'virtuous cycle of investment' could only be maintained if they were granted ownership of recordings for the full duration of copyright (2010: 5).

In making this argument, the trade body was ignoring the development of services deals, which had moved beyond being the preserve of seasoned performers. In 2016, Skepta's debut album was released via the label services company, Red Essential. In the same period, Stormzy entered into a services deal with Alternative Distribution Alliance for the release of his debut, *Gang Signs & Prayer*. (It has also been suggested that Taylor Swift's Universal contract is in the form of 'a long-term label services type deal' (Mulligan 2018).) The IFPI also overlooked the fact that each of the majors had purchased or set up distribution and services companies of its own. Sony acquired the Orchard in 2012; Warner set up the Alternative Distribution Alliance in the same year; Universal established Caroline in 2013.

More broadly, the role of traditional record companies was changing. They had formerly been oriented business-to-consumer, but recording artists were now leading the way in having 'interactive experiences with their fans' (Passerard and Cartwright 2019). As a result, rather than focusing on the needs of audiences, record companies were reoriented 'business-to-artist'; their main function was to act 'as financial and marketing companies' (Passerard and Cartwright 2019). In return, recording artists were using labels 'as accelerators rather than long-term partners' (Mulligan 2021a). They were also requesting a shorter transfer of rights.

The economics of ownership

In the *Investing in Music* series, the IFPI suggested that record companies would only have sufficient funds to invest in new music if given long-term assignment of copyright. This formula could now appear awry. In the years since the final report was issued, the lifetime assignment of copyright has less commonly been achieved, yet the profits of the largest companies have increased considerably (Hesmondhalgh et al. 2021: 123–8). Moreover, the major labels have managed to sign a larger number of artists than ever before. Sony Music, for example, has been investing in 'everything and anywhere' (Stassen 2021c).

There are, however, a number of reasons why record companies are continuing to prosper. In the first instance, they are deriving a significant proportion of their revenue from older copyright holdings. There are many heritage performers without the power or inclination to claim their intellectual property. Additionally, there are significant copyright catalogues the companies have refused to let go. Although Jay-Z, Rihanna and Frank Ocean have managed to gain rights ownership of their early recordings, most of the new agreements entered into by superstar artists are for future work only. This includes the surviving members of the Beatles, whose 1960's repertoire continues to be owned by the Parlophone label. The streaming era has, if anything, increased the profits from back catalogue. The ease of online distribution has meant a vast number of older recordings have been made available for consumption. It has been relatively inexpensive to do so, as record companies have not had to bear significant costs of manufacture, distribution, packaging or mechanical royalties. In addition, the costs of marketing and promoting these recordings are considerably lower than for new releases. The main rewards from this catalogue have usually gone to record labels rather than artists, as many of the latter are still being paid physical royalty rates.

Remastering provides a second, related explanation for the well-being of record companies. This is the process of returning to a master recording (and sometimes its component multi-track recordings) and reworking it to make a new final mix. There is aesthetic justification for remastering: it updates recordings for new ways of listening. Record companies derive economic benefits as well. Although the legislative status is unclear, the recording industry believes that a remastered recording warrants a new copyright if a change from the original is audibly apparent. With a new publication date, the period of copyright protection can be prolonged. Record companies can remove earlier versions of the recordings from circulation, ensuring the remasters have precedence. This provides them with a longer term in which to gain revenues from sales, downloading and streaming. In the United States, it has also helped them to gain performing rights remuneration from what would otherwise be regarded as pre-1972 recordings (Cooke 2018). In Britain and the European Union, it aids them in postponing the more costly effects of the 2011 term extension directive, namely its clean slate provisions and 20 per cent royalty for non-featured performers. As can be expected, remastering is most common for recordings nearing the end of their copyright term (the Beatles' repertoire, for example, was remastered in 2009 and given a (p) date of that year; the group's latter albums have subsequently been remastered again). The process does entail costs: aside from the expense of remastering, it might require renegotiation of the artists' royalty rates, as they can be regarded as having provided new work. The artists do not always have a strong negotiating position, however. This is because it is standard contracting practice that the company has ownership of the multi-track and final master recordings. Moreover, this 'physical' ownership is separate to the rights in the recordings and can reside with the company even if the artist manages to secure the return of copyright. This provides one reason why rights-holding artists might wish to partner with their former companies in respect of back catalogue.

A third reason for the companies' continued prosperity is that the industry has not been fully 'reshaped' (Mulligan 2020). Although the majors have acquired distribution companies, it is their traditional recording contracts, with the transfer of copyright, that remain their preferred model. Jason Iley, chairman and chief executive of Sony Music UK & Ireland, has spoken begrudgingly of high-profile artists who have signed with partner companies rather than directly to his label:

> Today, three of the most culturally important acts – Jorja Smith, AJ Tracey and Skepta – have chosen to sign to a distribution company. They want a bigger share of the revenue and that is their choice. With respect to them and their management, that is their decision. I clearly would prefer them to sign to Sony Music.
>
> (2021: Q252)

Although these artists have their independence, there is an explanation why others might opt for major company deals. As previously noted, while the openness of the internet has provided democratizing benefits for musicians, it has also meant there is more competition. Mulligan analysed trade figures for 2018 and found that DIY artists generated just 3 per cent of recording industry revenue, artists signed to service companies generated 5 per cent, and the share accorded to artists signed to traditional record companies amounted to 92 per cent (2019b: 13). The 3 per cent market share accorded to DIY distribution was divided between 3.7 million acts; the 5 per cent gained by services companies was distributed between 400,000 more. In order to escape this long tail, some artists desire the marketing expenditure only major labels can afford. This is where Page's 'make or buy' decision is crucial. These artists have to calculate whether the increased sales, exposure and streaming activity that can be gained by signing with a major will provide sufficient compensation for other aspects of their deals. They will have to accept lower royalty rates than could be gained by partnering with services companies. They will also usually have to accede to a longer transfer of rights: the opening negotiating point of major labels is still to request lifetime assignment (DCMS 2001: §44, §115).

A fourth reason for the record companies' good health is that, even in instances where they do not have full-term ownership of copyright, they still control the material during its most rewarding period of activity. Research conducted for the *Gowers Review* in 2006 indicated that 'most sound recordings sell in the ten years after release, and only a very small percentage continue to generate income, both from sales and royalty payments, for the entire duration of copyright' (2006: §4.33). Streaming has reaffirmed this pattern, with listener activity being concentrated on recordings from the most recent decade (Green 2020: 28). These ten years tend to come under the companies' purview, as the vast majority of their contractual agreements incorporate this span. In addition, recording contracts usually stipulate that an artist cannot re-record their material – whether for a rival label or for the artist's own company – within this period of greatest economic activity.

A final point is that, in addition to making money from rights ownership, the major record companies have found other ways to profit from copyright. They are gaining increasing influence as the distributors of titles, some of which they own but others they administer, such as the recordings derived from the services companies, DIY distributors, production companies and smaller labels with whom they partner. This catalogue is of such importance that alternative terminology has been favoured: the companies are now more regularly referred to as 'rights-holders' rather than 'rights owners'. These broader copyright holdings are vital in their agreements with online services. The major labels have tens of thousands of titles they can threaten to withdraw if the services do not offer them favourable terms. It is this overall catalogue that is employed when negotiating revenue shares, minimal guarantees and equity, and it is the market share gained by this wider catalogue that determines the payments from the services. It also signifies the status of the record company in comparison to its rivals and provides an indication of its worth to investors. Moreover, it is the deals and market shares achieved by the larger labels that encourage artists, distributors and production companies to sign with them in the first place, thus representing another virtuous cycle of investment that suits the majors' needs.

Services companies and DIY distributors have undoubtedly influenced the ways in which traditional record companies are operating. Will Ahdritz, the founder of AWAL, proclaimed that his company 'fundamentally chang[ed] the cost structure of recorded music business' (Ingham 2021e). However, these businesses have not yet undermined the status of major labels. In fact, it is services companies that have struggled rather than the other way round. AWAL, for example, had fundamental debts and was sold to Sony Music in 2021. In a related manner, some star artists who signed contracts with outside entities (such as Madonna, who partnered with Live Nation for her record releases) are turning to major label agreements, as are artists previously signed to independents (such as Adele, who moved from XL to Sony in partnership with her own label Melted Stone).

Rather than undermining its position, streaming has thus far provided rewards for the established recording industry. Globally, there was a year-on-year fall in trade revenues from 2001 to 2014 (IFPI 2022: 11). Since then there has been a steady revival, leading to 2021, when pre-inflation millennial revenues were surpassed (IFPI 2022: 22). It has been the major labels who have benefited the most. In 2021, they were generating US$2.5 million every hour (Ingham 2021a). In September of the same year, the Universal Music Group was floated on the Amsterdam stock exchange with an opening valuation of US$54.3 billion (Stassen 2021a). Counterintuitively, it is these financial gains that might end up causing the greatest detriment to their market shares. As Mulligan has indicated, rather than being gained from specialist skills of record production, record company revenue is increasingly derived from the provision of venture capital (Mulligan 2021a). Other financers are available. Tim Ingham has noted how in the wake of the Universal Music Group's flotation, '*everyone* wants in to music rights' (2021f. Emphasis in original). Investment companies had already begun to make their presence felt, but 'the giants of the financial world are now really waking up to the modern music business's true value – and they're throwing billions at it' (2021f). According to Ingham, these financers could transform the industry 'forever' (2021f).

Reform

Record companies are also facing campaigns for reform. On-demand streaming has produced a climate in which 'fared use' is pervasive (Bell 1998). Each time a recording is accessed, a payment has to be made. This has not made music scarce. In fact, it is now possible for the public to access the world's music for 'free', as it is advertisers who pay for the vast majority of streams. This includes the main output of the largest distributor, YouTube. Streaming activity does not equate with revenues, however. This is because advertising-supported services pay lower licensing rates than subscription services. Overall, the digital economy is underpinned by consumers. In 2021, subscription services were responsible for nearly three-quarters of the recording industry's global streaming revenues, with advertisers contributing the remainder (IFPI 2022: 11). Per capita spend on recorded music has been increasing as well. In 2022, Spotify claimed that, globally, the average adult 'is spending nearly double compared to during the peak CD era in 1999, and millions more people are spending' (Spotify 2022).

There are other aspects of the digital economy that might make copyright pessimists blanche. Although streaming has increased the tendency of artists to own their masters, to date it is record companies who have profited most from the revenue increase. Streaming operates at scale and favours those who have multiple copyright holdings rather than owners of individual titles. There have been parallel situations in the past, most notably in relation to the licensing of public performances and broadcasts. In these instances, however, individual copyright owners came together to form collecting societies, which have operated for them on a mutual and non-profit-making basis. Streaming is different. The making available right has enabled record companies and distributors to undertake licensing in lieu of collecting societies. As a result, artists are required to turn to these rights-holders to fulfil their collective needs.

Streaming is similar to public performance and broadcast in that licensing revenue is divided between artists in accordance with their overall share of listening activity. Yet it differs in three key respects. First, in the scale of activity.

In 2021, it was reported that Spotify alone had more than 70 million tracks on its platform, with a further 60,000 uploaded every day (Ingham 2021g). Second, in the fact that, unlike collecting societies, it is the goal of record companies and distributors to make a profit from their repertoire. They want a share of revenue that exceeds costs of administration. Third, in the diversity of artists' royalty rates. Collecting societies have provided fairly uniform divisions of revenue. In contrast, the agreements offered by record companies, distributors and services companies vary widely.

Streaming companies have been keen to outline their viability for musicians. For the year 2021, Spotify published data illustrating that over 1,000 artists had each 'generated' more than US$1 million from its service alone (Spotify 2022). The word 'generated' was carefully chosen, as the figures represent the total Spotify revenues for the recordings rather than the share the artists will receive. The most successful copyright-owning performers have done well in this environment, as they have been able to combine high royalty rates with a high volume of activity. This includes the 14,700 DIY artists who each generated more than US$10,000 from Spotify in 2021 (Spotify 2022). However, in this same year Spotify had over 8 million different artists on its service, out of whom it estimated 200,000 were 'professional or professionally aspiring recording acts' (Spotify 2022). For the majority of these performers, the coupling of high streaming activity and sustainable payments has been hard to achieve. This has led artists to complain that streaming is 'broken' (Dredge 2020b) and artist organizations to talk of a need to 'fix' the system of payments (Cooke 2020). Given the increase in trade revenues and rise in consumer spending, these complaints have received a sympathetic ear from authorities and politicians. WIPO reported back that there is a 'systemic problem' that is penalizing performers (Castle and Feijóo 2021: 10). The British government launched an inquiry into the economics of music streaming (UK Parliament 2021).

Some of the campaigns have been spearheaded by heritage artists, with those who have been accorded physical royalty rates for online services feeling most aggrieved. This ill-feeling has been more pronounced among those who have not recouped their balances, as the micro payments from streaming have been unlikely to get them on even terms. A number of solutions have been explored and proposed. In the United States, artists have pointed towards the 1976 Copyright Act's termination rules and insisted that recording rights be returned to them after a period of thirty-five years. Some have launched cases against their labels, while others have reached out of court agreements. Prince was in the latter camp, making a settlement with the Warner Music Group shortly before he died. This deal finally secured him ownership of his early recordings, but his former label gained exclusive licensing rights in return (Collins 2014). In Europe there have been calls for a reversion right that would operate similarly. If implemented, it might in some instances be more effective than American termination measures, as continental contracting practice indicates a clear transfer of rights, rather than stating they will be regarded as assigned only if found not to be work made for hire. In other instances, it might be weaker, as European legislation tends to posit record companies as the original authors. Thus, the artists may have no rights to revert.

Performers have in addition campaigned for the 'contract adjustment mechanism' that is outlined in the European Council's 2019 Copyright Directive. When implemented in local laws, they hope it will enable them to claim 'appropriate and fair remuneration... when the remuneration originally agreed turns out to be disproportionately low compared to all the subsequent relevant revenues' (EC 2019: art. 20). Due to UK's departure from the European Union, it will not implement this Directive. Local trade bodies have nevertheless pushed for heritage artists to be paid 'the same royalty rate on old recordings as most new artists are on newer recordings' (MMF and FAC 2021). Meanwhile, some record labels have acted on their own initiative. This includes Britain's largest independent record company, the Beggars Group, which revised its contracts so a 25 per cent digital royalty is the base rate for all artists, new and old. Reflecting the artist-centric focus of the contemporary industry, Beggars said this was 'the fair and right' thing to do (Ingham 2019d). Some multinational companies have moved in a similar direction. In 2020, following the death of George Floyd and the return to prominence of the Black Lives Matter movement, BMG pledged to 'review all historic contracts' of artists of colour to address 'inequities or anomalies' (Ingham 2020b). In 2021, the Sony Music Group declared it would 'not apply' the unrecouped balances of any artists who signed contracts in the previous millennium (Cooke 2021). In 2022, the Warner Music Group and Universal introduced similar policies.

Non-featured performers have also felt hard done by. On-demand streaming operates similarly to radio. It triggers a communication to the public right and its playlists provide a comparable form of listening. It is also threatening to take radio's place: Spotify has ambitions of 'sucking listeners away' (Dredge 2021a). Yet on-demand streaming differs from broadcast in that there is no equitable remuneration. Faced with this potential reduction to their payments, non-featured performers have campaigned for reform. In 2015, FIM proposed that on-demand streaming should be regarded as representing a fifty/fifty split between the reproduction right and making available right, with the latter element being subject to equitable remuneration (Trubridge 2015). This suggestion fed into the Fair Internet for Performers (FIFP) campaign, launched the same year. FIFP is an alliance of performers' organizations that has sought equitable rights for streaming services within European law. Its crusade initially coincided with an EU investigation into the 'contentious grey area' of the making available right (EC 2015: 9). FIFP had little success, however. When the EU introduced its Copyright Directive in 2019, it made no mention of the making available right or of equitable remuneration. The Directive instead contains the 'fair remuneration' of its contract adjustment mechanism, which FIFP suggested 'may prove useless in practice and not help those performers who are most in need' (FIFP 2017a: 2).

As can be expected, this campaign did not receive backing from record companies, who would lose out if their rights-holders share of streaming revenues was pegged to 50 per cent. Featured artists were also initially reluctant to provide support. FIFP speak on behalf of 'performers who simply transfer all their rights to the producer for a single payment' and have thus been targeted towards non-featured performers (FIFP 2017b). In Britain, the Featured Artists' Coalition (FAC) placed itself alongside record companies, arguing that exclusive rights are 'stronger and better' than equitable remuneration (Aguilar 2018: 170).

There has been a reversal. Prior to 2020, many featured artists had already been concerned about revenues from streaming. This feeling was exacerbated when the coronavirus pandemic put their earnings from live music on hold. Despite it being the supposed 'age of the artist', there was a sense that royalties from online services were 'never going to add up' (Mulligan 2021b). In Britain, a significant crusade was led by Tom Gray of the band Gomez. As well as playing a large part in inaugurating a governmental inquiry into the economics of streaming, his 'broken record' campaign brought together a number of high-profile artists to write to Prime Minister Boris Johnson and demand a 'two word' change to the CDPA (Paine 2021). If implemented, it would result in equitable remuneration being applied to the making available right.

The signatories to Gray's letter include Lily Allen, Jazzie B, Kate Bush, the Chemical Brothers, Roger Daltry, Brian Eno, Peter Gabriel, David Gilmour, John Paul Jones, Kano, Linton Kwesi Johnson, Mark Knopfler, Annie Lennox, Roots Manuva, Laura Marling, Paul McCartney, Laura Mvula, Stevie Nicks, Orbital,

Jimmy Page, Robert Plant, Chris Rea, Tim Rice, Robert Smith and Sting. Their support could be considered odd. Equitable remuneration has been indicative of legislative weakness. It was initially granted to performers as a companion to the neighbouring rights of producers, suggesting they should receive at least some form of payment in respect of recorded performances. Neighbouring rights, in turn, have been viewed as a secondary form of intellectual property, awarded to master rights-holders and performers because they have not been deemed worthy of authorial recognition. Equitable remuneration would provide these featured artists with little flexibility in comparison to having exclusive controls. It could also put them in a worse situation financially.[5]

There is nevertheless a sense of shared interests. Musicians are harking back to the co-operative spirit that underpinned the original creation of performers' rights. Their target has been different, however, in that record companies as well as licensees are in their sights. Gray's letter to Boris Johnson states, 'For too long, streaming platforms, record labels and other internet giants have exploited performers and creators without rewarding them fairly. We must put the value of music back where it belongs – in the hands of music makers' (Paine 2021). Equitable remuneration is the one form of recording revenues administrated in a truly collective fashion. It has also been safeguarded from contractual transfer. In this respect, it has some assured financial benefits for featured artists, as it cannot be recouped from rights-holders advances.

Few advocates have proposed that equitable remuneration should be implemented for the entirety of on-demand streaming revenues. One suggestion is to apply it to the making available element of streaming only, albeit that the extent of that element is not legislatively defined (Trubridge 2015). Others have proposed that it be restricted to 'passive' algorithmic activity (CC Young 2020). A further idea, implemented in Spain and endorsed by a WIPO study, is for a supplementary 'streaming remuneration' right that would work alongside the

---

[5] If contemporary rates were to be applied, the performers' remuneration would be limited to 50 per cent of the revenues, with the other half going to the rights-holders. This would offer an improvement for most artists with traditional recording contracts, but a lower rate than others currently achieve. The payments would be overseen by collecting societies, which could prove costly. Societies charge administration rates. They do not have the negotiating power of exclusive rights-holders: they have to offer blanket licences (and thus cannot threaten to withdraw their material); their licensing agreements can be referred to governmental tribunals (resulting in poorer terms than could be achieved on the open market). Some featured artists could therefore be worse off if equitable remuneration were implemented for streaming. In addition to the possibility of lower revenue shares, they would in many cases have to divide the remuneration with non-featured performers, whereas this is not the case with their current payments.

rights of reproduction and making available (Castle and Feijóo 2021). For the remainder of their revenues, as well as the money generated by physical sales, downloading, synchronization and digital sampling, the ideal of many featured artists is still to gain authority by owning copyright. In doing so, they will cast themselves as corporate authors.

A creative sound recording copyright

One striking feature of the proposals for reform is that none of them has sought to address the fundamental imbalance in music copyright legislation. The Berne Convention awards ownership of rights in musical works to their composers. The term is tied to their lifetimes. They are formalist rather than physicalist: you do not have to copy a work exactly in order to plagiarize it. The Rome Convention and the WPPT treat sound recordings differently. Ownership is given to producers. The term is linked to dates of production. The rules of plagiarism remain resolutely physicalist. Even in the United States, where there is some recognition of sound recordings as creative works, the rights take on an industrial hue due to work made for hire rules. None of the stakeholders in contemporary debates has suggested it is time, finally, to reward the originators of sound recordings. There have been no calls for recordings to be embraced by Berne or for the WPPT to recognize creative authorship, nor have there been any demands to exempt sound recordings from works made for hire legislation and for the United States Copyright Act to restrict ownership to the recording artists 'whose performance is captured' and to studio personnel responsible for 'capturing and electronically processing the sounds' (SJC 1971: 5).

Proposals have been made by legal scholars, however. Lionel Bently believes the law is in need of modification so it can 'reflect the peculiar features of popular music, in particular the importance of sound' (2009: 196). He has therefore suggested an 'original works of sound' copyright category that would match the copyright in musical compositions in respect of 'duration, moral rights, and what constitutes copyright infringement' (2009: 196). This copyright would be awarded to the performer-writers of recordings, reflecting Bently's belief that the musical arrangement that arises during the recording process is a form of composition (2009: 196). He has maintained that this categorization would 'save copyright law from being asked to invent "musical works" (and, indeed, "performances") in circumstances… where the musical artefact is created in the recording studio (and subsequently marketed, appreciated and consumed) by way of such recording' (2009: 196). The resultant 'works of sound' copyright would be wide-ranging. Bently believes it would remove the need for a songwriting copyright for popular music as well as the equitable remuneration rights of performers. He has nevertheless suggested that a producer-owned sound recording copyright should exist alongside it (2009: 196).

Bently's conception would appear to have a number of advantages for the creators of sound recordings. Their work would gain the same legislative status as musical compositions. Authorship would be awarded in respect of creativity. The music makers would therefore not have to compete with recording companies for the initial ownership of rights. The copyright would also commonly last longer than it does now, as it would be tied to their lifetimes rather than dates of production. Yet there are a number of reasons why it might be resisted. At a practical level, it would require an overhaul of legislation that could be unrealistically ambitious. In comparison to the 'two-word' change that artists have advocated to expand the use of equitable remuneration, Bently's suggestion would require a re-writing of international copyright treaties, followed by updates to national laws.

There are conceptual difficulties as well. The 'works of sound' copyright is rooted in a distinct period of recording history and a particular way of making records. Bently envisions recordings being created in 'totality' in professional studios, where musicians simultaneously combine the acts of composition, performance and production in developing their work (2009: 185). This overlapping mode of creation was perhaps true of some progressive rock groups of the 1970s, but is now generally restricted to artists creating electronic music from scratch on digital audio workstations. Elsewhere, rather than coalescing, the division of labour has widened. As the twenty-first century has elapsed, there have been fewer self-contained groups creating material in studio settings. The credits for composition and performance have consequently diverged. Bently provides some insurance against this, outlining how 'Popular music that is created in the old-fashioned way, where the song is developed outside the studio and later recorded will generate two works: "musical work" and "original work of sound"' (2009: 185). The distinctions between the two are not necessarily clear-cut, however, and would pose difficult decisions about licensing arrangements and fees. They would also prove problematic in respect of cover versions. It would need to be decided whether the new version is utilizing the musical work copyright, the work of sound copyright or both.

It would also need to be determined whether cover versions warrant original works of sound copyrights of their own.

Another concern with Bently's proposal is that it would result in an expansion of legislation. Any increase to the term would raise alarm bells with copyright pessimists (even if its effects might be moot, given that, if undertaken repeatedly, the remastering process already has the potential to extend the duration of sound recording copyright indefinitely). In addition, there is evidence that recording artists might have concerns about a separate aspect of 'ratcheting up' the law (Sell 2010). Recording practice has developed in a physicalist context, providing musicians with the freedom to mimic timbres and production techniques. Few artists would want to close down these opportunities by acknowledging a copyright in which the 'form' of a sound recording could be protected and therefore infringed (Barron 2006: 113). This can be discerned from the 'Blurred Lines' copyright case (*Williams v Bridgeport Music* 2013). Although centred on compositional rights, it has offered a scenario in which the 'feel' of a recording can be protected by law. Rather than supporting this position, a significant number of musicians signed an amicus brief against it (Gardner 2016).

In a different respect, Bently overestimates the importance of copyright's classifications. Although his works of sound categorization would enhance the reputation of recordings within legislation, it would make little difference to their standing elsewhere. The biases of the law have not affected the economics of the music industries. In most countries, the revenues for recording rights exceed those for music publishing rights. In 2020, for example, the total global revenues from uses of sound recording copyright were valued at US$21.1 billion, while those for musical works were valued at US$11.4 billion (Dredge 2021b). In addition, recording rights-holders have a more prominent role and are usually first to the table in respect of online licensing agreements (Cooke 2016b: 32, 54).

Legislation has also had limited influence when it comes to aesthetic regard. Although the creativity of studio work has rarely been acknowledged in law, interest in the 'art of record production' has nevertheless grown (Frith and Zagorski-Thomas 2012). Furthermore, even though sound recording copyright overlooks the artistry of performers, this has not meant that its acquirement has belittled their status. In fact, some artists may have gained greater respect by obtaining copyright on economic grounds than they would for receiving it in respect of creativity. This is perhaps most notable in relation to artists of colour, particularly those working in genres where art and business are entwined. Music copyright can accurately be critiqued for having a Eurocentric view of creativity and for overlooking the skills of performance. This has, however, been most evident in the legislation and case law for compositions. Sound recording copyright, in contrast, has been demonstrative of financial acumen. As such, it has provided a platform on which these biases can be overturned.

A further reason why music makers might not unify behind a creative sound copyright is that the effects would be uneven. Martin Kretschmer and Friedemann Kawohl have argued that once artists become successful, their legal interests tend to 'align' with those of corporations (2004: 44). Sound recording can be regarded as the prime example of this: recording artists have needed to portray themselves as business-like entities to secure ownership of rights. During the work made for hire hearings that took place in 2000, Hilary Rosen warned that if sound recording copyright was to be recognized on artistic rather than economic grounds, this would pluralize claims to ownership, with studio producers, engineers and non-featured performers all demanding their share (HJC 2000: 129). As well as leading to a wider division of royalties, she maintained this would problematize licensing procedures, as each owner would need to be contacted to authorize the use of a recording. The RIAA have continued with this line of reasoning, arguing that it is because of the centralized control of master rights that recordings are effectively licensed to online services. Compositions, in comparison, have 'multiple co-owners' and 'frequent changes ownership', which is why they have been more likely to get tied up in disputes (USCO 2016a: 127). It is the RIAA's argument that any recording artists who have managed to gain copyright by configuring themselves as a record companies would be foolish to campaign for a legislative system that recognizes their creative work.

Conclusion

This leaves us with the possibility for an extremely pessimistic reading. Sound recording copyright leaves intact many of the failings of copyright legislation. It makes steady encroachments on the public domain; it replaces fair use with a policy of 'fared use'; it favours big corporations rather than the creators of works. It then compounds these problems while adding difficulties of its own. Practices have become entrenched and there is little inclination for a fundamental overhaul of legislation. Consequently, the creative impulse of this copyright has been negated. Music makers cast themselves as businesses to acquire ownership. They do so in a self-serving manner, being content to dispossess other artists as long as their own interests can be secured. Against this background, the larger majority of music makers are treated punitively and it is record companies that reap the main rewards from investing in copyright.

Yet, for those who believe that music makers should be the recipients of this copyright, there are reasons to be hopeful. The maintenance of underlying categories has not meant there is inertia. Sound recording copyright and performers' rights have proved adaptive, both in relation to the tweaking of their measures and in the ability of their terminology to embrace different recipients. The move towards artist ownership has been both widespread and generative. The turn to licensing has enabled a larger cohort of musicians to claim control of their rights. Set against a background of DIY rights-holders, artists with services agreements and superstar performers proclaiming the virtues of owning the masters, it is now more common for musicians to gain concessions when negotiating traditional label deals. Although the default starting position of major record companies is still to request lifetime assignment of rights, this is matched by a standard response from artist representatives. They want a transfer of shorter duration and are seeking licence rather than assignment.

Overall, the tide does appear to be turning. We are moving towards a situation in which all new contracts for featured artists will provide them with at least some opportunity for owning copyright, whether this is from the outset or deferred. Moreover, the improved terms in these agreements are helping to encourage revisions elsewhere. First, record companies are introducing voluntary measures in respect of legacy contracts. In some instances, the recoupment of heritage artists is being waived; in others, their royalties are being raised. As well as needing to appear performer-friendly in the age of the artist, the companies are hoping to resist government intervention and hence are implementing these measures in preference to having their control of copyright curtailed. Second, the situation for non-featured performers might also be improved. They face a possible decline in their broadcast payments and are being denied equitable remuneration for on-demand streaming. Featured artists are, however, providing support. In doing so, they are demonstrating a combination of altruism and self-interest akin to the record companies' voluntary measures. They are advocating equitable remuneration for streaming, even though it might not be of immediate financial benefit to them. The proposals are nuanced, however, and would enable featured artists to balance a portion of revenues for which they negotiate their royalties with a portion that has a fixed rate and which cannot be recouped. Lastly, there is evidence of greater recognition for the creative work of studio producers and engineers. The United States Copyright Act was updated in 2018 to provide them with a share of remuneration from digital subscription radio services. This is made in respect of their 'creative contribution to the creation of the sound recording' (1976: §114).

Are these developments good for the wider ecosystem of recorded music? In addition to protecting authors, copyright is supposed to stimulate creativity. Record companies have played upon this notion, making dire warnings about the consequences for new music if they lose ownership of their back catalogues. They have argued that, should they be deprived of its rewards, they will not have sufficient funds for future investment. If this theory were true, we could be in the early stages of an endgame. The combined impact of shorter copyright transfer, increased royalty rates, further equitable remuneration and uptake of offers from their rivals could eventually place a squeeze on record company profits and lead to their demise. Are we in a situation, then, in which artists' desire to own copyright could work against the interests of art? This seems unlikely. Musicians will continue to make recordings whether or not there are record companies. Where the companies are correct, however, is in arguing that they have taken the lead in the funding and marketing of recordings. It is arguable they have been good at it too. For as long as this continues, there will be a need for them. Moreover, as well as having sufficient profit margins to accommodate higher royalties and reduced copyright terms, the current financial well-being of record companies provides evidence they could go further. The industry can bear a situation in which all featured artists have ownership of their masters.

Glossary

adaptation right: One of the **rights** given to the authors of **works**. This right embraces arrangements, translations and the conversion of works from one copyright category to another. In most countries, there is no adaptation right for sound recordings or performances.

advances: Expense payments made to creators that are usually **recoupable** from **royalties**. It is common practice for record companies to pay recording artists personal advances (covering their living expenses) and recording advances (covering the costs of making the recording).

AFM (American Federation of Musicians): The primary union for musicians in the United States and Canada, founded in 1896.

AHRA (Audio Home Recording Act) (1992): United States Act that introduced a levy on the sale of digital audio-recording devices, imposed the **SCMS** and has **anti-circumvention measures**.

anti-circumvention measures: Laws that prohibit the circumvention of technological barriers put in place to prevent unauthorized use of digital goods.

assignment: A transfer of **rights** in which ownership passes from one party to another.

author: In relation to **copyright**, the author is commonly regarded as the original owner of the **work**. Different parties can be regarded as authors, including **creators** (for **musical works**) and **producers** (for **sound recordings**).

authors' rights: Derived from the French *droit d'auteur*, this term is used in relation to **copyright** laws in **civil law** countries. In comparison with copyright in **common law** countries, there is a stronger focus on the authorship of **works**. The rights in **sound recordings**, **broadcasts** and **performances** are therefore separated into the category of **neighbouring rights**.

basket of rights: The array of different **rights** granted to **authors** and **performers**.

BBC (British Broadcasting Corporation): The national broadcaster of the UK. Founded in 1922 as the private British Broadcasting Company, it became the public service British Broadcasting Corporation in 1927.

Berne Convention for the Protection of Literary and Artistic Works: The principal international agreement governing **rights** in **literary works** and artistic works, including **musical works**. First agreed in Berne in 1886, with subsequent revisions in Paris (twice), Berlin, Rome, Brussels and Stockholm.

BIRPI (United International Bureaux for the Protection of Intellectual Property): Founded in 1893, BIRPI administered international **intellectual property** agreements, including the **Berne Convention** and the **Rome Convention** until 1970, when it was superseded by **WIPO**.

blanket licence: Provides the licensee with access to the entire catalogue of works belonging to the **rights-holder**.

bootleg: A **sound recording** that is reproduced and distributed by someone other than the **record company** with whom the artist is contracted; bootlegs are derived primarily from live recordings and studio outtakes.

BPI (British Phonographic Industry): A trade body of the British recording industry, representing the three **major record labels** and over 400 independent record companies.

broadcast right: One of the **rights** given to **authors**, **producers** and **performers**; addresses both audio and audio-visual broadcasting.

business-to-business: A term used within the **music industries** to refer to revenues that are derived from transactions between **rights-holders** and **licensees**. Although consumers frequently get to hear the music that derives from these transactions, they do not pay for it directly.

business-to-consumer: A term used within the **music industries** to refer to revenues that are derived from direct transactions with consumers.

CDPA (Copyright, Designs and Patents Act 1988): The current UK legislation for **copyright**, designs and **patents**.

CISAC (International Confederation of Societies of Authors and Composers): An international organization that campaigns for legal protection for **authors** and **composers**, and provides a network for their **collecting** societies, founded in 1926.

civil law: A legal system founded in continental Europe in which a codified system serves as the primary source of the law.

collecting society: Also known as Collective Management Organizations (CMOs), the music industries' collecting societies administer revenues relating to different **rights**. For composers, lyricists and publishers, there are **performing rights** and **mechanical right** societies. For **featured artists**, **non-featured performers** and **record companies**, there are **performing rights** societies.

common law: A legal system, originating in England, in which law is established through precedents set by judicial decisions.

common law copyright: A form of copyright that provides protection in instances where statutory legislation does not exist.

communication to the public right: This term has various uses but usually incorporates the **broadcast right** and the **making available right**. It can also encompass the **public performance right**.

composer: The person responsible for the melodic, harmonic, rhythmic and timbral aspects of a musical work. See also **lyricist**.

compulsory licensing: A provision within legislation that enables the licensee to employ **intellectual property** without having to gain the **rights-holder**'s consent, usually in return for a standard fee.

connected rights: See **neighbouring rights**.

copyright: A form of **intellectual property** that embraces **literary works**, dramatic works, **musical works**, artistic works, **sound recordings**, films, broadcasts and typographical arrangements.

creative commons: A non-profit organization founded in 2001, which through its **licences** aims to facilitate greater access to **works**.

creator: Within copyright law it is common for the creator to be regarded as the **author** of literary, dramatic, musical or artistic **works**. Outside of the United States, where **performers** and **studio personnel** are held to be creators, it is less common for creativity to determine authorship of **sound recording copyright**.

DAB (Digital Audio Broadcasting): The international standard for digital radio broadcasting.

DAT (Digital Audio Tape): A digital format for studio recording and home recording, introduced by Sony in 1987.

de minimis: Latin term meaning 'pertaining to minimal things'. In copyright, it establishes thresholds below which the law should not be enforced.

derivative right: US term for the **adaptation right**. In America, this right does address sound recordings.

direct licensing: Licensing agreements that are undertaken by record companies and music publishers rather than through their **collecting societies**.

distribution right: One of the **rights** given to **authors**, **producers** and **performers**. In some territories this right is restricted to the distribution of physical copies of works; in other territories it can embrace electronic distribution, such as the **making available** of works.

distributor: Within the **recording industry**, this term was originally applied to companies and individuals who transferred recordings between manufacturers and retailers. Online distributors specialize in transferring digital recordings between **rights-holders** and DSPs.

DRM (Digital Rights Management): Addresses various means of restricting access to digital content.

droit d'auteur: See **authors' rights**.

DSP (Digital Service Provider): An organization such as a streaming company or downloading company that provides online access to content.

equitable remuneration: A provision within copyright law which ensures that authors, producers and performers are paid fairly for particular uses of their work. Within the **music industries**, its most notable use is derived from measures in the **Rome Convention** and WPPT which outline how **producers** and **performers** should be paid for **broadcast** and **public performance**.

exclusive: In copyright law this term is most commonly used in relation to **rights** that **authors**, **producers** and **performers** have the sole authority to utilize. This exclusivity can be **licensed** or **assigned**. In contracting terms, this term refers to contracts that bind the contracting party so they can only deal with the contractor in relation to the subject matter covered in the agreement.

fair dealing: These measures provide exemptions to the use of exclusive **rights** in the UK and some countries of the British Commonwealth. In the UK fair dealing can apply in the case of research, private study, criticism, review, quotation, news reporting, parody, caricature and pastiche.

fair use: A US doctrine that permits use of copyright material without having to require permission. Uses include commentary, criticism, parody, reporting, research and scholarship.

featured artists: Artists under whose names **sound recordings** are released. When contracted **exclusively** to **record companies**, **production companies** or **services companies**, featured artists are usually paid a combination of **royalties** and **advances**. See also **non-featured performer**.

federal law: Law created by the federal government of a country. See also **state law**.

FIFP (Fair Internet for Performers): An alliance of performers' organizations that seeks equitable rights legislation for streaming services within European law, founded in 2015.

FIM (International Federation of Musicians): The international organization for musicians' unions and their equivalent representative organizations, founded in 1948.

fixation: Employed in the **Rome Convention** and the **WPPT** in reference to the capture of sounds in a **recording**.

formalist: A term utilized by Anne Barron to refer to copyright protection that expands beyond the physical manifestation of the **work** to protect the general form of the author's expression. In such cases, the rights in works can be infringed even if not copied exactly. See also **physicalist**.

free-rider: A person or entity who, in the absence of copyright protection, is able to copy someone else's work and price it less expensively because they do not have to bear risk-taking costs of production.

heritage artist: A **featured artist** who has had a long career and might be subject to a **legacy contract**.

IFPI (International Federation of the Phonographic Industry): Founded in 1933, the IFPI is the international trade organization for the **recording industry**.

ILO (International Labour Organization): An international agency founded in 1919. It sets standards, policies and programmes with approval from workers, employers and governments.

independent artist: A **recording artist** who self-releases their work.

independent company: Any record or publishing company that is not defined as a **major**. This ranges from micro enterprises to large vertically and horizontally integrated corporations.

independent producer: Within the recording industry, this can refer to: (a) an individual or company that works separately to a **record company** and negotiates with them for the use of **sound recordings** they have initiated and had responsibility for; (b) a **studio producer** who, rather than working in-house, is employed on a freelance basis to oversee recording sessions. Some independent producers undertake both roles. See also **producer**.

intellectual property: A branch of law that embraces **copyright, patents**, trademarks and trade secrets.

inter-company licensing: Licensing agreements that take place between record companies.

legacy contract: An old contract that has inferior terms when compared with a contemporary contract.

licence: In a **copyright** context this term refers to: (a) the transfer of **rights** from the original **author** to a **rights-holder** with a difference from **assignment** in that the author retains underlying ownership; (b) the permission granted to by a rights-holder to a licensee to use the work.

life of copyright: The overall duration of the copyright **term**.

literary work: The first form of creative practice protected by copyright law, this category has embraced literary creations that are written, spoken and sung, including lyrics and, prior to the development of the separate category of **musical works**, the scores of compositions.

live music: A sector of the **music industries** and a type of musical activity that refers to performances that take place in-person, this term was popularized by musicians' unions in the mid-twentieth century. Although live music occurs synchronously, it can be recorded for deferred use.

lyricist: The person responsible for setting words to music. See also **composer**.

major company: Within the **music industries** this term refers to companies that have the greatest international market share and which are usually part of multinational corporations. As of 2022, the **recording industry** majors are Universal Music Group, Sony Music Entertainment and Warner Music Group. The **music publishing** majors are Sony Music Publishing, Warner Chappell and Universal Music Publishing. See also **independent company**.

making available right: One of the **rights** given to **authors, producers** and **performers**, it is used in relation to downloading and on-demand streaming.

master recording: Commonly shortened to 'master', this term originally referred to the master disc that formed the basis of duplicative manufacture. Although this use has been retained, it has been superseded by use of master to refer to the final **mix** (or **fixation**) of a recording that will be utilized across different recording formats.

master rights: A term used by music makers and music companies to refer to the rights in recordings. See also **sound recording copyright**.

mechanical right: A **right** awarded to the authors of **musical works** in respect of the use of their compositions in sound recordings and other 'mechanical' reproduction devices, such as music boxes and player pianos. Although some copyright legislation includes a distinct mechanical right, this use of works is now commonly addressed as an aspect of the **reproduction right**.

mix: The process of combining and optimizing the sounds from multi-track recording sessions into a final recording that will be employed across different recording formats.

MMC (Monopolies and Mergers Commission): A British public body that had responsibility for investigating mergers, markets and other inquiries relating to industrial and commercial practice. Founded as the Monopolies and Restrictive Practices Commission in 1949, it was superseded by the Competition Commission in 1999, which itself became the Competition and Markets Authority in 2014.

moral rights: These rights exist separately to the economic **rights** of authors and performers, and include the right to be identified as the author, the right to object to derogatory treatment of the work and the right to object to false attribution. At an international level, the moral rights of authors were first addressed in the 1928 revision of the **Berne Convention** and those of performers in the 1996 **WPPT**. Although they cannot be **assigned**, these rights can be waived. They tend to have greater recognition in **civil law** than **common law**.

MPA (Music Publishers Association): In Britain and the United States, the same name has been given to trade bodies looking after the interests of music publishers. The British MPA was founded in 1881; the American one in 1895.

MU (Musicians' Union): An organization, founded in 1893, which represents musicians working in all sectors of the British **music industries**.

musical work: A copyright category addressing the melodic, harmonic, rhythmic and timbral aspects of music composition. In some territories, this type of **work** also embraces lyrics; in others, lyrics are addressed as **literary works**.

music industries: Used in reference to the **recording industry, music publishing** industry and **live music** industry, this term was popularized by the academics Martin Cloonan and John Williamson to indicate that the music business is multiple rather than singular and that these sectors can have opposing points of view.

music publishing: A sector of the music industries. Composers and lyricists contract with music publishers to oversee various uses of their works. The term 'publishing' is derived from an original focus on the publication of sheet music, but there is now commonly a greater focus on **mechanical, synchronization, public performance, broadcast** and online **licensing**.

NAB (National Association of Broadcasters): US trade body that represents the interests of radio and television broadcasters, founded in 1923.

NAPA (National Association of Performing Artists): US organization founded in 1934 by bandleader Fred Waring to campaign for **performing rights** for musicians. Now defunct.

national treatment: A principle within international law, including **intellectual property** law, that requires countries to give the same protection to foreigners as to locals.

neighbouring rights: Although this term is sometimes used in reference to **sound recording rights** and **performers rights**, particularly their **broadcast** and **public performance** aspects, it more correctly refers to legislation in **civil law** countries whereby **rights** in **sound recordings**, broadcasts and **performances** (and sometimes films and databases) do not classify as **authors' rights** and are instead viewed as rights that 'neighbour' those in **creative works**. Also known as **related rights** and **connected rights**.

non-featured performers: Performers such as **session musicians**, orchestral musicians and backing singers who, in contrast to **featured artists**, are not contracted **exclusively**.

options: Music contracts generally last for an initial term, which is calculated in relation to the delivery of an agreed number of recordings or songs. At the conclusion of this term there are usually one or more options, which the music company, rather than the recording artist or songwriter, can exercise to extend the duration of the contract. These further option periods will also usually be calculated in relation to set numbers of recordings or songs.

patent: A form of **intellectual property** that addresses inventions.

performers: In addition to **featured artists** and **non-featured performers**, the **performers' rights** of intellectual property law embrace dramatic performers.

performers' rights: The **Rome Convention** provides a performer with rights to prevent the **broadcast, fixation** and **reproduction** of recordings of their performances, and **equitable remuneration** in respect of the **broadcast** and **public performance** of recordings of their performances. The **WPPT** provides a performer with economic rights in respect of the **reproduction, distribution, rental** and **making available** of recordings of their performances; **equitable remuneration** in respect of the **broadcast** and **public performance** of recordings of their performances; and the **moral right** to be identified as the performer.

performing rights: The collective name for the **public performance, broadcast** and **making available rights**.

personal advances: See **advances**.

phonogram: Term used in the **Rome Convention, Phonograms Convention** and **WPPT** for a **sound recording**. Phonogram also provides the initial for the (P) symbol that signifies the owner of sound recording rights.

Phonograms Convention (The Convention for the Protection of Producers of Phonograms Against Unauthorized Duplication of their Phonograms): A 1971 international agreement addressing the unauthorized duplication and distribution of **sound recordings**.

physicalist: A term utilized by Anne Barron to refer to copyright protection that is limited to the exact copying of a **work**. See also **formalist**.

PPL (Phonographic Performance Limited): The British **collecting society** operating on behalf of **sound recording rights-holders** and **performers** in respect of their

public performance and **broadcast rights**. Founded in 1934, it is owned by British record companies.

producer: Within copyright law this term refers to the person or legal entity who takes the initiative and has responsibility for the **fixation** of a **sound recording**, and in consequence is given ownership of **sound recording copyright.** See also **independent producer** and **studio producer.**

production company: **Recording industry** production companies work in conjunction with or on behalf of **featured artists** to make **sound recordings** they aim to **license** or **assign** to **record companies** in exchange for **royalties.**

PRS (Performing Right Society): This British **collecting society** operates on behalf of its **composer, lyricist** and **publisher** members in respect of their **public performance, broadcast** and **making available rights.** Founded in 1914, it has been known as PRS for Music since 2009.

public domain: When **intellectual property** law is not applicable to creative **works,** they are regarded as being in the public domain. They can attain this status because the **term** of the rights has expired, the rights have been forfeited or waived or the work might be otherwise be unprotected.

public performance right: One of the **rights** given to **authors, producers** and **performers**; addresses the use of the work in venues, cinemas, shops, restaurants, workplaces and other public places. In some territories, this right encompasses the **broadcast right.**

publisher: See **music publishing.**

record company: Any of the major or independent companies that releases recorded music.

recording: See **sound recording.**

recording advances: See **advances.**

recording artists: See **featured artists** and **non-featured performers.**

Recording Artists' Coalition: An American organization representing the interests of **featured artists**, founded in 2000 by the artists Sheryl Crow and Don Henley.

recording industry: Traditionally referring to the work of **record companies**, the term recording industry can be extended to embrace all holders of **sound recording copyright**, including **production companies, services companies, distributors** and **rights-holding** artists.

recoupment: Within the **music industries**, it is common that expenses forwarded to a creator by a contracting company will be paid back through the recoupment of the same amounts from the creator's royalties. Within the **recording industry** this commonly includes all **advances,** tour support, half of video costs and in some instances marketing expenditure. In profit-share deals, all costs (with the possible exception of overheads) are jointly borne by creator and company before royalties are paid. Recoupment is differentiated from loans in that a creator will not usually have to pay back any outstanding amounts if their contract is terminated.

remaster: The process of making a new version of a master recording. The remaster can, in some instances, be granted a copyright and publication date of its own.

rental right: One of the **rights** given to **authors, producers** and **performers**; addresses instances where the work is accessed on terms that it will or may be returned.

reproduction right: One of the **rights** given to **authors, producers** and **performers**; addresses the reproduction of the work in any material form, including storing the work by electronic means and making copies which are transient or are incidental to other uses of the work.

RIAA (Recording Industry Association of America): A trade body of the **recording industry** representing the majority of recorded music sold in the United States, founded in 1952.

rights: In copyright law this term refers to the economic **reproduction, distribution, rental, performing** and **adaptation rights** of **authors, producers** and **performers**, and the **moral rights** of authors and performers. The economic rights are usually granted **exclusively** but can be subject to **compulsory licensing** provisions.

rights-holder: A company or individual who is entitled to exploit the **rights** in a **work** or **performance**. They can be the original owner of the rights or can hold them via **licence** or **assignment**.

Rome Convention for the Protection of Performers, Producers of Phonograms and Broadcasting Organizations (1961): The first international agreement representing the interests of **performers**, broadcasters and **producers**.

Royalties: Royalty contracts indicate that the individual or company transferring their assets (such as **copyright**) does so in return for an agreed percentage of revenues (their royalties).

SCMS (Serial Copy Management System): A copyright protection system, endorsed by the **AHRA**, that prevents digital technologies such as **DAT** from making multiple copies of the same recording.

service provider: See **DSP**.

services company: Although some of these companies are owned by major record companies, they offer an alternative form of agreement. They provide limited advance funds to their contracted **featured artists**, but in return pay high royalty rates and do not seek ownership of copyright.

session musicians: Although this term can now embrace backing singers and is sometimes used in reference to **live music**, its most common employment has been in relation to musicians who make instrumental contributions at recording sessions and who, in contrast to **featured artists**, are employed on a freelance basis and paid fixed sums rather than **advances** and sales **royalties**. See also **non-featured performers**.

sound recording: Any acoustic, electronic or digital recording of sound that can be audibly reproduced.

sound recording copyright: A category of copyright that addresses **rights** accorded in respect of the fixation of **sounds** in a **recording.** This copyright is separate to the rights that **composers** and **lyricists** have in respect of recordings of their **work.** In most countries, it is also separate to **performers' rights.** See also **master rights.**

state law: The body of law created by a federated state. It can be distinguished from the **federal law** that applies to the whole federation of which the state forms a part.

studio producer: Has responsibility for overseeing the recording process in recording studios. See also **independent producer** and **producer.**

subsist: In relation to intellectual property, this term means that it is valid, enforceable and unexpired.

synchronization: Within the **music industries** this term is used in reference to the synchronization of sound recordings with visual media, including film, television, advertisements and computer games. Synchronization is usually addressed under the **reproduction right** rather than having a distinct **right** of its own.

term: In copyright law this refers to the duration of the rights, which can be calculated in accordance with the life of the author (as with **musical works**) or by the date of publication (as is the main tendency with **sound recording copyright** and **performers' rights**).

UNESCO (United Nations Educational, Scientific and Cultural Organization): A branch of the United Nations that seeks international cooperation in education, arts, science and culture. Founded in 1945, it was one of the co-organizers of the **Rome Convention.**

unfair competition: This law addresses misleading, deceptive, dishonest, fraudulent, coercive or unconscionable practices that enable businesses to gain competitive advantage in the market.

WCT (WIPO Copyright Treaty): An international agreement adopted by member states of **WIPO** in 1996, addressing advances in information technology since the last amendment of the **Berne Convention** in 1979. Known collectively with the **WPPT** as the 'internet treaties', these agreements introduced the **making available right.**

WIPO (World Intellectual Property Organization): Founded in 1967, WIPO develops international policy in relation to intellectual property, and oversees international treaties, including the **Berne Convention, Rome Convention, Phonograms Convention, WCT** and **WPPT.**

work: Used in copyright law to refer to **literary, musical,** dramatic and artistic creations. Practice has varied in respect of whether **sound recordings** are classified as works.

work made for hire: Within United States copyright law, there are two categories of work made for hire: (1) a work prepared by an employee within the scope of their employment; (2) a work specially ordered or commissioned for use as part of either a motion picture or other audio-visual work, a contribution to a collective work, a translation, a supplementary work, a compilation, an instructional text, a test, or as answer material for a test, or an atlas. If agreed in writing with the employee or independent contractor, the employer or commissioner can be regarded as the **author** of the **work**.

WPPT (WIPO Performances and Phonograms Treaty): An international agreement adopted by member states of **WIPO** in 1996, addressing advances in information technology since the **Rome Convention** of 1961. Known collectively with the **WCT** as the 'internet treaties', these agreements introduced the **making available right**.

Timeline

1710	Statue of Anne (UK): Commonly regarded as the world's first copyright legislation. Rights are granted to 'published books and other writings' for a period of fourteen years, which can be renewed for fourteen more years, after which books enter the public domain.
1740	*Gyles v Wilcox* (UK): Holds that an adaptation is not an infringement of a copyright work.
1760s–1770s	Battle of the Booksellers (UK): London booksellers seek a perpetual common law copyright; Scottish booksellers seek confirmation of the concept of the public domain.
1774	*Donaldson v Beckett* (UK): Establishes that common law copyright existed in principal, but has been superseded by the Statute of Anne with its limited term of copyright.
1777	*Bach v Longman* (UK): Establishes that musical notation is a form of writing that can be protected under the Statute of Anne.
1787	Constitution (US): 'Congress shall have Power… To promote the Progress of Science and useful Arts, by securing for limited Times to Authors and Inventors the exclusive Right to their respective Writings and Discoveries.'
1790	Copyright Act (US): First federal copyright legislation in the United States, addresses 'maps, charts and books'. Musical scores are not mentioned directly but are held to be books. The copyright term lasts for fourteen years, after which it can be renewed by the original copyright owner for a further fourteen years.
1791	*Decret rendu sur la Pétition des Auteurs dramatiques* (France): First legislation to create a performing right.
1814	Copyright Act (UK): Creates a new copyright term which lasts for the longer of twenty-eight years or the life of the author.
1831	Copyright Act (US): Notated music is formally incorporated in American copyright law.

1833	Dramatic Literary Property Act (UK): Includes the first performing right in British legislation.
1835	*D'Almaine v Boosey* (UK): Holds that an adaptation is an infringement of a musical work.
1842	Copyright Act (UK): Notated music is formally incorporated into British copyright law, where it gains a performing right in addition to a reproduction right. The term of copyright is extended to life of the author plus seven years and a minimum of forty-two years from publication.
1877	Thomas Edison introduces sound recording via his cylinder-based phonograph.
1886	Berne Convention: The first international copyright agreement establishes the principal of national treatment. It does not include a mechanical right for musical works and does not grant any rights to sound recordings.
1887	Emile Berliner introduces the gramophone disc.
1897	Copyright Act (Public Performance of Musical Compositions) (US): Musical works gain a public performance right.
1898	Valdemar Poulsen introduces the first magnetic recorder.
1908	*White-Smith v Apollo* (US): Holds against the immediate imposition of a mechanical right and instead suggests a legislative review of this subject.
1908	Berlin Revision of the Berne Convention: Introduces a mechanical right for musical works and a right in respect of the public performance of mechanical reproductions of musical works. The revised Convention includes copyright protection for films, but rejects a proposal to protect sound recordings.
1909	Copyright Act (US): Establishes a mechanical right for compositions with compulsory licensing provisions. Does not create a sound recording copyright. The term of copyright is set at twenty-eight years, renewable for a further twenty-eight years. The Act introduces 'work made for hire' criteria by which a company can own the copyright of its employees. Case law establishes that the criteria can be applied to commissioned works.

1910   Copyright Act (Germany): Establishes a mechanical right for compositions with compulsory licensing provisions. Creates the world's first copyright for sound recordings, which are regarded as adaptations of musical works. The rights are granted to performers but case law establishes that they are transferred to record companies by automatic assignment.

1911   Copyright Act (UK): Musical works are recognized as a distinct type of copyright work and gain a mechanical right with compulsory licensing provisions. A reproduction right is established for 'records, perforated rolls, and other contrivances by means of which sounds may be mechanically reproduced'. Although granted on creative grounds, the right is awarded to the 'makers' of recordings, which can be a 'body corporate'. The term of copyright for literary, dramatic, musical and artistic works lasts for the life of author plus fifty years; the term for sound recording copyright lasts for fifty years from the making of the master recording.

1925   Electric recording introduced in the UK and US.

1925   *Remick v. American Automobile Accessories* (US): Establishes that the performing right includes broadcasts.

1925   Dramatic and Musical Performers' Protect Act (UK): Criminalizes the unauthorized recording of live performances.

1927   *Messager v BBC* (UK): Establishes that the performing right includes broadcasts. Although reversed on appeal, it is reconfirmed in *Performing Right Society v Hammonds Bradford Brewery* (1934).

1928   Rome Revision of the Berne Convention: Introduces a broadcast right, which stipulates that composers and lyricists should receive 'equitable remuneration'. The Italian organizers propose incorporating sound recording copyright within the Convention on grounds that recordings are adaptations of musical works; the British delegate proposes that sound recordings are recognized as original works. Neither proposal is accepted, but the Conference suggests that governments find ways of protecting the interests of performers.

1933	First international congress of the recording industry held in Rome, leading to the formation of the IFPI.
1934	Meeting between IFPI and CISAC in Stressa at which it is agreed that, rather than seeking for sound recordings to be recognized as creative works within copyright legislation, record companies will campaign for neighbouring rights.
1934	*Gramophone Company v Carwardine and Company* (UK): Establishes that sound recordings have performing rights, leading to the formation of PPL in the same year.
1934	NAPA is founded in the United States with the goal of gaining performing rights for musicians.
1936	Copyright Law (Austria): First legislation to address the neighbouring rights of record manufacturers and performers.
1939	Italian performers' rights convention results in the Samaden Proposal, which suggests that broadcast revenue for sound recordings should take the form of an equitable remuneration to be divided between record companies and featured artists.
1942–1944	AFM strike (US) results in the establishment of a levy on sales of sound recordings, which will be used to support musicians who are negatively affected by the advances of recorded music.
1946	Agreement between PPL and MU (UK): PPL revenues are divided 67.5 per cent to record companies, 20 per cent to featured artists and 12.5 per cent to the MU in support of musicians who have been negatively affected by the advances of recorded music.
1947	Tape recording technology introduced in recording studios.
1948	Brussels Revision of the Berne Convention: Musicians' unions campaign for performers' rights to be recognized within the Convention; the recording industry campaigns for sound recording rights to be recognized within the Convention. Both requests are denied but the Conference recommends studies on these subjects, based on the Samaden Proposal.
1948	Foundation of FIM, which seeks to restrict and gain compensation for the use recordings in public performance and broadcast contexts.
1948	Columbia Records introduces the 33 1/3 rpm long-playing record.

1949	Reel-to-reel tape recorders are made available for domestic use.
1949	RCA Victor introduces the 45 rpm single record.
1956	Copyright Act (UK). Sound recordings are not regarded as original creative works; the copyright is instead awarded to the 'maker'.
1961	Rome Convention: First international agreement for the rights of producers, performers and broadcasters. Phonogram producers (defined as 'the person who, or the legal entity which, first fixes the sounds of a performance or other sounds') have an exclusive reproduction right for their sound recordings; broadcasters have an exclusive right for their radio productions; performers gain the 'possibility of preventing' the 'fixation' of their performances in recorded form without their consent. In respect of the performing rights, the Convention suggests that broadcasters should pay an equitable remuneration to phonogram producers and performers. The term of rights is a minimum of twenty years.
1962	Philips introduces the compact tape cassette.
1964	A consortium of American companies introduces the eight-track cartridge.
1971	Public Law 92–140 (US): The first federal law for sound recording copyright provides a reproduction right and distribution right, but no performing rights. Rights are granted in respect of the creativity of recording artists and studio personnel, but in most instances are claimed by record companies and production companies as work made for hire. Prior to 1971 there had been six public laws in the United States, which gradually increased the renewal period of copyright so the term could last for its initial twenty-eight-year period plus a maximum extension of thirty-four years.
1971	Phonograms Convention: International agreement to protect record companies against unauthorized manufacture and distribution. Ownership of sound recording copyright is awarded to the 'producer', defined as 'the person who, or the legal entity which, first fixes the sounds of a performance or other sounds'.

1976	Copyright Act (US): Sound recordings gain a derivative right in addition to the reproduction and distribution right. They are not granted any performing rights. Work made for hire legislation is amended: employers can claim ownership of rights in their employees' work, but ownership of commissioned works is restricted to nine categories and does not include sound recordings. The term of copyright is life plus fifty years for works; seventy-five years from publication for work made for hire. The assignment of rights for works can be terminated after thirty-five years; works for hire rights cannot be terminated. Pre-1972 sound recordings continue to receive protection via state law rather than federal law, but it is determined that their term of protection will last until 2067.
1982	Philips and Sony introduce the compact disc.
1982	BPI launches the 'home taping is killing music: and it's illegal' campaign in the UK.
1984	Record Rental Amendment Act (US): Introduces rental rights for sound recordings.
1987	Sony introduces DAT.
1988	MMC *Collective Licensing Report* (UK): Terminates the agreement between PPL and the MU.
1988	CDPA (UK): Sound recordings are classified as 'works' and authorship is granted to 'the person by whom the arrangements necessary for the making of the recording… are undertaken'. Includes performers' rights in respect of the unauthorized recording of live performances.
1989	United States adheres to the Berne Convention.
1992	Sony introduces the MiniDisc and Philips introduces the Digital Compact Cassette (DCC).
1992	Audio Home Recording Act (US): Imposes a levy on the sale of digital recording technologies such as DATs, MiniDiscs and DCCs; stipulates that manufacturers of the hardware for these technologies include the SCMS; has anti-circumvention measures that prevent tampering with the SCMS.

1992	Rental Directive (EU): Provides rental rights for authors, phonograph producers and performers. Outlines performing rights for phonograph producers and performers which stipulate that broadcasters and venues pay equitable remuneration.
1993	Trade-Related Aspects of Intellectual Property Rights (TRIPs): International agreement enables countries to reinforce their intellectual property laws by imposing trade restrictions on other areas of economic activity.
1993	The Fraunhofer Society publishes the standard for the MP3.
1993	Copyright Duration Directive (EU): Harmonizes the terms of rights in the EU at life plus seventy years for literary, dramatic, musical, artistic, cinematographic and audiovisual works, and fifty years from publication for sound recordings, performances and broadcasts.
1995	Digital Performance Right in Sound Recordings Act (US): Establishes a performing right for sound recordings for digital subscription and interactive services. Licensing revenue for digital broadcasts is split 50 per cent to the rights-holders; 45 per cent to featured artists; 2.5 per cent to non-featured performers; and 2.5 per cent to backing singers. Revenue for on-demand streaming can be split according to contract.
1995	No Electronic Theft Act (US): Private individuals can be prosecuted for the uploading and downloading of digital files.
1996	Copyright and Related Rights Regulations (UK): Incorporates the EU Rental Directive into the CDPA. Authorship of a sound recording is granted to the 'producer', defined using the authorial criteria of the CDPA. Performers gain exclusive reproduction, distribution and rental rights, and equitable remuneration for broadcast and public performance.
1996	In the UK, PPL is granted the responsibility for handling public performance and broadcast revenues relating to recordings. It adopts a 50/50 split between producers and performers; the performers' share is split two-thirds to featured artists and one-third to non-featured performers.

1996	The WCT and WPPT introduce the making available right. The WPPT also introduces moral rights for performers.
1998	Term Extension Act (US): Increases the term of copyright to life plus seventy years for authorial works, and ninety-five years from publication for work made for hire.
1998	Digital Millennium Copyright Act (US): Outlines US policy for implementing the WCT and WPPT.
1999	Napster is launched.
1999	Satellite Home Viewer Extension Act (US): Adds sound recordings to the list of commissioned work made for hire.
2000	The US House Judiciary Committee holds hearings in relation to the Satellite Home Viewer Extension Act, and as a result sound recordings are removed from the list of commissioned work made for hire.
2000	*A&M Records v Napster* (US): Holds that Napster could be found liable for vicarious infringement of copyright.
2001	Information Society Directive (EU): Outlines policy for implementing the WCT and WPPT.
2003	Copyright and Related Rights Regulations (UK): Incorporates the EU Information Society Directive into UK law.
2003	Launch of Apple's iTunes store in the US; it is launched in the UK the following year.
2003	In the US, the RIAA launches its campaign to pursue individual file sharers for copyright infringement.
2003	Launch of The Pirate Bay in Sweden.
2005	YouTube is launched.
2006	Launch of The Pirate Party in Sweden.
2006	Spotify founded in Sweden; it is launched in the UK in 2009, and in the US in 2011.
2006	The Performances (Moral Rights, etc.) Regulations (UK): Incorporates the WPPT into UK law in respect of moral rights for performers.
2011	Term Extension Directive (EU): Extends the term of sound recording copyright in the EU to seventy years from publication. Unrecouped balances of performers are waived after fifty years; featured artists gain a 'use it or lose it' clause; non-featured performers are entitled to 20 per cent of revenues in the last twenty years of the term.

2013	The Copyright and Duration of Rights in Performances Regulations (UK): Implements the 2011 EU Term Extension Directive.
2018	CLASSICS Act (US): Establishes that pre-1972 sound recordings can receive remuneration for digital broadcasting; reduces the common law copyright term for these recordings.
2018	Allocation for Music Producers Act (US): Updates the US Copyright Act so that studio producers, mixers and sound engineers can receive a share of remuneration for digital broadcasting.
2019	Copyright Directive (EU): Includes a contract adjustment mechanism and right of revocation.
2021	Economics of Music Streaming (UK): Governmental inquiry looks at the impact of streaming on revenues of performers and songwriters.

Bibliography

Abrams, H. B. (2010), 'Copyright's First Compulsory License', *Santa Clara High Technology Law Journal*, 26 (2): 215–52.

AEPO-ARTIS (2018), 'Performers' Rights in International and European Legislation: Situation and Elements for Improvement', October. Available online: https://www.aepo-artis.org/usr/files/di/fi/2/AEPO-ARTIS-Study-2018---Performers%E2%80%99-Rights-in-International-and-European-_20181161711.pdf (accessed 18 October 2021).

Aguilar, A. (2018), '"We Want Artists to Be Fully and Fairly Paid for Their Work": Discourses on Fairness in the Neoliberal European Copyright Reform', *JIPITEC*, 9: 160–78.

Alderman, J. (2001), *Sonic Boom: Napster, P2P and the Battle for the Future of Music*, London: Fourth Estate.

Allbritton, C. (1999), 'Prince: Don't Trust the Net', *Wired*, 20 July. Available online: https://www.wired.com/1999/07/prince-dont-trust-the-net/ (accessed 11 August 2020).

Alloway, N. (1983), 'Activities and Achievements', in J. Borwick (ed), *The First Fifty Years: Celebrating the Anniversary of IFPI*, 7–13, London: Brooks Design Partnership.

Anderson, C. (2009), *The Longer Long Tail*, London: Random House Business Books.

Anderson, T. (2004), '"Buried under the Fecundity of His Own Creations": Reconsidering the Recording Bans of the American Federation of Musicians, 1942–1944 and 1948', *American Music*, 22 (2): 231–69.

'Anka Buys Rights Back from Para' (1965), *Billboard*, 16 March: 6.

Arditi, D. (2020a), 'The Global Music Report: Selling a Narrative of Decline', in R. Osborne and D. Laing (eds), *Music by Numbers: The Use and Abuse of Statistics in the Music Industries*, 74–89, Bristol: Intellect.

Arnold, R. (2015), *Performers' Rights*, 5th edn, London: Sweet & Maxwell.

'Artists, Representatives Speak Out on New Amendment' (2000), *Billboard*, 22 January: 123.

Asor (1878), 'Phonograph', *English Mechanic*, 4 January: 404.

Atkinson, B. (2007), *The True History of Copyright: The Australian Experience 1905–2005*, Sydney: Sydney University Press.

Attali, J. (1985), *Noise: The Political Economy of Music*, Minneapolis and London: University of Minnesota Press.

AWAL (2018), 'Maintaining Rights to Your Masters and Why It Means Everything', *Hypebot*, 11 October. Available online: http://www.hypebot.com/hypebot/2018/10/maintaining-rights-to-your-masters-and-why-it-means-everything.html (accessed 11 August 2020).

Bach v Longman (1777), 2 Cowper 623.

Banas, E. (2020), 'Nikki Sixx Sells His Shares of Motley Crue Catalog to Music Investment Company', *WMMR*, 3 September. Available online: https://wmmr.com/2020/09/03/nikki-sixx-sells-his-shares-of-motley-crue-catalog-to-music-investment-company-2/ (accessed 7 December 2021).

Barfe, L. (2004), *Where Have All the Good Times Gone: The Rise and Fall of the Record Industry*, London: Atlantic Books.

Barr, K. W. (2016), 'Music Copyright in the Digital Age: Creators, Commerce and Copyright – An Empirical Study of the UK Music Copyright Industries', PhD thesis, Glasgow: University of Glasgow.

Barron, A. (2004), 'The Legal Properties of Film', *Modern Law Review*, 67 (2): 177–208.

Barron, A. (2006), 'Copyright Law's Musical Work', *Social and Legal Studies*, 15 (1): 101–27.

Beaumont-Thomas, B. (2021), 'MPs and Music Industry Bodies Criticise Pay of Universal Head Lucian Graine', *Guardian*, 10 November. Available online: https://www.theguardian.com/music/2021/nov/10/mps-and-music-industry-bodies-criticise-pay-of-universal-head-lucian-grainge (accessed 15 November 2021).

Belam, M. (2016), 'REM's Michael Stipe and Mike Mills at the Borderline', *Guardian*, 18 November. Available online: https://www.theguardian.com/music/musicblog/2016/nov/18/rem-michael-stipe-and-mike-mills-at-the-borderline-live-interview (accessed 22 October 2021).

Bell, T. W. (1998), 'Fair Use vs. Fared Use: The Impact of Automated Rights Management on Copyright's Fair Use Doctrine', *North Carolina Law Review*, 76 (2): 557–620.

Bently, L. (2009), 'Authorship of Popular Music in UK Copyright Law', *Information, Communication & Society*, 12 (2): 179–204.

Berlin Act (1908), *Revised Berne Convention for the Protection of Literary and Artistic Works*, 13 November. Available online: https://www.keionline.org/wp-content/uploads/1908_Berne_Convention.pdf (accessed 1 November 2021).

Berliner, E. (1888), 'The Gramophone: Etching the Human Voice', *Journal of the Franklin Institute*. Available online: https://www.loc.gov/item/berl0179/ (accessed 19 July 2019).

Berne Convention (1886), *Convention Concerning the Creation of an International Union for the Protection of Literary and Artistic Works*, 9 September. Available online: https://www.keionline.org/wp-content/uploads/1886_Berne_Convention.pdf (accessed 1 November 2021).

Bettig, R. V. (1996), *Copyrighting Culture: The Political Economy of Intellectual Property*, Boulder: Westview Press.

Blume, J. (2014), '10 Things You Need to Know about Placing Music on TV and in Films', *BMI*, 25 April. Available online: https://www.bmi.com/news/entry/10_things_you_need_to_know_about_placing_music_on_tv_and_in_films (accessed 13 November 2020).

Boosey, W. (1911), 'The Copyright Bill: Attitude of the Labour Party', *The Times*, 1 May: 4.

Boosey, W. (1931), *Fifty Years of Music*, London: Ernest Benn Ltd.

Brannigan, P. and I. Winwood (2014), *Into the Black: The Inside Story of Metallica, 1991–2014*, London: Faber and Faber.

Brauneis, R. (2014), 'Musical Work Copyright for the Era of Digital Sound Technology: Looking beyond Composition and Performance', *GW Law School Public Law and Legal Theory Paper No. 2014-4*. Available online: http://ssrn.com/abstract=2400170 (accessed 18 July 2019).

Brennan, M. (2020), *Kick It: A Social History of the Drum Kit*, Oxford: Oxford University Press.

Broven, J. (2009), *Record Makers and Breakers: Voices of the Independent Rock 'n' Roll Pioneers*, Urbana: University of Illinois Press.

Brown, M. (2008), *Tearing Down the Wall of Sound: The Rise and Fall of Phil Spector*, London: Bloomsbury.

Brylawski E. F. and A. Goldman, eds (1976), *Legislative History of the 1909 Copyright Act*, South Hackensack: Fred B. Rothman & Co.

'Campaign Stirs Other Issues' (2004), *Music Week*, 24 July: 7.

Caramanica, J. (2016), 'Frank Ocean Is Finally Free, Mystery Intact', *New York Times*, 15 November. Available online: https://www.nytimes.com/2016/11/20/arts/music/frank-ocean-blonde-interview.html?_r=0 (accessed 12 August 2020).

Carson, D. (2010), 'Making the Making Available Rights Available – 22nd Annual Horace S. Manges Lecture, February 3, 2009', *Columbia Journal of Law and the Arts*, 33 (2): 135–64.

Castle, C. and C. Feijóo (2021), *Study on the Artists in the Digital Music Marketplace: Economic and Legal Considerations*, Geneva: WIPO.

CC Young (2020), 'Written Evidence Submitted by CC Young', *Economics of Music Streaming*, 24 November. Available online: https://committees.parliament.uk/work/646/economics-of-music-streaming/publications/written-evidence/ (accessed 9 November 2021).

Century Communications v Mayfair Entertainment (1993), EMLR 335.

Chafee, Z. (1945), 'Reflections on the Law of Copyright: II', *Columbia Law Review*, 719: 719–38.

Chapple, S. and R. Garofalo (1977), *Rock 'n' Roll Is Here to Pay: The History of Politics of the Music Industry*, Chicago: Nelson-Hall.

Charlie Rose (2000), [TV programme] PBS, 12 May. Available online: https://charlierose.com/videos/19757 (accessed 1 November 2021).

Christman, E. (2021), 'Bruce Springsteen in Talks to Sell Recorded Music Catalog to Sony Music', *Billboard*, 2 November. Available online: https://www.billboard.com/pro/bruce-springsteen-talks-sony-music-sell-recorded-music-catalog/ (accessed 30 November 2021).

Cloonan, M. (2007), *Popular Music and the State in the UK*, Aldershot: Ashgate.

Collins, W. (2014), 'Prince's WMG Deal Steams from U.S. Laws that Support Master Recording Copyright Termination', *Hypebot*, 25 April. Available online: https://www.hypebot.com/hypebot/2014/04/princes-warner-brothers-deal-a-result-of-us-law-supporting-master-recording-copyright-termination.html (accessed 24 July 2019).

Commission of the European Communities (1988), *Green Paper on Copyright and the Challenge of Technology: Copyright Issues Requiring Immediate Action*, 7 June, Brussels: Commission of European Communities.

Commission of the European Communities (1995), *Copyright and Related Rights in the Information Society*, 19 July, Brussels: Commission of the European Communities.

Congressional Budget Office (CBO) (2004), 'Copyright Issues in Digital Media', August. Available online: https://www.cbo.gov/publication/15911 (accessed 18 July 2019).

Conot, R. (1979), *Thomas A. Edison: A Streak of Luck*, New York: Da Capo.

Constitution of the United States (1787), available online: https://www.archives.gov/founding-docs/constitution-transcript (accessed 1 November 2021).

Cooke, C. (2015), *Dissecting the Digital Dollar: Full Report*, London: Music Managers Forum.

Cooke, C. (2016a), 'Too Much Ambiguity in Sony's Streaming Deals for Summary Judgement on 19's Sales v Licence Litigation, Says Judge', *Complete Music Update*, 30 September. Available online: https://completemusicupdate.com/article/too-much-ambiguity-in-sonys-streaming-deals-for-summary-judgement-on-19s-sales-v-licence-litigation-says-judge/ (accessed 30 April 2020).

Cooke, C. (2016b), *Dissecting the Digital Dollar Part Two: Full Report*, London: Music Managers Forum.

Cooke, C. (2018), 'Remastering Doesn't Always Create a New Copyright, Appeals Court Says in Pre1972 Royalties Case', *Complete Music Update*, 22 August. Available online: https://completemusicupdate.com/article/remastering-doesnt-always-create-a-new-copyright-appeals-court-says-in-pre-1972-royalties-case (accessed 2 April 2022).

Cooke, C. (2020), 'Musicians' Union and Ivors Academy Call for Government Intervention to "Fix Streaming"', *Complete Music Update*, 11 May. Available online: https://completemusicupdate.com/article/musicians-union-and-ivors-academy-call-for-government-intervention-to-fix-streaming/ (accessed 12 October 2021).

Cooke, C. (2021), 'Artist and Management Community Welcome Sony Music's Decision to Pay Royalties to Artists on Unrecouped pre-2000 Record Deals', *Complete Music Update*, 14 June. Available online: https://completemusicupdate.com/article/artist-and-management-community-welcome-sony-musics-decision-to-pay-royalties-to-artists-on-unrecouped-pre-2000-record-deals/ (accessed 27 June 2021).

Cooper, J. L. and K. L. Burry (2001) 'The Work Made for Hire Conundrum', in T. G. Donovan (ed), *Talent in the New Millennium: Reports Presented at the Meeting of the International Association of Entertainment Lawyers, MIDEM 2001, Cannes,* 1–11, Antwerp: Maklu.

Copyright Act (1842), *An Act to Amend the Law of Copyright*. Available online: http://www.copyrighthistory.org/cam/tools/request/showRepresentation?id=representation_uk_1842 (accessed 1 November 2021).

Copyright Act (1909), *An Act to Amend and Consolidate the Acts Respecting Copyright*. Available online: https://www.copyright.gov/history/1909act.pdf (accessed 1 November 2021).

Copyright Act (1911), Available online: https://www.legislation.gov.uk/ukpga/Geo5/1-2/46/contents (accessed 1 November 2021).

Copyright Act (1956), Available online: https://www.legislation.gov.uk/ukpga/1956/74/contents/enacted (accessed 1 November 2021).

Copyright Act (1976), *Copyright Law of the United States (Title 17)*. Available online: https://www.copyright.gov/title17/ (accessed 1 November 2021).

Copyright, Designs and Patents Act (CDPA) (1988), Available online: https://www.legislation.gov.uk/ukpga/1988/48/contents (accessed 1 November 2021).

'Copyright in Gramophone Records: The Bill through Committee' (1911), *The Times*, 14 July: 7.

'The Copyright Issue which the Industry Music not Ignore' (2004), *Music Week*, 24 July: 6–7.

Copyright Law (1936), *Federal Law on Copyright in Literary and Artistic Works and Related Rights*. Available online: https://wipolex.wipo.int/en/legislation/details/124 (accessed 1 November 2021).

The Copyright and Related Rights Regulations (CRRR) (2003), Available online: https://www.legislation.gov.uk/uksi/2003/2498/contents/made (accessed 1 November 2021).

da Costa, J. F. (1976), 'Some Reflexions on the Rome Convention', *Copyright*, 12 (3): 80–4.

Countryman, V. (1949a), 'The Organized Musicians I', *University of Chicago Law Review*, 16: 56–86

Countryman, V. (1949b), 'The Organized Musicians II', *University of Chicago Law Review*, 16: 239–97.

Creative Commons (n.d.), 'About the Licenses'. Available online: https://creativecommons.org/licenses/ (accessed 16 March 2022).

Cummings, A. S. (2010), 'From Monopoly to Intellectual Property: Music Piracy and the Remaking of American Copyright, 1909–1971', *The Journal of American History*, 97 (3): 659–81.

Currier, F. (1909), *The House Report 1 on the Copyright Act of 1909*, February. Available online: https://ipmall.law.unh.edu/sites/default/files/hosted_resources/lipa/copyrights/The%20House%20Report%201%20on%20the%20Copyright%20Act%20of%201909.pdf (accessed 1 November 2021).

D'Alton, L. J. (2012), 'A Critical Historical Analysis of the Public Performance Right', PhD thesis, University of Western Ontario.

D'Almaine v Boosey (1835), 1 Younge and Collyer 288.

Dannen, F. (2003), *Hit Men: Power Brokers and Fast Money Inside the Music Business*, London: Helter Skelter.

The Dave Clark Five and Beyond: Glad All Over (2015), [TV Programme], BBC2, 14 February.

Davies, G. (2012), 'The 50th Anniversary of the Rome Convention for the Protection of Performers, Producers of Phonograms and Broadcasting Organisations: Reflections on the Background and Importance of the Convention', *Queen Mary Journal of Intellectual Property*, 2 (3): 206–24.

Demers, J. (2006), *Steal This Music: How Intellectual Property Law Affects Musical Creativity*, Athens and London: University of Georgia Press.

Denisoff, R. S. (1975), *Solid Gold: The Popular Record Industry*, New Brunswick and London: Transaction.

Department for Culture, Media and Sport (DCMS) (2000), *Consumers Call the Tune: The Impact of New Technologies on the Music Industry*, London: DCMS.

Digital, Culture, Media and Sport Committee (DCMS) (2001), 'Economics of Music Streaming: Second Report of Session 2021–22', *House of Commons Digital, Culture, Media and Sport Committee,* 15 July. Available online: https://committees. parliament. uk/work/646/economics-of-music-streaming/publications/ (accessed 24 May 2022).

Digital Performance Right in Sound Recordings Act (1995), *Public Law 104–39,* 1 November. Available online: https://www.govinfo.gov/link/plaw/104/public/39 (accessed 1 November 2021).

The Disrupters: The Music Industry and the Digital Revolution (2016), [Film] UK: The Economist Films. Available online: https://www.youtube.com/watch?v=aqz3DaisBz8 (accessed 1 November 2021).

Donovan, N. (2013), 'If CDs Cost £8 Where Does the Money Go?', *BBC*, 26 August. Available online: https://www.bbc.co.uk/news/magazine-23840744 (accessed 28 April 2020).

Doyle, T. (2014), 'His Name Is Prince… And He Is Funky', *Q*, December: 74–9.

Dredge, S. (2020a), 'Kanye West Offers Guidelines for Recording and Publishing Deals', *Music Ally*, 21 September. Available online: https://musically.com/2020/09/21/kanye-west-offers-guidelines-for-recording-and-publishing-deals/ (accessed 12 October 2021).

Dredge, S. (2020b), '#BrokenRecord: "It's about Saying We All Recognise This Is Problematic"', *Music Ally*, 18 May. Available online: https://musically.com/2020/05/18/brokenrecord-its-about-saying-we-all-recognise-that-this-is-problematic/ (accessed 12 October 2022).

Dredge, S. (2021a), 'Spotify CEO Daniel Ek Talks Bollywood, Creators and Battling Radio with Live Features', *Music Ally*, 23 February. Available online: https://musically.com/2021/02/23/spotify-daniel-ek-bollywood-creators-radio/ (accessed 9 November 2021).

Dredge, S. (2021b), 'Global Value of Music Copyright Grew 2.7% to $32.5bn in 2020', *Music Ally*, 17 November. Available online: https://musically.com/2021/11/17/global-value-music-copyright-grew-in-2020/ (accessed 16 March 2022).

Eames, F. (1934), 'Property in Music: A Performer's Rights', *The Times*, 27 March: 10.

Eggertsen, C. (2019), 'What Are Masters and Why Do Taylor Swift & Other Artists Keep Fighting for Them?', *Billboard*, 3 July. Available online: https://www.billboard.com/articles/business/8518722/taylor-swift-masters-artists-ownership-labels-rights-prince (accessed 22 October 2021).

Ehrlich, C. (1989), *Harmonious Alliance: A History of the Performing Right Society*, Oxford and New York: Oxford University Press.

Ellis-Peterson, H. (2016), 'Mercury Prize 2016 Goes to Skepta's *Konnichiwa*', *Guardian*, 15 September. Available online: https://www.theguardian.com/music/2016/sep/15/mercury-prize-2016-goes-to-skeptas-konnichiwa (accessed 12 August 2020).

Espiner, T. (2016), '"Bowie Bonds": The Singer's Financial Innovation', *BBC*, 11 January. Available online: https://www.bbc.co.uk/news/business-35280945 (accessed 11 August 2020).

European Commission (EC) (2015), *Towards a Modern, More European Copyright Framework*, Brussels: European Commission.

European Council (EC) (2001), *Directive 2001/29/EC on the Harmonisation of Certain Aspects of Copyright and Related Rights in the Information Society*.

European Council (EC) (2011), *Directive 2011/77/EU amending Directive 2006/116/EC on the Term of Protection of Copyright and Certain Related Rights*.

European Council (EC) (2019), *Directive (EU) 2019/790 of the European Parliament and of the Council of 17 April 2019 on Copyright and Related Rights in the Digital Single Market*.

European Economic Community (EEC) (1992), *Council Directive 92/100/EC of 19 November 1992 on Rental and Lending Right and on Certain Rights Related to Copyright in the Field of Intellectual Property*.

European Economic Community (EEC) (1993), *Council Directive 93/98/EEC of 29 October 1993 Harmonising the Term of Protection of Copyright and Certain Related Rights*.

Fair Internet for Performers (FIFP) (2017a), 'Comments on the Proposed Directive on Copyright in the Digital Single Market'. Available online: https://www.aepo-artis.org/usr/files/di/fi/7/FAIR-INTERNET-extended-comments-to-proposed-Directive-on-Copyright-April-20_20174121230.pdf (accessed 1 November 2021).

Fair Internet for Performers (FIFP) (2017b), 'Europe's Performers Call on MEPs to Rebalance Copyright and Guarantee a Fair Remuneration from Streaming and Download Services', 11 January. Available online: https://www.fair-internet.eu/europes-performers-call-on-meps-to-rebalance-copyright-and-guarantee-a-fair-remuneration-from-streaming-and-download-services/ (accessed 24 July 2019).

Ficsor, M. (1997), 'Copyright for the Digital Era: The WIPO Internet Treaties', *Columbia-VLA Journal of Law & the Arts*, 21 (3/4): 197–224.

Fleischer, R. (2015), 'Protecting the Musicians and/or the Record Industry? On the History of "Neighbouring Rights" and the Role of Fascist Italy', *Queen Mary Journal of Intellectual Property*, 5 (3): 327–43.

Forde, E (2012) 'Digital Roadkill', *The Word*, March: 29–30.

Forde, E. (2019), *The Final Days of EMI: Selling the Pig*, London: Omnibus Press.

Forde, E. (2021), 'BMG's Ben Katovsky on the DCMS Streaming Inquiry and the Future of Music Publishing', *Synchtank*, 1 September. Available online: https://www.synchtank.com/blog/the-synchtank-interview-bmgs-ben-katovsky-on-the-dcms-streaming-inquiry-and-the-future-of-music-publishing/ (accessed 3 October 2021).

Frith, S. (1978), *The Sociology of Rock*, London: Constable.

Frith, S. (1987), 'The Making of the British Record Industry 1920–64', in J. Curren, A. Smith and P. Wingate (eds), *Impacts and Influence: Essays on Media Power in the Twentieth Century*, 278–90, London and New York: Routledge.

Frith, S. (1988), 'Copyright and the Music Business', *Popular Music*, 7 (1): 57–75.

Frith, S. (1993), 'Introduction', in S. Frith (ed), *Music and Copyright*, ix–xiv, Edinburgh: Edinburgh University Press.

Frith, S. (2000), 'Music Industry Research: Where Now? Where Next? Notes from Britain', *Popular Music*, 19 (3): 387–93.

Frith, S. (2001), 'The Popular Music Industry', in S. Frith, W. Straw and J. Street (eds), *Cambridge Companion to Pop and Rock*, 26–52, Cambridge: Cambridge University Press.

Frith, S. (2004), 'Music and the Media', in S. Frith and L. Marshall (eds), *Music and Copyright*, 2nd edn, 171–88, Edinburgh: Edinburgh University Press.

Frith S. and L. Marshall (2004), 'Making Sense of Copyright', in S. Frith and L. Marshall (eds), *Music and Copyright*, 2nd edn, 1–18, Edinburgh: Edinburgh University Press.

Frith, S. and S. Zagorski-Thomas (2012), *The Art of Record Production: An Introductory Reader for a New Academic Field*, Farnham: Ashgate.

Frith, S., M. Brennan, M. Cloonan and E. Webster (2019), *The History of Live Music in Britain, Volume 2: 1968–1984: From Hyde Park to the Hacienda*, Abingdon and New York: Routledge.

Gardner, E. (2016), '"Blurred Lines" Appeal Gets Support from More Than 200 Musicians', *Hollywood Reporter*, 30 August. Available online: https://www.hollywoodreporter.com/business/business-news/blurred-lines-appeal-gets-support-924213/ (accessed 18 October 2021).

Garnett, K., G. Davies and G. Harbottle (eds) (2011), *Copinger and Skone James on Copyright*, 16th edn, vol. 1, London: Thomson Reuters (Legal) Ltd.

Gelatt, R. (1977), *The Fabulous Phonograph 1977–1977*, 2nd edn, London: Cassell.

Giblin, R. (2011), *Code Wars: 10 Years of P2P Software Litigation*, Cheltenham, UK and Northampton, US: Edward Elgar.

Gillett, C. (1983), *The Sound of the City*, 2nd edn, London: Souvenir Press.

Gitelman, L. (1997), 'Reading Music, Reading Records, Reading Race: Musical Copyright and the U.S. Copyright Act of 1909', *Musical Quarterly*, 81 (2): 265–90.

Gitelman, L. (1999), *Scripts, Grooves, and Writing Machines: Representing Technology in the Edison Era*, Stanford: Stanford University Press.

Goehr, L. (1992), *The Imaginary Museum of Musical Works: An Essay in the Philosophy of Music*, Oxford: Clarendon Press.

Goldstein, P. (1994), *Copyright's Highway: From Gutenberg to the Celestial Jukebox*, New York: Hill and Wang.

Goodman, F. (2015), *Allen Klein: The Man Who Bailed Out the Beatles, Made the Stones, and Transformed Rock & Roll*, Boston and New York: Eamon Dolan.

Goodman, L. (2017), *Meet Me in the Bathroom: Rebirth and Rock and Roll in New York City 2001–2011*, London: Faber & Faber.

Gorrell Committee (1909), *Report of the Committee on the Law of Copyright*, London: His Majesty's Stationery Office.

Gorrell Committee (1910), *Minutes of Evidence Taken before the Law of Copyright Committee*, London: His Majesty's Stationery Office.

'Government Must Hear Music's Voice' (2006), *Music Week*, 4 March: 8–9.

Gowers, A. (2006), *Gowers Review of Intellectual Property*, Norwich: Her Majesty's Stationery Office.

Gramophone Company Advertisement (1915), *Talking Machine News and Side Lines*, November: 304–5.

Gramophone Company v Carwardine and Company (1934), Ch. 450.

'Gramophones and Copyright: Mr. Buxton's Proposals' (1911), *The Times*, 12 July: 12.

The Great Rock 'n' Roll Swindle (1980), [Film] Dir. Julien Temple, UK: Virgin Films.

Green, C. (ed) (2017), *2017 All about the Music: Recorded Music in the UK*, London: BPI.

Green, C. (ed) (2020), *2020 All about the Music: Recorded Music in the UK*, London: BPI.

Greenfield, S. and G. Osborn (1998), *Contract and Control in the Entertainment Industry*, Aldershot: Ashgate.

Greenfield, S. and G. Osborn (2004), 'Copyright Law and Power in the Music Industry', in S. Frith and L. Marshall (eds), *Music and Copyright*, 2nd edn, 89–102, Edinburgh: Edinburgh University Press.

Gregory Committee (1952), *Report of the Copyright Committee, 1951*, London: His Majesty's Stationery Office.

Grey, E. (1909), *Correspondence Respecting the Revised Convention of Berne for the Protection of Literary and Artistic Works*, London: His Majesty's Stationery Office.

Hamilton, M. A. (1987), 'Commissioned Works as Works Made for Hire under the 1976 Copyright Act: Misinterpretation and Injustice', *University of Pennsylvania Law Review*, 135: 1281–320.

Hanley, J. (2017), 'United We Stand', *Music Week*, 9 October: 22–37.

Hanley, J. (2021), 'The Music Week Interview: Merck Mecuriadis', *Music Week*, 1 September: 34–9.

Harris, J. (2004), *The Last Party: Britpop, Blair and the Demise of English Rock*, London: Harper Perennial.

Harrison, A. (2011), *Music: The Business: The Essential Guide to the Law and the Deals*, 5th edn, London: Virgin.

Henn, H. ([1956] 1960), *The Compulsory License Provisions of the U.S. Copyright Law*, Washington: United States Government Printing Office.

Henry Hadaway v Pickwick Group (2015), EWHC 3407.

Hesmondhalgh, D. (1998), 'Post-Punk's Attempt to Democratise the Music Industry: The Success and Failure of Rough Trade', *Popular Music*, 16 (3): 255–74.

Hesmondhalgh, D. (2013), *The Cultural Industries*, 3rd edn, London: Sage.

Hesmondhalgh, D., R. Osborne, H. Sun and K. Barr (2021), *Music Creators' Earnings in the Digital Era*, Newport: Intellectual Property Office. Available online: https://www.gov.uk/government/publications/music-creators-earnings-in-the-digital-era (accessed 10 October 2021).

Higgs, J. (2012), *The KLF: Chaos, Magic and the Band Who Burned a Million Pounds*, London: Phoenix.

Hill, L. F. (1978), 'An Insight into the Finances of the Record Industry', *Three Banks Review*, 118: 28–45.

Hirsch, P. M. (1971/2), 'Processing Fads and Fashions: An Organization-Set Analysis of Cultural Industry Systems', *American Journal of Sociology*, 77: 639–59.

Holland, B. (2000), 'RIAA's Involvement Goes Back 10 Years', *Billboard*, 29 July: 1, 103.

House Judiciary Committee (HJC) (1965), *Copyright Law Revision: Hearings Eighty-Ninth Congress First Session on H.R. 4347, H.R. 5680, H.R. 6831, H.R. 6835 Bills for the General Revision of the Copyright Law, Title 17 of the United States Code, and for Other Purposes*, Washington: US Government Printing Office.

House Judiciary Committee (HJC) (1967), *Copyright Law Revision: Hearings, Ninetieth Congress, First Session, Pursuant to S. Res. 37, on S. 597*, Washington: US Government Printing Office.

House Judiciary Committee (HJC) (1971), *Prohibiting Piracy of Sound Recordings: Hearings, Ninety-Second Congress, First Session, on S. 646 and H. R. 6927*, Washington: US Government Printing Office.

House Judiciary Committee (HJC) (1976), *Copyright Law Revision: Report Together with Additional Views to Accompany S. 22*, Washington: US Government Printing Office.

House Judiciary Committee (HJC) (1978), *Performance Rights in Sound Recordings*, Washington: US Government Printing Office.

House Judiciary Committee (HJC) (1994), *Performers' and Performance Rights in Sound Recordings*, Washington: US Government Printing Office.

House Judiciary Committee (HJC) (1995), *Digital Performance Right in Sound Recordings: Report to Accompany H. R. 1506*, Washington: US Government Printing Office.

House Judiciary Committee (HJC) (1996), *Digital Performance Right in Sound Recordings Act of 1995, Hearings, Hundred Fourth Congress, First Session, on H. R. 1506*, Washington: US Government Printing Office.

House Judiciary Committee (HJC) (2000), *United States Copyright Office and Sound Recordings as Work Made for Hire, Hearings, One Hundred Sixth Congress, Second Session, Serial No. 145*, Washington: US Government Printing Office.

Humphries, S. J. (1934), 'Property in Music: The Rights of a Performer', *The Times*, 13 April: 10.

Iley, J. (2021), 'Oral Evidence', *Economics of Music Streaming, House of Commons 868*, 19 January. Available online: https://committees.parliament.uk/work/646/economics-of-music-streaming/publications/oral-evidence/ (accessed 9 November 2021).

Ingham, T. (2012), 'Given Half a Chance', *Music Week*, 16 March: 1, 3.

Ingham, T. (2013), 'Editorial: Clearing up a Spot of Bother', *Music Week*, 19 July: 2.

Ingham, T. (2015), 'What Will Record Deals Look Like in the Future?', *Music Business Worldwide*, 19 November. Available online: https://www.musicbusinessworldwide.com/what-will-record-deals-look-like-in-the-future/ (accessed 2 May 2020).

Ingham, T. (2018a), 'Sony Music Isn't Robin Hood – It's Being Much Smarter Than That', *Music Business Worldwide*, 15 June. Available online: https://www.musicbusinessworldwide.com/sony-music-isnt-robin-hood-its-being-much-smarter-than-that/ (accessed 30 April 2020).

Ingham, T. (2018b), 'How Much Will Artists Get Paid from the Major Labels' Spotify Profits?', *Music Business Worldwide*, 5 April. Available online: https://www.musicbusinessworldwide.com/how-much-will-artists-be-paid-from-the-major-labels-spotify-profits/ (accessed 2 May 2020).

Ingham, T. (2019a), 'Taylor Swift: Scooter Braun Has "Stripped Me of My Life's Work"', *Music Business Worldwide*, 30 June. Available online: https://www.musicbusinessworldwide.com/taylor-swift-scooter-braun-has-stripped-me-of-my-lifes-work/ (accessed 12 August 2020).

Ingham, T. (2019b), 'Rob Stringer Talks Sony's Strategy, Tencent/Universal… And Why Music Is Worth More Than "2 Minutes of Someone Snoring in Lapland"', *Music Business Worldwide*, available online: https://www.musicbusinessworldwide.com/rob-stringer-talks-strategy-tencent-and-why-sonys-music-is-worth-more-than-2-minutes-of-someone-snoring-in-lapland/ (accessed 29 March 2021).

Ingham, T. (2019c), 'Streaming Platforms Are Keeping More Money from Artists than Ever (and Paying Them More, Too)', *Rolling Stone*, 9 April. Available online: https://www.rollingstone.com/music/music-features/streaming-platforms-keeping-more-money-from-artists-than-ever-817925/ (accessed 2 May 2020).

Ingham, T. (2019d), 'Could Music Companies Help Black Artists by Adjusting Old Record Deals', *Rolling Stone*, 8 June. Available online: https://www.rollingstone.com/pro/features/music-black-artists-old-record-deals-1011447/ (accessed 21 November 2020).

Ingham, T. (2020a), 'Kanye West's War against Record Contracts Could Actually Work – For Kanye Anyway, *Rolling Stone*, 21 September. Available online: https://www.rollingstone.com/pro/features/kanye-west-universal-masters-war-1064225/ (accessed 12 December 2020).

Ingham, T. (2020b), 'BMG Pledges to Review Historical Record Contracts "Mindful of the Music Industry's Shameful Treatment of Black Artists"', *Music Business Worldwide*, 11 June. Available online: https://www.musicbusinessworldwide.com/bmg-to-review-historic-record-contracts-mindful-of-the-music-industrys-shameful-treatment-of-black-artists/ (accessed 20 June 2020).

Ingham, T. (2021a), 'The Major Music Companies Now Turn Over $2.5 Every Hour – And Will Generate More Than $20bn between Them This Year', *Music Business Worldwide*. Available online: https://www.musicbusinessworldwide.com/major-music-companies-now-turn-over-2-5m-every-hour-and-will-generate-more-than-20bn-between-them-this-year/ (accessed 13 September 2021).

Ingham, T. (2021b), 'Warner Music Group Is Worth $10bn More Than It Was a Year Ago', *Music Business Worldwide*, 22 October. Available online: https://www.musicbusinessworldwide.com/warner-music-group-is-worth-10bn-more-than-it-was-a-year-ago/ (accessed 8 June 2022).

Ingham, T. (2021c), 'Warner Music Spends over $100m to Buy David Guetta Recordings Catalog', *Music Business Worldwide*, 17 June. Available online: https://www.musicbusinessworldwide.com/warner-music-spends-over-100m-to-acquire-david-guetta-recordings-catalog/ (accessed 3 October 2021).

Ingham, T. (2021d), 'The Name's Bonds. Music Bonds', *Music Business Worldwide*, 19 October. Available online: https://www.musicbusinessworldwide.com/the-names-bonds-music-bonds/ (accessed 8 June 2022).

Ingham, T. (2021e), 'Would AWAL Really Have Thrived Had It Not Been Sold to Sony Music', *Music Business Worldwide*, 16 September. Available online: https://www.musicbusinessworldwide.com/would-awal-really-have-thrived-had-it-not-been-sold-to-sony-music-kobalt/ (accessed 12 October 2021).

Ingham, T. (2021f), 'Here. Come. The. Giants', *Music Business Worldwide*, 7 October. Available online: https://www.musicbusinessworldwide.com/here-come-the-giants/ (accessed 12 October 2021).

Ingham, T. (2021g), 'Over 60,000 Tracks Are Now Uploaded to Spotify Every Day: That's Nearly One per Second', *Music Business Worldwide*, 24 February. Available online: https://www.musicbusinessworldwide.com/over-60000-tracks-are-now-uploaded-to-spotify-daily-thats-nearly-one-per-second/ (accessed 21 June 2021).

International Federation of the Phonographic Industry (IFPI) (2003), *The WIPO Treaties: 'Making Available' Right*, London: IFPI.

International Federation of the Phonographic Industry (IFPI) (2010), *Investing in Music: How Music Companies Discover, Develop and Promote Talent*, London: IFPI.

International Federation of the Phonographic Industry (IFPI) (2012), *Investing in Music: How Music Companies Discover, Nurture and Promote Talent*, London: IFPI.

International Federation of the Phonographic Industry (IFPI) (2014), *Investing in Music: How Record Companies Discover, Nurture and Promote Talent*, London: IFPI.

International Federation of the Phonographic Industry (IFPI) (2016), *Investing in Music: The Value of Record Companies*, London: IFPI.

International Federation of the Phonographic Industry (IFPI) (2022), *Global Music Report 2022*, London: IFPI.

International Labour Office (ILO) (1939), *International Labour Conference Twenty-Sixth Session, Geneva 1940: Rights of Performers in Broadcasting, Television and the Mechanical Reproduction of Sounds*, Geneva: International Labour Office.

International Labour Organization, United Nations Educational Scientific and Cultural Organization, and United International Bureaux for the Protection of Intellectual Property (ILO, UNESCO and BIRPI) (1968), *Records of the Diplomatic Conference on the International Protection of Performers, Producers of Phonograms and Broadcasting Organizations*, Belgium: ILO, UNESCO, BIRPI.

International Labour Organization, United Nations Educational Scientific and Cultural Organization, and World Intellectual Property Organization (ILO, UNESCO and WIPO) (1982), *Model Law Concerning the Protection of Performers, Producers of Phonograms and Broadcasting Organizations with a Commentary on It*, Belgium: ILO, UNESCO, WIPO.

Jaszi, P. (1991), 'Toward a Theory of Copyright: The Metamorphoses of "Authorship"', *Duke Law Journal*, 40 (2): 455–502.

Joe Budden Podcast (2018), [Podcast], YouTube. Available online: https://www.youtube.com/watch?v=bI-mvYUC-88&feature=youtu.be (accessed 12 August 2020).

Johns, A. (2009), *Piracy: The Intellectual Property Wars from Guttenberg to Gates*, Chicago and London: The University of Chicago Press.

Jones, D. (2017), *David Bowie: A Life*, London: Preface.

Jones, G. (1985), 'The Gramophone Company: An Anglo-American Multinational, 1898–1931', *The Business History Review*, 59 (1): 76–100.

Jones, M. (n.d.), 'Radio Licence: The History of UK Radio Licence', available online: https://www.radiolicence.org.uk/history/ (accessed 18 October 2021).

Jones, M. L. (1997), '*Organising Pop: Why So Few Acts Make Pop Music*', Ph.D thesis, University of Liverpool.

Jones, M. L. (2014), 'Revisiting "Music Industry Research": What Changed? What Didn't?', in L. Marshall and D. Laing (eds), *Popular Music Matters: Essays in Honour of Simon Frith*, 45–60, Farnham: Ashgate.

Kealy, E. R. (1979), 'From Craft to Art: The Case of Sound Mixers and Popular Music', *Sociology of Work and Occupations*, 6 (1): 3–29.

Keightley, K. (2003), 'Cover Version' in J. Shepherd, D. Horn, D. Laing, P. Oliver and P. Wicke (eds), *Continuum Encyclopedia of Popular Music of the World. Volume I: Media, Industry and Society*, 614–17, London and New York: Continuum.

Kernfeld, B. (2011), *Pop Song Piracy: Disobedient Music Distribution Since 1929*, Chicago and London: University of Chicago Press.

Knopper, S. (2009), *Appetite for Self-Destruction: The Spectacular Crash of the Record Industry in the Digital Age*, London: Simon & Schuster.

Kordosh, J. (1987), 'Fab! Gear! The George Harrison Interview (Part 1)', December. Available online: http://beatlesnumber9.com/creem.html (accessed 9 November 2021).

Kot, G. (2009), *Ripped: How the Wired Generation Revolutionized Music*, New York: Scribner.

Kretschmer, M. (2008), 'Creativity Stifled? A Joined Academic Statement on the Proposed Copyright Term Extension for Sound Recordings', *European Intellectual Property Review*, 9: 341–7.

Kretschmer, M. and F. Kawohl (2004), 'The History and Philosophy of Copyright', in S. Frith and L. Marshall (eds), *Music and Copyright*, 2nd edn, 21–53, Edinburgh: Edinburgh University Press.

Lainer, J. (2010), *You Are Not a Gadget: A Manifesto*, London: Allen Lane.

Laing, D. (2004), 'Copyright, Politics and the International Music Industry', in S. Frith and L. Marshall (eds), *Music and Copyright*, 2nd edn, 70–85, Edinburgh: Edinburgh University Press.

'The Law of Copyright' (1908), *Phono Trader and Recorder*, July: 74.

Leeds, J. (2001), 'Record Labels, Artists Reach Services Accord', *Los Angeles Times*, 8 November. Available online: https://www.latimes.com/archives/la-xpm-2001-nov-08-fi-1527-story.html (accessed 20 August 2020).

Legge 22 Aprile 1941 N. 633 (1941), *Protezione del diritto d'autore e di altri diritti connessi al suo esercizio*. Available online: http://www.interlex.it/testi/l41_633.htm (accessed 1 November 2021).

Leiber, J. and M. Stoller with D. Ritz (2009), *Hound Dog: The Leiber & Stoller Autobiography*, London: Omnibus Press.

Lessig, L. (2004), *Free Culture: How Big Media Uses Technology and the Law to Lock Down Culture and Control Creativity*, New York: Penguin.

Lewisohn, M. (2013), *All These Years Volume 1: Tune In*, London: Little, Brown.

Lewis-Young, J. (1907), 'The History of Talking Machines', *Phono Trader and Recorder*, January: 576–80.

Leyshon, A. (2014), *Reformatted: Code, Networks, and the Transformation of the Music Industry*, Oxford: Oxford University Press.

Lord Kilbracken (1987), 'Copyright, Designs and Patents Bill', *Hansard, HL Deb*, 30 November, vol. 490, col. 886–91. Available online: http://hansard.millbanksystems.com/lords/1987/nov/30/copyright-designs-and-patents-bill-hl-1 (accessed 2 November 2021).

Love, C. (2000), 'Courtney Love Does the Math', *Salon.com*, 14 June. Available online: https://www.salon.com/2000/06/14/love_7/ (accessed 21 April 2020).

Lydon, M. (2004), *Ray Charles: Man and Music*, updated edn, New York and London: Routledge.

Macaulay, T. B. (1841), 'Copyright', Hansard, HC Deb, 5 February, vol. 56, col. 347–8. Available online: https://hansard.parliament.uk/commons/1841-02-05/debates/2cd5b5f7-326a-4402-87c1-2d54c16c0b9b/Copyright (accessed 1 November 2021).

Maconie, S. (1999), *Blur: 3862 Days*, London: Virgin.

Malt, A. (2021), 'Taylor Swift May Have Prompted Stronger Re-record Restrictions at Labels, while Publishing Could Limit Reach of Ashanti Re-records', *Complete Music Update*, 18 November. Available online: https://completemusicupdate.com/article/taylor-swift-may-have-prompted-stronger-re-record-restrictions-at-labels-while-publishing-could-limit-reach-of-ashanti-re-records/ (accessed 20 November 2021).

Marshall, L. (2005), *Bootlegging: Romanticism and Copyright in the Music Industry*, London: Sage.

Marshall, L. (2013), 'The Structural Functions of Stardom in the Recording Industry', *Popular Music and Society*, 36 (5): 578–96.

Martland, P. (2013), *Recording History: The British Record Industry 1988–1931*, Lanham: Scarecrow Press.

Masouyé, C. (1981), *Guide to the Rome Convention and to the Phonograms Convention*, Geneva: WIPO.

Mayer, A. M. (1878), 'On Edison's Talking-Machine', *Popular Science Monthly*, April: 723.

McNamara (2011), 'What Microsoft Paid the Stones to Help Launch Windows 95', *Networkworld*, 29 June. Available online: https://www.networkworld.com/article/2220097/what-microsoft-paid-the-stones-to-help-launch-windows-95.html (accessed 19 October 2021).

Miège, B. (1989), *The Capitalization of Cultural Production*, New York: International General.

Millard, A. (1995), *America on Record: A History of Recorded Sound*, Cambridge: Cambridge University Press.

Mnookin, S. (2007), 'Universal's CEO Once Called iPod Users Thieves. Now He's Giving Songs Away', *Wired*, 27 November. Available online: https://www.wired.com/2007/11/mf-morris/ (accessed 5 May 2020).

Monopolies and Mergers Commission (MMC) (1988), *Collective Licensing: A Report on Certain Practices in the Collective Licensing of Public Performance and Broadcasting Rights in Sound Recordings*, London: Her Majesty's Stationery Office.

Monopolies and Mergers Commission (MMC) (1994), *The Supply of Recorded Music: A Report on the Supply in the UK of Pre-recorded Compact Discs, Vinyl Discs and Tapes Containing Music*, London: Her Majesty's Stationery Office.

Mulligan, M. (2018), 'Taylor Swift, Label Services and What Comes Next', *MIDiA*, 22 November. Available online: https://www.midiaresearch.com/blog/taylor-swift-label-services-and-what-comes-next (accessed 12 August 2020).

Mulligan, M. (2019a), 'Big Machine (Inadvertently) Just Did a Promo Ad for Label Services Deals', *Music Industry Blog*, 1 July. Available online: https://musicindustryblog.wordpress.com/2019/07/01/big-machine-inadvertently-just-did-a-promo-ad-for-label-services-deals/ (accessed 12 August 2020).

Mulligan, M. (2019b), *Music Publishing: A Full-Stack Revolution*, London: MIDiA Research.

Mulligan, M. (2020), *Insurgents and Incumbents: How the 2020s Will Remake the Music Business*, London: MIDiA Research.

Mulligan, M. (2021a), 'Labels Are Going to Become More Like VCs Than They Probably Want to Be', *Music Industry Blog*, 30 July. Available online: https://www.midiaresearch.com/blog/labels-are-going-to-become-more-like-vcs-than-they-probably-want-to-be (accessed 11 October 2021).

Mulligan, M. (2021b), 'The Paradox of Small', *Music Industry Blog*, 18 June. Available online: https://www.midiaresearch.com/blog/the-paradox-of-small (accessed 16 October 2021).

Music Managers' Forum (MMF) (n.d.). *Digital Deals Comparison Calculator*, Available online: https://themmf.net/digitaldollar-comparisoncalculator-form/ (accessed 20 June 2020).

Music Managers Forum and Featured Artists Coalition (MMF and FAC) (2021), 'Written Evidence Submitted by the Music Managers Forum and Featured Artists Coalition', *Economics of Music Streaming*, 21 January. Available online: https://committees.parliament.uk/work/646/economics-of-music-streaming/publications/written-evidence/ (accessed 9 November 2021).

'The Musical Copyright Situation' (1909), *Phono Trader and Recorder*, May: 724–6.

Musicians' Union Executive Committee (1947), *Report to Conference*, London: Musicians' Union.

Napier-Bell, S. (2014), *Ta-Ra-Ra-Boom-De-Ay: The Dodgy Business of Popular Music*, London: Unbound.

Negus, K. (1992), *Producing Pop: Culture and Conflict in the Music Industry*, London: Arnold.

Negus, K. (1999), *Music Genres and Corporate Cultures*, London: Routledge.

Newman, M. (2016), 'Inside Prince's Career-Long Battle to Master His Artistic Destiny', *Billboard*, 28 April. Available online: https://www.billboard.com/articles/news/cover-story/7348551/prince-battle-to-control-career-artist-rights (accessed 21 July 2021).

Nimmer, M. B. (1963), *Nimmer on Copyright: A Treatise on the Law of Literary, Musical and Artistic Property, and the Protection of Ideas*, New York: Matthew Bender.

Norman, P. (2001), *The Stones*, London: Sidgwick & Jackson.

O'Dair, M. (2014), *Different Every Time: The Authorised Biography of Robert Wyatt*, London: Serpent's Tail.

Oldham, A. L. (2000), *Stoned*, London: Vintage.

Oldham, A. L. (2003), *2Stoned*, London: Vintage.

Oman, R. (1991), *Report on Copyright Implications of Digital Audio Transmission Services*, Washington: US Government Printing Office.

O'Riordan, J. and L. Gillon (2021), 'The Artist/Manager Relationship', in A. Harrison and T. Rigg (eds), *The Present and Future of Music Law*, 263–75, New York and London: Bloomsbury.

Osborne, R. (2012), *Vinyl: A History of the Analogue Record*, Farnham: Ashgate.

Osborne, R. (2014), 'Cover Me Badd', *Pop Bothering Me*, 1 October. Available online: https://richardosbornevinyl.blogspot.com/search?q=cover+versions (accessed 20 October 2021).

Osborne, R. (2019), 'Moby, Minstrelsy and Melville', in Z. Beaven, M. O'Dair and R. Osborne (eds), *Mute Records: Artists, Business, History*, 169–81, New York and London: Bloomsbury.

Osborne, R. (2021a), 'At the Sign of the Swingin' Symbol: The Manipulation of the UK Singles Chart', in R. Osborne and D. Laing (eds), *Music by Numbers: The Use and Abuse of Statistics in the Music Industries*, 20–38, Bristol: Intellect.

Osborne, R. (2021b), 'The Gold Disc: One Million Pop Fans Can't Be Wrong', in R. Osborne and D. Laing (eds), *Music by Numbers: The Use and Abuse of Statistics in the Music Industries*, 39–55, Bristol: Intellect.

Osborne, R. (2021c), '"I Am a One in Ten": Success Ratios in the Recording Industry', in R. Osborne and D. Laing (eds), *Music by Numbers: The Use and Abuse of Statistics in the Music Industries*, 56–71, Bristol: Intellect.

Page, W. (2021), *Tarzan Economics: Eight Principles for Pivoting through Disruption*, London: Simon & Schuster.

Paine, A. (2021), 'Paul McCartney, Kate Bush, Noel Gallagher, Kano, Stevie Nicks & Dozens More Artists Call on PM to "Fix Streaming"', *Music Week*, 20 April. Available online: https://www.musicweek.com/digital/read/paul-mccartney-kate-bush-noel-gallagher-kano-stevie-nicks-dozens-more-artists-call-on-pm-to-fix-streaming/083083 (accessed 29 June 2021).

Parker, N. (2006), 'A Raw Deal for Performers: Part 1 – Term of Copyright', *Entertainment Law Review*, 17 (6): 161–6.

Passerard, F. and P. Cartwright (2019), 'Business-to-Artist: Record Labels and Sub-labels in the Digital Age', *The Conversation*, 1 July. Available online: https://theconversation.com/business-to-artist-record-labels-and-sub-labels-in-the-digital-age-118950 (accessed 28 October 2021).

Passman, D. S. (2009), *All You Need to Know about the Music Business*, 7th edn, New York: Free Press.

Pater, W. (1877), 'The School of Giorgione', *Fortnightly Review*, October.

Peeler, C. D. (1999), 'From the Providence of Kings to Copyrighted Things (and French Moral Rights)', *Indiana International & Comparative Law Review*, 9 (2): 423–56.

Performing Right Society (PRS) (1956), 'Copyright Law Revision', *Performing Right*, September: 17–18.

Perry, A. (2021), 'Rock 'n' Roll Confidential: Merry Clayton', *Mojo*, October: 18.

Peterson, R. A. (1990), 'Why 1955? Explaining the Advent of Rock Music', *Popular Music*, 9 (1): 97–116.

Phonograms Convention (1971), *Convention for the Protection of Producers of Phonograms against Unauthorized Duplication of Their Phonograms*, 29 October. Available online: https://wipolex.wipo.int/en/text/288579 (accessed 1 November 2021).

Phonographic Performance Ltd (PPL) (2004), 'Seventy Years of PPL'. Available online: https://www.ppluk.com/Documents/70%20Years%20of%20PPL.pdf (accessed 7 November 2016).

Phonographic Performance Ltd (PPL) (2012), *Annual Review 2011: The Value of Music*, London: PPL.

Phonographic Performance Ltd (PPL) (2014), *Annual Review 2013: From Earth to Cosmos*, London: PPL.

Pop, I. (2014), 'The John Peel Lecture', *BBC*. Available online: https://www.bbc.co.uk/programmes/articles/1DBxXYBDJLt2xZgxjzCkLRg/bbc-music-john-peel-lecture-iggy-pops-keynote-speech-transcript (accessed 1 November 2021).

Popper, B. (2015), 'Jay Z Relaunches Tidal with Music's Biggest Artists as His Co-owners', *The Verge*, 30 March. Available online: https://www.theverge.com/2015/3/30/8314833/tidal-jay-z-streaming-music. (accessed 11 August 2020).

Porter, V. (1991), *Beyond the Berne Convention: Copyright, Broadcasting the Single European Market*, London: John Libbey.

Read, O. and L. W. Welch (1976), *From Tin Foil to Stereo: Evolution of the Phonograph*, 2nd edn, Indianapolis: Howard W Sams and Co.

Reel Stories: Sting (2021), [TV programme] BBC 2, 11 December.

Report of Committee (1928), *Copyright Royalty (Mechanical Musical Instruments) Inquiry*, London: His Majesty's Stationery Office.

Ricketson, S. and J. C. Ginsburg (2005), *International Copyright and Neighbouring Rights*, *vol. 1*, 2nd edn, Oxford: Oxford University Press.

Ringer, B. and H. Sandison (1989), 'United States of America', in S. M. Stewart and H. Sandison (eds), *International Copyright and Neighbouring Rights*, 2nd edn, vol. 1, 563–678, London: Butterworth & Co.

Ringer, B. A. ([1957] 1961), *The Unauthorized Duplication of Sound Recordings*, Washington: United States Government Printing Office.

Robertson, J. D. (1911a), 'The Copyright Bill: A Reply to Mr. Boosey', *The Times*, 2 May: 10.

Robertson, J. D. (1911b), 'Copyright Bill: The "Phonographic Industry"', *The Times*, 9 May: 4.

Robin Ray v Classic FM (1998), FSR 622.

Rome Act (1928), *International Convention for the Protection of Literary and Artistic Works*, 2 June. Available online: https://www.keionline.org/wp-content/uploads/1928_Rome_revisions_Berne.pdf (accessed 1 November 2021).

Rome Convention (1961), *International Convention for the Protection of Performers, Producers of Phonograms and Broadcasting Organisations*, 26 October. Available online: https://wipolex.wipo.int/en/text/289795 (accessed 1 November 2021).

Rose, M. (1993), *Authors and Owners: The Invention of Copyright*, Cambridge, MA and London: Harvard University Press.

de Sanctis, V. and V. de Sanctis (1989), 'Italy', in S. M. Stewart and H. Sandison (eds), *International Copyright and Neighbouring Rights*, 2nd edn, vol. 1, 448–67, London: Butterworth & Co.

Samuelson, P (1997), 'The U.S. Digital Agenda at WIPO', *Virginia Journal of International Law*, 37 (2): 369–440.

Sanjek, R. and D. Sanjek (1991), *American Popular Music Business in the 20th Century*, New York and Oxford: Oxford University Press.

Scaping, P. (1998), *BPI Yearbook 1998*, London: BPI.

Segal, V. (2014), 'The Outsider', *Q*, December: 92.

Sell, S (2010), 'The Global IP Upward Ratchet, Anti-counterfeiting and Piracy Enforcement Efforts: The State of Play', *PIJIP Research Paper Series*. Available online: http://digitalcommons.wcl.american.edu/research/15/ (accessed 14 September 2021).

Senate Judiciary Committee (SJC) (1971), *Creation of a Limited Copyright in Sound Recordings: Report to Accompany S. 646*, Washington: US Government Printing Office.

Sexton, P. (2017), 'State of the Union', *Music Week*, 24 July: 10–12.

Shafter, A. M. (1939), *Musical Copyright*, 2nd edn, Chicago: Callaghan and Company.

Sharon Osbourne Presents Rock 'n' Roll's Dodgiest Deals (2017), [TV programme] BBC4, 26 May.

Shaw, G. B. (1911), 'The Copyright Bill: Composers and Compensation', *The Times*, 4 May: 7.

Sherman B. and L. Bently (1999), *The Making of Modern Intellectual Property Law*, Cambridge: Cambridge University Press.

Slater v Wimmer (2012), EWPCC 7.

Smirke, R. (2014), 'Beggars Group's Martin Mills on Why He's Abandoning the 50/50 Streaming Split', *Billboard*, 2 May. Available online: https://www.billboard.com/biz/articles/6077399/beggars-group-martin-mills-streaming-money-reduction-spotify-revenue (accessed 24 July 2019).

Smith, C. (1997), *Creative Britain*, London: Faber and Faber.

Smith, D. (2021), 'BMG Purchases "Entire" Recorded Catalog of Mötley Crüe in Its "Largest Single Catalog Acquisition" Ever', *Digital Music News*, 30 November. Available online: https://www.digitalmusicnews.com/2021/11/30/motley-crue-bmg-deal/ (accessed 7 December 2021).

Smith, J. (2006), 'John Smith Supports Extend the Term!', *Music Week*, 25 March: 8.

Snapes, L. (2021), 'Olivia Rodrigo: I'm a Teenage Girl. I Feel Heartbreak and Longing Really Intensely', *Guardian*, 7 May. Available online: https://www.theguardian.com/music/2021/may/07/olivia-rodrigo-im-a-teenage-girl-i-feel-heartbreak-and-longing-really-intensely (accessed 14 September 2021).

Soul America: Amazing Grace (2008), [TV programme] BBC4, 4 September.

Sousa, J. P. ([1906] 2012), 'The Menace of Mechanical Music', in T. D. Taylor, M. Katz and T. Grajeda (eds), *Music, Sound and Technology in America: A Documentary History of Early Phonograph, Cinema, and Radio*, 113–22, Durham and London: Duke University Press.

Spotify (2022), 'Loud and Clear', *Spotify.com*, 24 March. Available online: https://loudandclear.byspotify.com/ (accessed 28 March 2022).

Springsteen, B. (2016), *Born to Run*, London: Simon & Schuster.

'Square, Inc. Announces Plans to Acquire Majority Ownership Stake in TIDAL' (2021), *Square*, 4 March. Available online: https://squareup.com/gb/en/press/tidal?country_redirection=true (accessed 18 November 2021).

Stahl, M. (2008), 'Recording Artists, Work for Hire, Employment, and Appropriation', *SSRN*, 23 October. Available online: https://papers.ssrn.com/sol3/papers.cfm?abstract_id=1288831 (accessed 19 July 2019).

Stahl, M. (2013), *Unfree Masters: Recording Artists and the Politics of Work* (Durham and London: Duke University Press).

Stahl, M. (2015), 'Tactical Destabilization for Economic Justice: The First Phase of the 1984–2004 Rhythm & Blues Royalty Reform Movement', *Queen Mary Journal of Intellectual Property*, 5 (3): 344–63.

Stassen, M. (2021a), 'Universal Music Group Goes Public: Sir Lucian Grainge Hails "Exciting Milestone in UMG's Storied History"', *Music Business Worldwide*, 21 September. Available online: https://www.musicbusinessworldwide.com/universal-music-group-goes-public-sir-lucian-grainge-hails-exciting-milestone-in-umgs-storied-history/ (accessed 12 October 2021).

Stassen, M. (2021b), 'Another $50+ Music Deal, as Primary Wave Buys Stake in Bing Crosby Estate', *Music Business Worldwide*, 11 October. Available online: https://www.musicbusinessworldwide.com/primary-wave-buys-stake-in-bing-crosby-estate-for-more-than-50m-report/ (accessed 12 October 2021).

Stassen, M. (2021c), 'Sony Spent $1.4bn on Music Acquisitions in the last Six Months… and Rob Stringer's Not Stopping There', *Music Business Worldwide*, 27 May. Available online: https://www.musicbusinessworldwide.com/sony-musics-spent-1-4bn-on-acquisitions-in-the-last-six-months-and-rob-stringers-not-stopping-there/ (accessed 3 October 2021).

Statute of Anne (1710), 'An Act for the Encouragement of Learning, by Vesting the Copies of Printed Books in the Authors or Purchasers of Such Copies, during the Times Therein Mentioned'. Available online: http://www.copyrighthistory.com/anne.html (accessed 1 November 2021).

Sterling, J. A. L. (1992), *Intellectual Property Rights in Sound Recordings, Film & Video: Protection of Phonographic and Cinematographic Recordings and Works in National and International Law*, London: Sweet and Maxwell.

Sterne, J. (2003), *The Audible Past: Cultural Origins of Sound Reproduction*, Durham and London: Duke University Press.

Stewart, S. (1983), 'The Years 1961 to 1979', in J. Borwick (ed), *The First Fifty Years: Celebrating the Anniversary of IFPI*, 15–19, London: Brooks Design Partnership.

Strauss, N. (2002), 'Record Labels' Answer to Napster Still Has Artists Feeling Bypassed', *New York Times*, 18 February. Available online: https://www.nytimes.com/2002/02/18/arts/record-labels-answer-to-napster-still-has-artists-feeling-bypassed.html (accessed 20 March 2020).

Stuart, D. K. (2017), 'Producer Agreements Are Stupid', in M. Halloran (ed), *The Musician's Business & Legal Guide*, 5th edn, 207–31, New York and London: Routledge.

Stutz, C. (2020), 'Kanye Speaks: West's Plan to "Re-think" the Music Industry', *Billboard*, 23 September. Available online: https://www.billboard.com/articles/business/9454350/kanye-west-speaks-plan-to-re-think-the-music-industry (accessed 12 December 2020).

Suisman, D. (2012), *Selling Sounds: The Commercial Revolution in American Music*, Cambridge, MA and London: Harvard University Press.

Sun, H. (2019), *Digital Revolution Tamed: The Case of the Recording Industry*, Basingstoke: Palgrave Macmillan.

Sutcliffe, P. (2016), 'Interregnum 1992–2003', *Mojo*, July: 63.

Sydnor, T. D. (2009), 'The Making-Available Right under U.S. Law', *Progress & Freedom Foundation Progress on Point Paper*, 16 (7): 1–47.

Symes, C. (2004), *Setting the Record Straight: A Material History of Classical Recording*, Middletown: Wesleyan University Press.

Talbot, M. (2006), 'Editorial: Creators Are Setting Term Agenda', *Music Week*, 29 April: 14.

Thompson, B. (2018), 'The Mojo Interview: John McLaughlin', *Mojo*, September: 33–7.

Thornton, S. (1995), *Club Cultures: Music, Media and Subcultural Capital*, Cambridge: Polity Press.

'Timeline' (n.d.), *The Musicians' Union: A Social History*. Available online: https://www.muhistory.com/contact-us/1991-2000/ (accessed 27 March 2020).

Toffler, A. (1980), *The Third Wave*, New York: William Morrow.

Toynbee, J. (2004), 'Musicians', in S. Frith and L. Marshall (eds), *Music and Copyright*, 2nd edn, 123–38, Edinburgh: Edinburgh University Press.

'Trade Topics' (1911), *Talking Machine News*, May: 77–8, 81, 83–4, 87.

'Trade Views Concerning the Act' (1912), *Talking Machine News*, January: 416–18.

Trubridge, H. (2015), 'Safeguarding the Income of Musicians', *WIPO Magazine*, May. Available online: https://www.wipo.int/wipo_magazine/en/2015/02/article_0002.html (accessed 24 July 2019).

UK Parliament (2021), 'Economics of Music Streaming'. Available online: https://committees.parliament.uk/work/646/economics-of-music-streaming/ (accessed 12 October 2021).

Ulmer, E. and H. H. von Rauscher (1989), 'Germany' in S. M. Stewart and H. Sandison (eds), *International Copyright and Neighbouring Rights*, 2nd edn, vol. 1, 414–47, London: Butterworth & Co.

United States Copyright Office (USCO) (2011), *Federal Copyright Protection for Pre-1972 Sound Recordings: A Report of the Register of Copyrights*, Washington: United States Copyright Office.

United States Copyright Office (USCO) (2016a), *Copyright and the Music Marketplace*, 2nd printing, Washington: United States Copyright Office.

United States Copyright Office (USCO) (2016b), *The Making Available Right in the United States: A Report of the Register of Copyrights*, Washington: United States Copyright Office.

'A United Voice' (2006), *Music Week*, 29 April: 1.

Vaidhyanathan, S. (2001), *Copyrights and Copywrongs: The Rise of Intellectual Property and How It Threatens Creativity*, New York and London: New York University Press.

Victoroff, G. (2017), 'Sampling', in M. Halloran (ed), *The Musician's Business & Legal Guide*, 5th edn, 48–54, New York and London: Routledge.

Voogt, B. (2019), 'The Indie Musician's Guide to Digital Distribution', *Heroic Academy*, 31 December. Available online: https://heroic.academy/indie-musicians-guide-to-digital-distribution/# (accessed 2 May 2020).

Wells, L. S. (2017), 'Independent Record Labels and Record Deals', in M. Halloran (ed), *The Musician's Business & Legal Guide*, 5th edn, 182–98, New York and London: Routledge.

Westminster Media Forum (2017), *The Future for Copyright and Design Rights Policy – Rights Management, Enforcement and the UK's Approach Post-Brexit*, Proceedings, 22 June.

Whitford, J. (1977), *Copyright and Designs Law: Report of the Committee to Consider the Law on Copyright and Designs*, London: Her Majesty's Stationery Office.

'Why It's Time for Action' (2004), *Music Week*, 24 July: 7.

Wikström, P. (2009), *The Music Industry: Music in the Cloud*, Cambridge: Polity Press.

Williams, P. (2008), 'A Music Revolutionary before the Revolution', *Music Week*, 3 May: 10.

Williamson, J. (2015), 'For the Benefit of All Musicians? The Musicians' Union and Performers' Rights in the UK', in A. Rahmatian (ed), *Concepts of Music and Copyright: How Music Perceives Itself and How Copyright Perceives Music*, 167–94, Cheltenham, UK and Northampton, US: Edward Elgar.

Williamson, J. and M. Cloonan (2016), *Players' Work Time: A History of the British Musicians' Union, 1893–2013*, Manchester: Manchester University Press.

WIPO Performances and Phonograms Treaty (WPPT) (1996), 20 December. Available online: https://wipolex.wipo.int/en/text/295477 (accessed 1 November 2021).

Witt, S. (2015), *How Music Got Free: What Happens When an Entire Generation Commits the Same Crime?* London: The Bodley Head.

World Intellectual Property Organization (WIPO) (1992), 'Preparatory Document for and Report of the First Session of the Committee of Experts on a Possible Protocol to the Berne Convention for the Protection of Literary and Artistic Works (Geneva, November 4 to 8, 1991)', *Copyright*, 2, February: 30–53.

World Intellectual Property Organization (WIPO) (1993), *Committee of Experts on a Possible Instrument for the Protection of the Rights of Performers and Producers of Phonograms, First Session, Geneva, June 28 to July 2, 1993*, Geneva: WIPO.

World Intellectual Property Organization (WIPO) (1994a), 'Committee of Experts on a Possible Instrument for the Protection of the Rights of Performers and Producers of Phonograms. Second Session, Geneva, November 8 to 12, 1993', *Copyright*, 2, February: 44–55.

World Intellectual Property Organization (WIPO) (1994b), 'Preparatory Document for the Third Session of the Committee of Experts on a Possible Instrument for the Protection of the Rights of Performers and Producers of Phonograms, Geneva, December 12 to 16, 1994', *Copyright*, 11, November: 241–76.

World Intellectual Property Organization (WIPO) (1995), 'Committee of Experts on a Possible Instrument for the Protection of the Rights of Performers and Producers of Phonograms Fourth Session, Geneva, September 4 to 8 and 12, 1995', *Industrial Property and Copyright*, 10, October: 363–96.

World Intellectual Property Organization (WIPO) (1999), *Records on the Diplomatic Conference on Certain Copyright and Neighboring Rights Questions*, Geneva: WIPO.

World Intellectual Property Organization (WIPO) (n.d.), 'Copyright'. Available online: https://www.wipo.int/copyright/en/ (accessed 16 March 2022).

'Years of Service' (2015), *Music Week*, 16 January: 8–10.

Yetnikoff, W. and D. Ritz (2004), *Howling at the Moon: Confessions of a Music Mogul in an Age of Excess*, London: Abacus.

Index